D0593560

THE LSO AT 70

THE LSO AT 70:

A History of the Orchestra

by

MAURICE PEARTON

ML
286.8
.L52
L6857
Cop. 1

SE 17 '75

MUSIC ROOM

LONDON
VICTOR GOLLANCZ LTD
1974

© Maurice Pearton 1974

ISBN 0 575 01763 5

Circ
Moore

Printed in Great Britain by
The Camelot Press Ltd, Southampton

For Hilde

LIST OF ILLUSTRATIONS

PREFACE

THE ORIGINAL INTENTION behind the planning and writing of this book was to publish a sequel to *London Symphony: Portrait of an Orchestra* by Hubert Foss and Noel Goodwin, which appeared at the time of the LSO's fiftieth anniversary, in 1954. The idea proved impracticable. The previous book was out of print and the publisher had gone out of business. There was thus no chance of a reprint to which a reader could conveniently be referred. It soon became clear that any account of developments in the last twenty years would require an extensive and detailed introduction, amounting to at least one-third of a book. Finally and conclusively, my vantage point differs from that of my distinguished predecessors. They were concerned with telling the history of the Orchestra largely in terms of the personalities associated with it. My interest focuses on what the development of the LSO demonstrates about public music-making in Britain during this century. The book is, in consequence, much more like a biography than a portrait. I mentioned this difference to Howard Snell and Alan Smyth in our initial conversation: their response—"so much the better, you can tell us what we look like from outside". To which Harold Lawrence subsequently added "warts and all". The reader will see that I have taken them at their word.

It is a commonplace of the biographer's task that not all aspects of his subject are of equal concern, and the focal point he adopts itself suggests what has to be left out. The LSO has given splendid concerts, ranging from the dazzling to the thought-provoking, under many more conductors than are named here. Similarly, the Orchestra has impinged on the lives of more musicians than have been consulted. It follows that any reader expecting a chronicle of glamorous occasions under sensational conductors, with "star" soloists before unfailingly rapturous audiences will be disappointed. This is an account of how an orchestra lives and works, its administrative as well as its artistic problems, and of the contribution it has made to the art and performance of symphonic music.

The sources are the Minute Books and other archives of the LSO, and diaries, letters and memoirs of those who have been concerned with the Orchestra, either as Members, or as impresarios or officials. These materials range from the ghoulish (LSO file: "*Joan of Arc at the Stake:* Requests for Complimentary Tickets") to the gossipy, but for the most part concern the problems of promoting concerts, players' fees and conditions, and the general politics of the arts. I have been privileged to refer to two unpublished volumes of memoirs: those of Wynn Reeves, for many years a Director of the LSO and Sub-principal Violin, and of Victor Olof, former violinist, conductor, orchestral organiser and artistic director of classical recordings. Written materials have been complemented by discussions with personalities involved either directly in the Orchestra or with the environment in which it operates. My thanks to all are recorded in the Acknowledgements. I am especially grateful to John Cruft, Director of Music, the Arts Council, who gave me much of his time to discuss not only the LSO in his day but also the whole development of the musical arts in this country, and to Alan Smyth, who also readily made time in a very busy schedule to answer questions about the workings of the Orchestra. I am in addition indebted to Miss Livia Gollancz who—surely unique among publishers—played the French horn in the LSO in a previous professional incarnation.

My thanks are also due to the Library officers of London University, the London Borough of Sutton, the Deutsches Kulturinstitut, and Morley College, who have provided printed materials. The personnel of the LSO office furnished documents and friendly encouragement. I am grateful to Miss Moira Webber for advice and assistance in research.

One final point: the Directors of the LSO *asked* me to undertake this book: they did not *commission* it. In consequence, neither they nor any other person mentioned above or in the Acknowledgements is responsible for the matters discussed or the opinions expressed.

MAURICE PEARTON

1974

ACKNOWLEDGEMENTS

The following were kind enough to supply information or discuss problems:

Miss Susan Alcock, William Alwyn, Miss Olive Baguley, Mrs Enid Blech, Lord Boothby, Adolph Borsdorf, Francis Bradley, Victor Busby, Miss Tamara Coates, George Christie, Hubert Cooter, Eugene Cruft, Miss Elsabie Daneel, Colin Davis, Antal Dorati, Mrs Gladys Dugarde, Mrs Sylvia East, Mrs Pat Elkin, Philip Emanuel, Leo d'Erlanger, E. Field, Ernest Fleischmann, Mrs Gladys Gibson, Peter Goodchild, Miss Marie Goossens, Arthur Hammond, T. Hazlam, Edward Heath, C. G. C. Hector, Miss E. B. Heemskerk, Roy Henderson, Mrs Joan Ingpen, Alan Jefferson, Maurice Johnstone, Paul Katz, Michael Kaye, Professor Josef Krips, Harold Lawrence, Mrs Mary Morris Lawrence, Miss Erda Lucas, Sir Jack Lyons, Miss Susan Mallett, George Mann, Neville Marriner, Muir Mathieson, Mme Doris Monteux, Sir Claus Moser, Reginald Mouat, H. Nightingale, Mrs Muriel Nissel, Victor Olof, D. C. Parker, Reginald Pound, André Previn, Professor Humphrey Procter-Gregg, Mrs Madeleine Wynn Reeves, Stephen Reiss, J. H. Roberts, Sheridan Russell, Lionel Salter, L. E. Simmonds, Boris Skidelsky, Malcolm Smith, Howard Snell, Jack Steadman, Paul Strang, Mrs Emmy Tillett, Sir Michael Tippett, Barry Tuckwell, Henri Van Marken, Miss Ella Vander Meerschen, Lord Howard de Walden, Edward Walker, Mrs Kate Wolff, Lady Jessie Wood, Dr Percy Young.

THE LSO AT 70

I

THE CONTEMPORARY ORCHESTRA, and the concert life it exists to serve, are alike creations of the last century. The London Symphony Orchestra, if chronology be strictly heeded, belongs to our century, but the time scales relevant to music differ from those of government and politics by which our reckoning is usually ordered, and the LSO's roots are as firmly in the nineteenth century as if it were as old as the orchestras in Berlin and Vienna, on which it was modelled.

By the time the LSO began its career, in 1904, the modern orchestra had taken on a particular size and character. The impetus had come from the opera house where demands for orchestral resources, particularly in regard to brass tone, had to match stage presentations aiming at maximum spectacle. The difference was not only one of size but one of kind. *Rienzi* and *Aïda* simply cannot be realised by forces suitable for *Die Entführung aus dem Serail*. The demands of the opera house were translated to the concert platform by a series of composers ranging from Berlioz to Mahler and Richard Strauss whose experiments in the world of sound called for larger numbers of performers. In the absence of our present-day electronic techniques, more complex patterns of sound could only be explored by using more players and a greater variety of instruments. The nineteenth-century composers also increased demands on their players' skills and concentration. Thus the pursuit of purely aesthetic ends affected the organisation and cost of performances. In these changes, the status and livelihood of the performing musician were necessarily involved.

Traditionally, in Europe, patronage derived from the Church or the Prince. Musicians were servants, required to perform at Mass or on social occasions, and they enjoyed whatever security *that* condition yielded: they might sit below the salt, but at least they had a place at the table. The Church still carries on this tradition. Since music is used as a medium of devotion, organists and choirs still receive training, opportunity and financial sustenance under its aegis. The Prince, however, has disappeared as a personal patron. His place, in music as well as government, has been taken by the characteristic institutions of the modern state: ministries, municipalities, committees. In consequence, patronage is now rarely individual but is institutional. Musicians are employed by associations or public authorities, often aided by professional management. Ministries of culture fund orchestras and opera companies, universities have string quartets in residence, foundations set up by industry for cultural purposes sponsor performances.

This change is comparatively recent, and has taken place at different speeds in different societies. Even Richard Strauss (1864–1949) began his conducting career as a member of the household of the Duke of Meiningen, but by the late nineteenth century this was an exception, if not an anachronism, and Strauss himself soon joined the ranks of conductors who might be, by title, Court officials, but who in practice were salaried professionals, on contract. In Britain, the Court had long ceased to play a leading role in the patronage of music. Although there was a Court Orchestra until the early years of this century, the title "Royal" indicated status confirmed rather than service expected. The Master of the King's (or Queen's) Musick did not ordinarily live at Court and only dined there ceremonially. The patronage of music devolved on private initiative. State support for music out of taxation—commonplace in continental Europe—only began in 1940, in consequence of "the collapse of all ordinary sources of theatre and music" in wartime. Before then, the giving of concerts and operas and other kinds of public music-making in Britain had been in the hands of groups of enthusiasts, concert societies, festival committees, civic leaders, individuals, who, for a variety of reasons, supported the performances of music out of their own resources. They still do.

Private sponsorship was not the only source of patronage; nor did it extend to full-time employment for musicians. The deficiencies in this respect were made up by patrons of cafés and restaurants, seaside resorts and theatres, all of which employed musicians extensively. The music hall has now gone from the scene, but at the turn of the century there were over fifty in London alone. With changes in taste, the type of operetta or musical play which filled Daly's Theatre and Drury Lane has also largely disappeared. Their contemporary counterparts usually require fewer—and different—players. In the last century, spas and seaside resorts were even more important to musicians since their seasons dovetailed with the activities of the winter concert societies and they could provide opportunities for playing works more akin to the classical repertoire with, perhaps, similar standards of performance. Whether the opportunities were realised or not depended on the musical director and his capacity to attract an audience. In all these cases, patronage stemmed from the audience and was translated into engagements by an agent or entrepreneur, familiarly known as an impresario.

This practice prevailed also in continental Europe, of course, but the broad difference remained that there the performance of serious music was considered an affair of the state which set the standards and the "tone", while in Britain it was an affair of those who happened to like music and were prepared to pay for it. In Britain there was only one remotely comparable organisation to the court, state and municipal orchestras of Europe, namely the Municipal Orchestra in Bournemouth, and that only for twenty-four players and from 1894. Otherwise, patronage came from the Victorian middle classes, exercising a preference for music through subscriptions or in promotional syndicates. Musicians ceased to be servants and therefore lost the assurance of continual employment; they became individual employees, subject to contract. In this situation, the musician had to look to himself for continuity of employment.

The main opportunities for serious music were provided by concert and choral societies, either in seasons of concerts, as those by the Hallé in Manchester or the Royal Philharmonic Society in London, or at festivals, as at Leeds, Birmingham, Norwich and other centres. All were private ventures. The leading societies had sufficient funds to pay the most eminent musicians of the day. Berlioz, writing for the *Journal des Débats*, noted that "over and above the regular subscribers [to the Hallé Society], there are four hundred people who pay half a guinea each *for the reversionary right to buy* any ticket that a regular subscriber may find himself unable to use".[1] In consequence of this scale of patronage, Britain became a Mecca for travelling virtuosi. Private societies commissioned new works, thus not only enlarging the repertoire but providing a possibly continuing source of employment, if the work established itself. These activities are still, happily, part of the British musical scene, but in the nineteenth century they represented essentially private initiative and private finance: they responded to enthusiasm and fashion and the state of public confidence. War scares and financial depressions adversely affected subscriptions. This characteristic, from the viewpoint of the nineteenth-century musician, meant that his career was haphazard and insecure. At best, he was engaged in an honoured profession; at worst, in casual labour. Accordingly, he developed certain professional responses.

The positive responses were adaptability and resource, particularly in sight-reading. Both Mendelssohn, who achieved an easy rapport with British players, and Wagner, who did not, reported favourably on their technical facility. The negative responses evoked far different comment. Both composers referred scathingly to the players' inability to achieve a real pianissimo or subtle gradations of tone, which, of course, could only result from regular playing together in rehearsal and performance. Under the system, any finely-shaded ensemble was virtually out of the question, since the players naturally had an incentive to play wherever the highest fees were currently being offered—typically by the big provincial festivals. This practice extended not only to performances but also to rehearsals, to which the players successfully claimed the right to send deputies, if so doing allowed them to fulfil better-paid engagements elsewhere. In this way the system whereby musicians appeared on individual or limited engagements worked against their employers. For concert promoters and conductors, the deputy system made rehearsal planning impossible and performances variable. The Treasurer of the Royal Philharmonic Society identified the problems, from bitter experience: "A, whom you want, signs to play at your concert. He sends B (whom you don't mind) to the first rehearsal. B, without your knowledge or consent, sends C to the second rehearsal. Not being able to play at the concert, C sends D, whom you would have paid five shillings to stay away."[2]

The deputy system was very much a London phenomenon since, for musicians in the provinces, opportunities to play in symphony concerts were more restricted and admission to the orchestra was, practically, the summit of ambition. If, as in Manchester, the players were on regular contract under a great conductor, the results could be excellent, as long as the season lasted. But even Hallé players were only hired for six months and spent the summer and early autumn in the seaside resorts of Lancashire and North Wales and at inland north country spas. Nevertheless, compared with musicians in other centres, the Hallé players were fortunate. Except for themselves and their colleagues at Bournemouth, British orchestras could offer, at best, *regular* employment. It could not, in the nature of things, be *permanent*. The eminence of a few ensured them a flow of pupils in academies but, as a general rule, musicians in Britain were constantly faced with a conflict between their artistic preferences and the facts of economic life.* The consequence for symphony orchestras was the deputy system.

Uncertainty was endemic: for conductors, it put a premium on minimum rehearsal, or none at all; among players it called for deftness of execution and an eye for the main chance. The entrepreneurial spirit was not confined to lay employers and organisers. It was customary in some quarters, particularly in resorts, for a conductor to be engaged, with responsibility for providing the band. Alternatively, players who themselves had favourable connections with concert societies and festival promoters often functioned on their behalf as sub-contractors among their colleagues who were not so well placed. In the profession such players are known as "fixers". In a somewhat different sphere of activity, individual conductors themselves sponsored concerts in which they engaged orchestras to play. Frequently, these occasions were prompted by a desire to introduce new works or to vary the standard repertoire. Eugene Goossens, Hamilton Harty and Thomas Beecham all

* Obviously, many musicians will not have experienced this as a dilemma but the assumption in the world of symphonic music is that they did—and still do.

at different times backed their judgement in this way. But in all cases, the opportunities for a musician to perform depended solely on the decisions of private individuals as to the value of music in their lives and therefore the amount of money they were willing or could be persuaded to lay out in engaging performers. Their decisions implied questions of taste and of standards, as well as of organisation and employment. Ultimately, of course, the proposition is still true. In a world of the tone-deaf or of the indifferent to music, symphony orchestras would lose their *raison d'être*. But, as we shall see, music is now recognised as a public good, not just a private indulgence, and the provision of music rests no longer solely on individual enthusiasm. At the beginning of this century, however, when the LSO made its debut, it rested on nothing else.

II

JUDGED FROM HIS effect on the future of concert-giving and of orchestral playing, the most important entrepreneur of his time was Robert Newman, a baritone who had turned to concert agency and management. In this role he became involved in 1893 in the promotion of Promenade Concerts at Covent Garden, following which he was appointed Manager of the newly-built Queen's Hall. The Hall, built by a private banker, Francis Ravenscroft, had a seating capacity of about 3,000, which made it one-third larger than its nearest rival, the St James's Hall in Piccadilly. The new hall opened its doors in November 1893, providing accommodation for concerts, recitals and public events. It became the centre of London's concert life—other than for chamber works—and its pre-eminence was confirmed in 1905 when the St James's Hall was demolished to make way for the Piccadilly Hotel. For the musical profession, unlike the public, the Queen's Hall was not a thing in itself, it was part of a complex of three institutions through which concert appearances took place. In close proximity were two indispensable adjuncts: Pagani's Restaurant, which in style and atmosphere was a smaller Café Royal for musicians, and The George public house on the corner of Mortimer Street and Great Portland Street. The restaurant was destroyed in 1940 in the same air raid which flattened the Queen's Hall: the pub survived, its importance to musicians having declined with the loss of the Hall. To generations of players, however, it was familiarly known as The Glue Pot—in reference to the difficulty orchestral managers usually experienced in extracting players in time for their cues. Restaurant and pub provided not only refreshment and recreation but also opportunities to get jobs: they constituted a labour exchange for the profession.

Newman's ambitions for the Queen's Hall ran to a "house"

orchestra and a regular series of concerts. To this end, he raised money from a famous laryngologist,* assembled an orchestra and appointed as conductor a former fellow student at the Royal Academy of Music, Henry J. Wood. The concerts were launched; the standard classical repertoire and new works in a winter series, with more popular programmes in the summer concerts, which in timing and programmes were an attempt to reach a new public. The summer "Promenade Concerts" have now burgeoned into an annual London Festival in all but name, with a repertoire commonly extending from medieval to contemporary music. But the beginnings were with Newman and Wood, in 1895, and with a programme of which the only "serious" item was the overture to *Rienzi*.

Wood, at the time of his appointment, had established a reputation in opera, but was an unknown quantity as a concert conductor. His quality as a trainer of orchestras soon became apparent. He made meticulous use of rehearsal time (assisted by Newman's habit of locking all the doors to prevent players withdrawing for a smoke, during *tacet* passages). Wood also held regular personal auditions for players, marked their parts in great detail, and inaugurated a tuning parade before rehearsing. These drills, which he carried out all his life, achieved substantial results but they implicitly accepted the prevailing conditions. Newman and Wood had to accept the deputy system for the Queen's Hall Orchestra, though neither liked it. Wood recalled in his memoirs that in September 1895, at the end of the first Promenade season, he found "an orchestra with seventy or eighty unknown faces in it. *Even my leader was missing*. Arthur Payne, deputy leader, told me of a certain

* Dr Cathcart. The *quid pro quo*, on Newman's part, was that the Queen's Hall Orchestra adopt the low or continental pitch (A = 439 vibrations per second) instead of the prevailing Philharmonic pitch (A = 452 vibrations per second), which Cathcart, on professional grounds, considered bad for singers. The Queen's Hall organ was tuned to this pitch, which has become standard. The sequel provides a telling detail of conditions at the time. The wind and brass players refused to buy instruments at the new pitch, since they had no assurance that it would be widely adopted. Cathcart therefore imported instruments from Belgium at his own expense for the first season, after which the players bought them from him.

music festival. My regular players were all there. Moreover, they would be absent for a week. . . . I made up my mind there and then to fight what is a bad principle."[1] He began by getting rid of the absent leader and promoting Payne, who continued to lead the Queen's Hall Orchestra after the "Proms" were over. The results marked a new chapter in British concert-giving, but Wood saw that no fundamental improvement could take place unless the "disastrously unprincipled" habit of deputising was ended.

Deputies, even if arranged, did not always arrive. Rehearsals, typically, might have to start without particular wind players, so that parts had to be hastily rewritten for the remaining players to double with some semblance of the full requirement of the score. This promoted skills in arranging instrumentation and sight-reading but could guarantee only an approximation to the composer's intentions. The concerts of the Lamoureux Orchestra from Paris at the Queen's Hall in 1896 publicly demonstrated the results which a more disciplined approach could yield. Discipline, however, depended on a player finding it more worth his while to attend rehearsals, as well as the concert. The Queen's Hall Orchestra was not too tempting an engagement. Wynn Reeves, a violinist who subsequently became Deputy Leader of the LSO and a Director and who led at Covent Garden for the opera seasons, recalled that the fees for the Proms were £2 10s a week for six rehearsals and six concerts of three hours. He thought himself "much better off deputising at Daly's Theatre at £2 10s a week *plus* 4d an evening, white tie money and no rehearsal. A white tie lasted easily for a week! So there was a clear 1s 8d a week for fares or cigarettes . . . or a quarter of a pound of Cadbury's chocolates for 3½d." For this reason, Reeves did not join the QHO and was therefore not among the founder-members of the LSO. Charles Crabbe, a cellist, who *did* join Wood's orchestra in 1898 and who left in protest when the players were told that they must play at the Proms or leave, turned to more lucrative opportunities at Covent Garden and also the Hotel Metropole which yielded £3 10s a week. In addition, he used to appear in theatre pits, especially at Daly's and Her Majesty's. In 1904 he joined the LSO. The demand for discipline made by Newman and Wood was, as they well knew, incompatible with current fee scales. They could compete with the theatres only if they could offer security of tenure.

By 1903, Newman and Wood, through building up a regular audience, were in a position to make the Queen's Hall Orchestra a permanent orchestra. They offered its players some hundred dates over about nine months of the year and a guaranteed minimum wage. Of necessity, absence, unless attested by a doctor's certificate, was not to be tolerated; players were to give up the right to send deputies in exchange for guaranteed employment. These possibilities were made known during 1903 but no action was taken until the following spring when Wood arrived at a rehearsal to find some 70 to 80 per cent of the orchestra composed of deputies. Newman appeared on the platform after the session and issued what was, in fact, an ultimatum: "Gentlemen, in future, there will be *no* deputies. *Good* morning."[2] Forty-six of his regular players promptly decided to resign and form an orchestra under their own management.

Newman's action was precipitate but the secession of the players was not quite the instantaneous reaction it appeared: the notion of forming and running their orchestra had been in the minds of some of the principals for some time and had been canvassed on tours during the year. It was resolved, in principle, in the train on the way back to London from the Kendal Festival. The proponents of independence were Adolf Borsdorf, T. R. Busby, H. Vander Meerschen and John Solomon, respectively First and Second Principal Horn, Fourth Horn and Principal Trumpet in Wood's orchestra. They were all established instrumentalists, with long-standing engagements at festivals and other concerts which filled their annual schedule. They had most to lose by acceding to Newman's and Wood's scheme.

Adolf Borsdorf was born in 1852 in Ditmannsdorf, in Saxony. The son of peasants, he learned to play the horn from the village shoemaker. Someone else taught him the violin but he also learned other crafts, including french polishing. As a boy, he used to tramp barefoot from village to village, playing at the inns, but in his late teens, he decided to study music and went to Leipzig where he supported himself by playing the viola in the pit band of the music hall. Borsdorf eventually got a post in the opera orchestra in Dresden but in the eighteen-eighties he came to London to play at Covent Garden. He married and remained in Britain for the rest of his life. In the early years, when engagements were scarce, he supported himself by french polishing coffins in a Soho basement. In music, however, he established himself as *the* superlative horn player in Glasgow and then London, and professional success, when it came, was secure.

T. R. Busby exemplified a different tradition. He had been born in Wellington Barracks in 1861, the son of a drum major in the Grenadier Guards. Thomas became a drummer boy in the same regiment and at the age of eighteen joined its band. He became known as an exponent of the French horn and left the army to pursue a career in the profession of music. He played in the private orchestra of Queen Victoria and established connections with resort impresarios, notably at Eastbourne. In London, Busby joined the Crystal Palace Orchestra, under August Manns—which brought him to the notice of Newman and Wood.

Henri van der Meerschen had come to London from his birthplace, Brussels, where he trained for the opera stage and took the French horn as second study. Belgium was famous for wind players and a Conservatoire background was in itself a guarantee of quality. The musical environment was described by a fellow student, Eugene Goossens, in the early chapters of his memoirs *Overture and Beginners*. Vander Meerschen (as he came to spell his name for the benefit of the English) arrived in London in response to an invitation from Eugene Goossens' father to join the orchestra of the Carl Rosa Opera Company, which he conducted for many years. As with Borsdorf, marriage helped to make the move permanent: Vander Meerschen's choice was Annetta Laubach, the company's principal contralto. He settled in Glasgow but was soon called to London to join the Queen's Hall Orchestra. Established there, he began the conventional player's life in concert orchestras and theatre pits. From then on, he was too busy even to take pupils!

John Solomon, the fourth founder, was born in 1864. He seems to have been much more withdrawn from his colleagues than the other three, but was universally respected as a man and as a master of his instrument. Older players still recall his characteristic phrasing. John Solomon became Professor of the Trumpet at the Royal Academy of Music and was regularly on call for the Royal Orchestra for Queen Victoria and King Edward VII.

Immediately after Newman's *démarche*, the dissident players met in The Glue Pot (where else?) to decide what to do. A more formal meeting took place on 19th May 1904 in St Andrew's Hall, Newman Street, when Busby outlined a comprehensive scheme for self-management, including a draft constitution and a programme of work. The scheme was adopted unanimously and was referred to Hans Richter, with whom Borsdorf had had a professional relationship dating from his days in Dresden. Richter approved but stipulated that there should be one hundred players and offered his services for the inaugural concert. His tremendous prestige was thus at the disposal of the new venture.

These matters had been brewing for some time: Newman's action merely gave the dissidents the signal to go. They made it quite clear that no personality conflicts were involved: they merely wished to maximise their professional opportunities as they saw them. Many years later, in a letter to Wood, at the time of his Jubilee in 1938, John Solomon recalled their frame of mind:

> . . . I don't know whether you ever had the history of that break [i.e. the secession]. May I be allowed as a culprit to tell you how deeply sorry we were for it but the truth is that all our old players built up a connection such as best concerts, festivals and many other engagements which we had been forced to accept, not knowing what would happen for the future, as when you made such a success after a few years, you might have been snapped up either abroad or elsewhere, and the QH Orchestra would have been abandoned or smashed up. Consequently we would have been stranded, both QH and outside engagements. . . . I was very upset at the time of leaving you because I was happy in my work and position as Principal with you. . . .[3]

This was true as far as it went but it necessarily and tactfully omitted the vital factor in the dissidents' thinking. While they appreciated Wood's qualities as a trainer, they did not think he commanded those sympathies and interpretative insights which carry a conductor to the pinnacles of his profession. They felt that in eight years they had discovered all there was to discover about Henry Wood in this respect. The Queen's Hall Orchestra was Wood's. Accordingly, accepting Newman's offer would have tied them to a conductor with an immensely detailed knowledge of the Orchestra, who was a first-rate disciplinarian and a second-rate interpreter. This they wanted to avoid. Newman unwittingly presented them with the opportunity.

Nevertheless, the dilemma set out by John Solomon was genuine, in that even if Wood had been as imaginative as he and his colleagues required, their employment could still have been abrogated if Wood were translated elsewhere. In fact, as applied to Wood himself, the dissidents' reasoning was false: his career remained in Britain. Wood was the quintessential Cockney. It was, as his biographer remarks, "a necessity of his nature that he should be London-centred. Nowhere else in the world could he experience the same comforting sense of belonging."[4] Wood never joined the club of international travelling conductors, nor held foreign appointments, though after the First World War he was offered the conductorship of the Boston Orchestra. However, even had they possessed this insight, the players could hardly have been expected to tie their careers to Wood or any other conductor who at a rather different level was subject to the same capricious conditions as themselves. The players preferred to be directly and collectively dependent on the market for their professional services, rather than on the reactions of conductors or agents. The new collective entity was registered as the "London Symphony Orchestra".

The new Orchestra's first concert took place on Thursday, 9th June 1904, at 3 p.m.—the hour being chosen because many of the players were engaged to appear at Covent Garden that evening. The programme contained two overtures, *Die Meistersinger* and *Die Zauberflöte*, a Bach suite, Elgar's *Enigma Variations*, a Liszt rhapsody and Beethoven's Fifth. Wood was in the audience. He did not record his feelings on being publicly taken to task in the LSO's advertising. The posters referred to the orchestra as "consisting of recently resigned members of the Queen's Hall Orchestra and other eminent soloists". The programme book was more explicit:

> The recent decision of the Directors of the Queen's Hall Orchestra regarding the employment of Deputies imposes conditions on its most prominent Members that they find it impossible to accept. About half the Band has in consequence felt it necessary to resign. These performers, being, however, unwilling to lose touch with a public that has for many years showed the most generous appreciation of their abilities, have formed an organisation of their own under the title of
>
> THE LONDON SYMPHONY ORCHESTRA
>
> and have obtained the co-operation of a sufficient number of other Instrumentalists to complete an Orchestra which they venture to think is second to none in Europe. . . .
>
> The objects of the London Symphony Orchestra will be similar to those of the Queen's Hall Orchestra—that is to say, it will give Concerts of its own and will be open to accept engagements to play at Concerts given by others. . . .
>
> This new venture will be carried on as in Berlin and in Vienna, where the Members of the Orchestra of the Philharmonic Societies are their own directors.* As such, they elect their own conductors and therefore form something akin to a Musical Republic. . . .

The statement concluded by expressing the belief that the standing of the members of the LSO was such that eminent musicians would not hesitate to appear as conductors, instancing by way of support for this view, that Hans Richter was conducting the first concert. At the end of the rehearsal, Richter gave the new orchestra a watchword. "But gentlemen for you to be successful there must be discipline, artistic discipline." The performance bore him out: discipline was evident, but so were other qualities; brilliance, precision and

* The LSO Directors omitted to mention that in Berlin the players had legally bound themselves to remain inviolably together!

nobility of string tone were those most frequently remarked by contemporaries.

It is important to recall that what the LSO was doing was *new* in Britain. Formally, the players who appeared on the platform were all shareholders in the company which saw that they got there. The company, styled "The London Symphony Orchestra Ltd", became the entrepreneur, the employer of conductors and soloists for its own promotions and the negotiator of terms for its members in concerts sponsored by others. Through their elected Board of Directors, the players took their employment into their own hands and were ultimately responsible for the policies followed. This basic arrangement has ruled ever since (though there have been times when the Directors have had to make compromises which abridged their working independence). Even now (1974) the Principal Conductor only attends Board meetings on request and for specific items on the agenda. Neither does he select or engage soloists. This pattern of relationships has been emulated by other orchestras in Britain, when existing sources of patronage have ceased and players have been driven to reorganise or disband, notably the London Philharmonic in 1939, the Royal Philharmonic Orchestra in 1963 and the Philharmonia, after the withdrawal of Walter Legge in 1966. For Britain then, the LSO pioneered a new form of organisation and, incidentally, nailed a cherished fallacy that musicians are too otherworldly to manage their affairs.

In 1904 it might have seemed that the secessionists had put their worldliness, expressed in the desire for income, before a concern for artistic results. In the event, they were able satisfactorily to combine the two. The new orchestra included the former Leader of the Queen's Hall Orchestra, Arthur Payne, and other principals, that is those who had already established themselves professionally—which in itself guaranteed a certain quality in the various departments. This nucleus had recruited, in addition, former colleagues like Charles Crabbe who had shared the same orchestral background, so that only one-fifth of the LSO had not undergone the training which Wood had given the Queen's Hall Orchestra. A minimum *esprit de corps* was therefore built into the new orchestra from the start. It was sustained by the fact that now the players themselves were responsible for standards of performance through their control of recruitment. If a player was not adequate, they had only themselves to blame; if the inadequacy became general, then the LSO would lose engagements. These were, and are, the consequences of orchestral self-government. It is not surprising that the minutes of the meetings of the Board of Directors over the seventy years of the LSO's existence, consistently reflect problems of discipline and standards.

The Directors deliberately reinforced these advantages by choosing the leading conductors of the day, Richter and Artur Nikisch, who already had a public following and whose authority and insight stamped themselves on the performances. Richter, born at Györ in 1843, stood squarely for the German classics, especially Beethoven and Wagner, for whom he had worked as copyist. Richter became one of the Wagner entourage. He played on the staircase at Triebschen and participated in the first Bayreuth Festival. His first appearance in England was at the Wagner Festival in 1877, gaining him a reputation which was consolidated by frequent visits and which in 1899 prompted the Directors of the Hallé Society to appoint him as chief conductor. In Britain Richter and the German repertoire were synonymous. He was regarded as the indisputable authority on Wagner in all matters of interpretation, particularly tempi. He championed Elgar but his sympathies did not extend to contemporary French compositions. To the petitions organised by Hallé subscribers he bluntly replied, "There is no French music."

Wynn Reeves left no comment on Richter's handling of the LSO, but sketched his experience of Richter at Covent Garden. "He had magnificent poise and mastery of every detail. He never glanced at the score and yet gave every important cue without fuss. He had a gadget on the side of the desk containing a moist sponge into which he meticulously dipped his thumb before turning each page. During the ten seasons I played under him I remember him making only one mistake. In Act III of *Tristan und Isolde*, Isolde's first words on her entry are 'Ich bin's', preceded by two silent beats. For some unaccountable reason on this one occasion Richter omitted to indicate the two silent beats, a thing we were quite unprepared for. The result was utter chaos for some bars . . . if this had happened with any other conductor the orchestra would have jumped to the conclusion that he had omitted to indicate the two beats and would automatically have skipped them, but we had got into the habit of depending absolutely on Richter's infallibility."

Nikisch was Hungarian-born like Richter, but in Szent-miklos, which, unlike Györ, was remote from the orbit of Vienna. His tastes were wider and his career had taken him further afield, as Principal Conductor of the Boston Symphony Orchestra and as visitor to St Petersburg, where he persuaded audiences of the value of the *Pathétique* after the disastrous première under the composer.

Nikisch became identified as the *romantische Klanglyriker* of the time. Wynn Reeves recalled: "The Orchestra gloried in playing for him! He was the only conductor I can remember who was asked by them to continue the rehearsal after time was up. . . . He had a wonderful sense of phrase and also a grasp of a symphony or any great work he was conducting; in fact he gave a revealing performance of practically everything he touched. . . ."

Through his classes in Leipzig, Nikisch influenced a whole generation of conductors, notably, from the British point of view, Albert Coates and Adrian Boult. With Richter, a performance was a massive didactic experience, with Nikisch, an essay in the lyrical and the dramatic. Nikisch summed up this difference: "Richter was a German-Hungarian: I am a Hungarian-Hungarian."

These two were supported by other *chefs d'orchestre* like Wassily Safonoff from Moscow, and Fritz Steinbach from Cologne, whose contemporary fame has not been transmuted into legend in Britain, perhaps because they did not have the same opportunities as Richter and Nikisch to impress themselves on audiences over a comparable period of time. Safonoff, who dispensed with a baton, provided the Russian element in the LSO seasons—a function subsequently associated with Albert Coates. Wynn Reeves recalled that Safonoff "was especially fine in Tchaikovsky. His readings were less mawkish than most conductors and by refraining from wallowing he often got more excitement with his manly approach. . . . He was a religious man, and invariably crossed himself before going on the platform." Steinbach like Richard Strauss had been conductor of the Duke's orchestra at Meiningen, which he brought to London in 1902, but at the time of his association with the LSO he was Director of the Conservatoire in Cologne. Reeves thought him "one of the most inspiring" of the conductors of the Orchestra during his (Reeves') time. "It was generally agreed that he was the greatest in Brahms. It is inconceivable to me to this day that so much of the beauty he revealed in the Brahms symphonies has not been carried on by at least one or other of the conductors who heard him and is now completely lost. His concerts were sold out as soon as announced, and the enthusiasm of the audience knew no bounds."*

The new Directors settled to the task of running their new organisations, the company and the Orchestra. The essentials of orchestral management, before the First World War, were the same as they are now, though the detailed problems are now far more complex and on a larger scale. The Directors had to ensure engagements and to develop and discipline the Orchestra. The players' previous common experience and the choice of conductors made establishing the LSO in the world of music relatively easy. Nevertheless, the LSO had entered a competitive field. Both the manner of its founding and the form of government adopted were a challenge to orthodoxy; it was a "Musical Republic" among Royal Autocracies. At this time and for long afterwards, musicians could only earn fees by appearing in front of an audience (sessions in studios were to come) and the LSO had to share London's patronage with the re-formed Queen's Hall Orchestra, with the New Symphony Orchestra from 1905, and with the Beecham Symphony Orchestra, from 1909. Moreover, the concerts of the Royal Philharmonic Society continued to be the accepted yardstick of musical standards and social prestige alike.

The LSO's qualities were continuously demonstrated under

* Reeves records that Wood attended a Steinbach concert, occupying his usual seat in the Grand Circle at the Queen's Hall, "complete with scores, blue pencil and stop watch; at the end of the Symphony he looked at his stop watch and said to his friend, 'There you are, what did I say? Exactly the same time as I take to the second and yet he fills his halls and mine are half empty.' "

a variety of conductors and could not be denied. Perhaps the most piquant tribute to its artistic success in these formative years was paid by Robert Newman, who, in 1908, offered his Proms to his former employees, in place of the Queen's Hall Orchestra. The offer was refused. Other impresarios and concert societies were gratifyingly anxious to provide the new orchestra with opportunities to perform. By name and origin, the Orchestra was identified with London, where, apart from Queen's Hall, it appeared in the pit at Covent Garden in 1907 under Franz Schalk, of the Vienna Opera, and Nikisch. It was, however, soon in demand for tours of the provinces which at that time enjoyed a more autonomous and identifiable life than they do now. The LSO appeared on this vigorous scene. An assiduous concert-goer, not the least of whose services to literature has been a portrait of the LSO, recalls the impression it made in his native Bradford. "I had been brought up symphonically on the Hallé—a very solid orchestra playing under the even solider Hans Richter and the solidest German masterworks. Then one night some strangers arrived and at once changed the whole atmosphere of St George's Hall . . . charging it with electricity and apparently filling it with colour from the palest purest blue to menacing clouds of indigo and violet sheets of lightning. These sorcerers from the South, for whom nobody had prepared me, were the LSO conducted by Nikisch."[5] J. B. Priestley was, most probably, attending a concert on a tour organised by Percy Harrison, a well-known Birmingham impresario who regularly engaged the Orchestra from its first season onwards for that purpose. "Harrison tours" comprised subscription concerts in the main provincial centres, Birmingham, Glasgow and the Yorkshire manufacturing towns.

It was during these tours that the LSO cemented its relationship with Elgar, then Professor of Music at Birmingham University. His *Introduction and Allegro for Strings* and *Sea Pictures* became stock items in the repertoire. The Orchestra gave the first London performance of his First Symphony under Richter in December 1908 and the première of the Second, on 24th May 1911, under Elgar himself (in a performance which was a comparative failure). Elgar became friendly with several members of the Orchestra, particularly with W. H. Reed, who became Leader in 1908 in succession to Arthur Payne and who was consulted by Elgar in the writing of his violin concerto. The work received its first performance at an LSO concert on 29th May 1911, with Kreisler as soloist and Nikisch conducting. It is a curious comment on the alleged inaccessibility of Elgar to continental Europeans that two out of three of his major symphonic works were launched by two Hungarians and a Viennese!

That season was also memorable in the annals of the Orchestra in that it saw the retirement of Hans Richter from concert life in Britain. His farewell programme, on 10th April 1911, was characteristic: the Overture *Die Meistersinger*, the Third Brandenburg, the Brahms Haydn Variations, *Cockaigne* and Beethoven's Seventh Symphony. The programme notes summed up Richter's quality: "The distinction of Dr Richter's work is the outcome of his high ideals and exceptional abilities." Wynn Reeves' conclusion was, simply, that he "was one of the greatest musicians I have ever played under, with a wonderful insight into whatever he was interpreting . . . he never descended into the slightest hint of effect for effect's sake". Richter took his farewells in Germany and retired to Bayreuth, where he died in 1916.

Richter had been the LSO's principal conductor in that he conducted the majority of its own promotions: his artistic integrity and towering prestige in the profession ensured that his was the dominant influence over the LSO in its opening seasons. For a successor, the Directors turned not to Nikisch, for reasons which have not been minuted, but to Elgar. He accepted, but conducted only six concerts in the 1911–12 season and on the autumn "Harrison tour". Elgar had no discernable influence on repertoire and the question of training did not arise.

Touring by the Orchestra was not confined to the leading cities in the United Kingdom. At the time the LSO was founded, the term "entente cordiale" crept into discussions of relationships between Britain and France—six years earlier they had been anything but "cordiale". The LSO contributed to the cultural aspect of this reversal of feeling and attitudes. In January 1906, the Orchestra accompanied the Leeds Festival Choir to Paris, giving two concerts in the Théâtre du

Châtelet, a house comparable in size and seating capacity with Drury Lane, and then the home of the Colonne Orchestra. The conductors were Stanford, Colonne himself and André Messager, composer of opéra-comique and for many years conductor at Covent Garden. The programmes offered a *mélange* of established music from the two countries plus works from the German repertoire: a Bach motet and the Sanctus from the B minor Mass, Strauss' *Don Juan* and Beethoven's Ninth. Of the English contribution, Parry's *Blest Pair of Sirens* still holds a place, as does, more precariously, Elgar's *King Olaf*. The other works, notably Stanford's *Requiem* and *Irish Symphony*, Cowen's *Scandinavian Symphony*, Mackenzie's music for *The Tempest* are now of interest only to musical antiquarians.

The concerts were packed and the audiences cheered. The attack and precision of the LSO made a great impression. Messager commented that the Orchestra's "most remarkable feature is the astonishing balance and precision of the string instruments"—which was especially in evidence during the adagio in the Ninth Symphony. But though the performances were acclaimed, the concerts did little for the cause of British composers on the Continent. M. D. Calvocoressi, authority on French and Russian music and second in command to Diaghilev at the outset of his career, was also in his lifetime standing unofficial counsellor to the French on English music. He reports that "the modern British works . . . created so unfavourable an impression that thenceforth none of the French conductors who sometimes consulted me on the subject of new works suitable for their programme would consider doing an English work. They simply refused to believe that, on so important an occasion, the organisers could have failed to select the very best and most live of the contemporary British output."[6] The judgement reflected deep cultural differences. In England "enthusiasm and apathy, approval and disapproval rubbed along together without much friction", whereas in France "it was of paramount importance to oppose the influence of musical officialdom . . . the upholder of what was supposed to be the true French musical tradition and official distributor of musical education".[7]

Five years later, Members received notice of an even more ambitious nature, a trip to the United States and Canada, at the nomination of Artur Nikisch. The jet aircraft has made such ventures a comparative commonplace—the LSO will be undertaking its thirteenth US tour in 1974—but in 1912 a journey for an orchestra from London to Wichita, Kansas was an exacting and exciting feat.

The Orchestra left Euston on 28th March 1912 and embarked on the White Star liner *Baltic*. This itself represented a last-minute change since the original bookings had been made on the new White Star liner, the *Titanic*, and had been altered to suit Howard Pew, the American agent in charge of the tour. The Orchestra learned of the disaster to the *Titanic* when they arrived. Wynn Reeves recalls that the *Baltic* was "most comfortable except for a wretched slow roll, which gave me my first and only attack of sea-sickness. After a day or two the orchestra settled down and decided to give a concert; this took place in the first class saloon and in spite of a heavy sea was well attended. Arthur Payne who conducted supported himself with one arm round a pillar, while the other held Miriam Timothy's harp. There were one or two awkward moments—the first oboe making a hurried exit in the middle of a solo."

In America, the schedule did not work out quite as smoothly as expected. Reeves, quite clearly, had not forgotten:

> We soon started on our fantastic tour of thirty-one concerts and thousands of miles to be completed in twenty-one days, living on the trains which were scheduled to arrive at important towns in time for all meals which we had at the best hotels. Needless to say we were at times hopelessly late and had to make do at a small station buffet. We slept thirty-two in each carriage which had most comfortable bunks. We were called each morning by darky attendants with "All up for breakfast". On dressing hurriedly we found occasionally that we had a mile to walk to the hotel. Meanwhile the attendants shut the bunks up having made the beds.
>
> On one particular occasion we received notification that the train was hopelessly late and that we could not get to the hotel at which our breakfast was ordered. I was deputed to represent four of my friends at the coming fight when we arrived at the small station buffet. As soon as the train

> stopped, I streaked across to the buffet seizing all I could see, removing glass covers in ten seconds, by which time the buffet was being mobbed. The proprietor came dashing out from behind the counter brandishing a revolver and shouted, "I refuse to serve another thing until I know who is paying for this." We looked at the counter which by this time was as stripped as if it had been attacked by a swarm of locusts. We assured the proprietor that Mr Fales, the millionaire who was running the tour, would pay, and returned to the train. The loot for my party consisted of four sandwiches, four sticks of chocolate and a bottle of some mineral or other. When we were on time we could go to the hotels, always the best in town and the food was excellent. The only means of getting a bath on the tour was at these hotels and there was always a great many applications.

In this fashion the LSO visited the major centres between the East Coast and the Middle West, and in Canada. The Orchestra took four programmes comprising works by Beethoven (*Egmont* and *Leonore No. 3* Overtures, Fifth Symphony), Tchaikovsky (*Francesca da Rimini*, *Pathétique* Symphony), Wagner (Overtures *Tannhäuser*, *Die Meistersinger*; "Waldweben" from *Siegfried* and "Prelude and Liebestod" from *Tristan und Isolde*), with one piece each from Brahms (First Symphony), Strauss (*Don Juan*), Weber (Overture *Oberon*) and Liszt (Hungarian Rhapsody No. 1). The proportions reflected popular demand. Nikisch had wished to include the *Enigma Variations* and the A flat Symphony of Elgar, but opposition from potential subscribers in the United States kept the programmes to what Nikisch on arrival called "tried and true" compositions. He added that there were few novelties worthy of performance, although he freely admitted that *Der Rosenkavalier* was a most marvellous score, and that Debussy had succeeded in writing most beautiful music even if it were different. Asked about Schoenberg, Nikisch threw up his hands. "If I had to conduct music of that character, I should change my profession."

The first Carnegie Hall concert was not sold out, neither was the appearance at Cincinatti, but on the rest of the tour, including the subsequent appearances in New York, full houses were the rule. Reeves recollected that audiences, as well as the LSO, suffered from the vagaries of touring:

> I think the wonderful patience of the audiences who were kept waiting at times for two or more hours impressed me as much as anything. We were assured that they were quite used to it and accepted it as something to be expected when artists were making long tours. This occurred at Montreal where we were due for an evening concert starting at 8 p.m. We did not reach the town until ten o'clock after which all our paraphernalia had to be taken to the hall—instruments, stands, music, stools, etc., to say nothing of the players. However, there was a fleet of lorries, manned by an army of assistants and the concert actually began at 10.30 p.m. which was a miracle. We were greeted most enthusiastically by an audience who had waited not less than two hours and a half.
>
> Our next concert was at Boston. We had left Montreal about four hours after schedule so of course were very late arriving for an afternoon concert and one of the most important of the tour. We arrived at the station an hour after we were due to begin so we were asked to go straight to the Hall, but we struck saying that we had had nothing to eat since leaving Montreal where we only had a cup of tea and a biscuit. We were all starving and it was preposterous of them to ask us to go straight on; we took the law into our own hands and spread out all over the town looking for a suitable restaurant. Here we did ourselves proud, arriving at the Hall about two hours after we were due to begin. Naturally this made us late for the evening concert and so on. Eventually we arrived back in New York more dead than alive for the last two concerts for which we had special rehearsals. Having a meal in the same hotel as on arrival and looking around at the Orchestra, it was impossible to imagine that these were the same men who had come off the boat to begin the tour.

Conditions for concerts were variable and could be hazardous. At Ottawa, the LSO found itself

> . . . playing in an enormous arena, with a capacity of about 23,000, evidently used to athletic and equestrian com-

> petitions. Half of it was screened off and our half was quite full and everything looked fine. Nikisch came in amid generous enthusiasm, the Duke of Connaught and his Suite leading the applause. Off we went but about the sixth bar we were joined by about a million birds residing in the roof who made such a tremendous din that we could hardly hear ourselves. Nikisch gave one look, took the bit between his teeth and tore through that programme as if the devil were at his heels, much to the joy of at least one of the first violins who loathed slow movements, greeting each one with a growling "Another b***** Adagio."

More sober episodes which Members recalled were official receptions by President Taft in the White House and by the Governor General in Ottawa. The LSO returned on the Dutch vessel *Potsdam*—making a precautionary detour after the *Titanic* disaster. The Orchestra were the only passengers, and relaxed. Wynn Reeves writes:

> The voyage lasted about twelve days. The weather was lovely and my friend Kinsey and I played chess practically all day, up in the prow of the boat. As we disembarked at Southampton, the ship's band played a March which Charles Woodhouse, our principal second violin, had composed and orchestrated especially for them. We heard the March until the boat was almost out of sight.

The final press comments stressed the attributes of the Orchestra which had impressed themselves on audiences throughout the tour: "vigour, force and temperamental impetuousness", muscular attack, the bigness of the LSO's tone, the climactic quality of its playing and shading of dynamics in the Romantic repertoire it played. Nikisch always said that the tone of the LSO remained in his head long after the concert was over. The North American tour must have given him much to enjoy in retrospect.

On its return from the USA, the Orchestra took part—one wonders with what undisclosed feelings—in the memorial concert for the victims of the *Titanic* disaster. The LSO was one of the seven orchestras in the Albert Hall which, totalling over five hundred musicians, played the solemn music commemorating the dead.

The conductors included Elgar, Wood, Beecham, Landon Ronald and Willem Mengelberg, of the Concertgebouw in Amsterdam, who had appeared with the LSO for the first time the previous February. He conducted the LSO later the following month, in June 1912, proving himself "a superb dictator, yet sympathetic and sensitive to a degree". It was to be another seventeen years before the Orchestra was to experience the full impact of these qualities and Mengelberg's superlative gifts as a trainer of orchestras.

At this time, in consequence of the epoch-making tour, the LSO went into a new venture—sound recording. The technique had been invented in the 1880s and had already gone through its first basic development from recording on cylinders to recording on discs. The former, which at the time was superior in quality of sound, remained for many years the favoured technique for commercial applications, in the form of dictation machines. For music the disc became standard, largely because multiple copies could easily be taken from one master. By 1912, the machine on which the discs were played, the gramophone, had ceased to be a curiosity and had become a serious economic proposition. The Gramophone Company—significantly The Gramophone and Typewriter Company at the outset—was founded at Hayes, Middlesex, in 1898. It was for this organisation that Nikisch and the Orchestra began to make recordings of items played on the American tour—the *Egmont* Overture and the conclusion of the Liszt Rhapsody. These titles were made using the acoustic techniques which were relied upon until 1925. Fred Gaisberg, the Chief Recorder of the Gramophone Company who supervised the session, recalled "virtuoso playing which was unique at that time", but the discs themselves scarcely convey that quality.

For musicians of the time, sound recording was merely an adjunct to their main work, though a few sensed the use of records as a form of publicity. Certainly, the LSO Directors would have been sceptical or astonished to be informed that their successors would compete to get into a recording studio and that the policies of record companies would come to have a dominant influence on many of the decisions they would have to take.

III

PUTTING THE LSO on the map of the concert world involved the Directors in the kind of activity they knew from experience: setting up and running the London Symphony Orchestra Ltd presented problems of a different order. The company had two principal objectives set out in the Memorandum of Association of 16th February 1905:

a. To carry on as a Joint Stock Company, Limited, the business of Orchestral Musicians in combination as an Orchestra under the title of "The London Symphony Orchestra" for the purpose of giving Symphony and other Concerts of high class music and of accepting and fulfilling engagements to perform at Concerts, Recitals, At Homes and other occasions and functions of every description where their services are desired.

b. To carry on either in connection with the business aforesaid, or as distinct and separate businesses, the business or businesses of Orchestral Musicians, Composers, Producers and Performers of all kinds of music, contractors for and providers of Musical Conductors and Directors, bands and musicians (vocal and instrumental) and public entertainers of all kinds, concert and musical agents, theatrical agents, theatre, music hall and concert room proprietors and lessees, box office proprietors and agents, publishers of musical dramatic and operatic works, foreign music importers, librarians, music engravers and printers, music rulers and copyists, manufacturers, repairers, and sellers of musical instruments of all kinds and any other business or businesses in connection with the above mentioned businesses customarily or usually carried on in connection therewith, or naturally incident thereto, or which may seem to the Company capable of being conveniently carried on in connection with the above or calculated directly or indirectly to enhance the value of or render more profitable any of the Company's property or undertaking.

In this comprehensive manner, the Directors claimed the widest possible options in the profession of music.

Other clauses follow from these two, setting out the right of the Company to enter into agreements, acquire and run property, raise funds and so on. The initial capital was established at £1,000 divided into 1,000 shares at £1 each: the right and obligation to purchase them was limited to "performing Members of the LSO" (curiously, such a member was not defined), each of whom was allotted ten shares. The Board of Directors comprised the four "Originators of the Orchestra", who were permanent, together with Ellis Roberts (violin), James Breeden (violin), E. F. James (bassoon), J. E. Hambleton (cello), and Charles Winterbottom (double bass). T. R. Busby was nominated Secretary. All but the Originators were required to retire at each AGM and present themselves for re-election in accordance with a stipulated procedure. The Directors were charged with the management of the Company, having "in particular . . . power to frame and enforce such rules and regulations as may seem to them reasonably necessary for the good government of the LSO and for the maintenance of the high standard of efficiency and excellence of performance which it has hitherto exhibited". Such rules had, however, to be open to discussion and amendment or rescission at any General Meeting of the Company.

In this way, the players set up the machinery for governing themselves and controlling the conditions of their employment. LSO Ltd became a public company whose shareholders were (and are) fully informed of the nature of its day-to-day activities and were in a position to make their presence felt. However, as experience was to show, this did not end the resentments and frustrations previously blamed on Newman and Wood; it merely changed their focus. At the same time, self-government extended the players' options. Under the previous regime, a player could either accept the conditions laid down by the management, or resign. Now, he had a voice in how the conditions were managed and resignation was the last resort. In between acceptance and resignation, there was much room for debate, seeking to influence opinion, finding support among like-minded colleagues—in a word, for politics. These processes could go on, not only as between the Members and the Board of Directors but within the Board itself, since its functions were exercised by a group of "not less than five or more than nine". So the LSO (and any self-governing orchestra) has had two lines of fracture built into its structure—one *between* the Directors and the Members, the other *within* the Board of Directors, whose divisions may be reflected among the Members.

This is as true in 1974 as it was in 1904. The more extreme forms of political behaviour are inhibited by the fact that both Board and Members of the Company are colleagues in the Orchestra and as such enjoy formal equality as artists. This feature makes the LSO Ltd unlike other public companies, which are necessarily organised hierarchically and where the rank and file do not enjoy equality with the Board of Directors. During the Orchestra's history, the sense of corporate identity has, on the whole, contained the natural divergence of views and prevented it from hardening into faction. But there have been exceptions to this rule and their effect has been devastating!*

The policy of the Company was to use its own promotions, predominantly at the Queen's Hall, to advertise the Orchestra's merits to concert societies and impresarios. To ensure that opportunities were created or followed up expeditiously, the Directors engaged the services of an agent, L. G. Sharpe, whose apprenticeship to the world of international celebrities had been served as a mate on windjammers. His prize artist was Paderewski. The policy of giving concerts to attract engagements drove the Directors to relying on guest conductors, as much as their explicit desire to escape from the Wood–Newman pattern on artistic grounds, since famous visitors were more likely to draw a capacity audience. This expectation was not always borne out. Richter once asked Tom Busby, in an interval, "What is the house like?"; "Not good, Doctor"; Richter, "Halve my fee".

* See below, pp. 77–81; 147–52; 176–9.

The LSO's own promotions were used to provide general finance for the Orchestra. Members customarily received no fee for their services, but relied on the success of the Orchestra to bring them a return through its engagements.

At the end of the Company's first year, the Chairman, at the General Meeting, reported that the progress of the LSO had been "quite phenomenal, not only from an artistic point of view but financially. The great name which the Orchestra had acquired . . . was a very valuable asset to the Company." The first year's activity, comprising fifty concerts, had enabled the Company to cover salaries totalling £3,000 and left £520 in hand. In the mild euphoria of the moment Ellis Roberts had slightly understated the relationship: the Orchestra was not *a* very valuable but *the* most valuable asset to the Company, in that if the Orchestra failed to attract the public, the Company would be necessarily forced out of the business for which it was set up. This remains the case.

The speed of the success was also important: it had been axiomatic from the outset that Members would not expect fees for the Company's own promotions—indeed, if they could not appear, the cost of a deputy would result in their subsidising these occasions—but already, in 1906, Richter was invited to conduct six concerts in the next season, and Members were to be guaranteed payment for four. This bred self-confidence and cohesion in the ranks of the players.

During the first decade or so, evidence of the continuing success of the venture was provided not only by the plaudits of audiences or the figures in the annual balance sheets but also in the gratifying list of applications from composers to have their works performed or at least run through at a general rehearsal; from conductors, including Dan Godfrey, who conducted the first permanent orchestra at Bournemouth; and from soloists, who offered fees to appear with the LSO (and were surprised when they were refused; this high-minded policy had to be abandoned, subsequently). Perhaps the most subtle indication of all was the suggestion by the press-cutting agency that the Orchestra might wish to raise its subscription.

To judge by the frequency of references in the Minutes, discipline was the most pressing problem for the management, particularly in regard to unpunctuality and failure to provide a deputy, lapses which evoked admonitions and fines. However, early in the Orchestra's career, the Directors came sharply up against the limits to their authority. The Board Minutes for 29th June 1906 record that Mr Caldwell (trumpet) "having been found guilty of misconduct on the concert platform", it was agreed that a letter be written him, that his services in connection with the London Symphony Orchestra would no longer be required, and that the money he had paid to take up shares as a Member would be refunded in due course. Within a fortnight, the Directors were meeting again to consider an agenda with only one item, namely a letter from Mr Caldwell's solicitors, in consequence of which the Directors promptly decided to withdraw their letter and issue the share certificates. The lesson was unmistakable: players could be disciplined; shareholders could not. Mr Caldwell continued to appear on public platforms with the Orchestra. It was by no means the last occasion on which relationships between the Board and the Members were (temporarily) conducted via their respective solicitors.

The LSO, from its inception, sought *quality*. The Members had, after all, left the Queen's Hall, in part, because they considered that Henry Wood would never live up to their artistic expectations. There were no native-born conductors in Britain whose standing in the profession approximated that of Richter, Nikisch and Steinbach. Hence, the aim of establishing an elite orchestra committed the Directors to conductors who had established themselves in the great school of Continental music. These set the style of the LSO's promotions. In adopting this policy, the Directors were also assuring themselves a public; they were not in a position to lose too much money on composers or conductors in whom they believed but the public did not. The public at the time was still vastly impressed by foreignness and over-inclined to consider a foreign passport a guarantee of quality.

But among musicians music has always been a more truly international profession than the public has sometimes been willing to allow and the Directors did not ignore emerging talent, even among their own countrymen.

In 1908, the LSO began its long and happily still continuing association with Leopold Stokowski, at that time organist of

St Bartholomew's, New York. His antecedents were firmly established in London and Oxford. The programme, which Stokowski repeated with the Orchestra sixty years later, comprised the Overture to *Die Meistersinger*, Debussy's *Prélude à l'après midi d'un faune*, the Violin Concerto by Glazounov, Brahms' First Symphony, and Tchaikovsky's *Marche Slave*. In the audience was Josef Szigeti, who, writing in 1949, still remembered "the already then Stokowskian sound of the London Orchestra in the concluding number . . . and the feline suppleness of the orchestral support that the young conductor gave to Zimbalist's playing of Glazounov's Concerto, then still a comparative novelty."[1] (Over sixty years later, the piece had passed through the cycle from novelty to rarity. Conductor and Orchestra were hard put to it in 1972 to find a violinist who could at short notice stand in for the soloist Silvia Marcovici at rehearsal.)

The same season saw the debut of another young conductor under LSO auspices, Thomas Beecham, then twenty-nine, who was on the eve of his triumphs at Covent Garden but who had already marked out those styles of music which remained his own. He conducted the LSO in part of a concert: *Carnaval Romain* and Holbrooke's prelude *Dylan*.

In the next season, 1909–10, the LSO "discovered" Kussewitzky (as he then transliterated his name), whose London debut included a Concerto for Orchestra by C. P. E. Bach, arranged for large orchestra by Maximilian Steinberg. This remained a characteristic Koussevitsky piece, when in later years he entered on his long association with the Boston Symphony Orchestra. In 1910, in the Queen's Hall, the rest of his programme comprised Beethoven, the *Egmont* Overture and Eighth Symphony, and Scriabin's *Poème de l'Extase*, a work with which, through the influence of other conductors from Russia such as Wassily Safonoff and Albert Coates, the LSO was to be identified as long as the Scriabin vogue lasted. In 1911, the Directors continued their policy by encouraging Hamilton Harty to conduct the Orchestra in his tone poem *With the Wild Geese*.

Koussevitsky and Stokowski typify those many conductors in the history of the LSO with whom it has given outstanding concerts, from its earliest days to the present. This is, after all, fulfilling one of the Orchestra's specific aims at its foundation. Beecham and Harty not only directed remarkable concerts but permanently affected the course of the Orchestra's development, as will be seen. In this respect, they were joined by another young conductor who emerged in the decade before the First World War, Willem Mengelberg.

In the first decade of its existence, the programmes in the LSO's own promotions were heavily weighted in favour of the German masters—Bach (today conspicuously absent), Beethoven, Weber, Brahms, Schumann, Wagner and Richard Strauss, whose tone poems were the *dernier cri* of orthodox musical taste. Otherwise, only Tchaikovsky's works were performed regularly, on a scale comparable with today, but then mainly the last three of the symphonies and *Francesca da Rimini*. Liszt and Saint-Saëns got more of a showing than they do at present, Mendelssohn, far less, being represented by two overtures and some piano pieces. Dvořák received similar casual treatment: the New World Symphony was performed only twice in ten years. Haydn and Mozart were featured hardly at all, except for the latter's G minor Symphony. The programme chosen to celebrate the 150th anniversary of Mozart's birth has a curious look:

28th January 1906

Overture . . . La Clemenza di Tito	Mozart
Concerto No. 17, in E♭, for two Pianos and Orchestra (No. 10 B & H New Edition)	Mozart
Deutsche Tänze	Mozart
Symphony No. 38 in D (Köchel No. 504) (The Prague Symphony—3 Movements)	Mozart
Overture . . . Olympia	Spontini

Solo Pianofortes—The Misses Mathilde and Adele Verne.
Conductor—Sir Charles Villiers Stanford.

These items would hardly be acceptable today for such an occasion. The change itself is a tribute to the educative work begun at this time by Stanford—he resurrected *Così fan tutte*—and by Thomas Beecham, first with the New Symphony Orchestra, founded at the end of 1905 and consciously modelled on the LSO, and then with the eponymous orchestra which Beecham himself set up in 1909.

The LSO adopted Elgar, as composer and conductor, giving concerts exclusively devoted to his works or with only one other item. Other native composers were thinly represented, though Holbrooke as well as Harty conducted his own compositions. This was, it seems, as much as any other concert-giving organisation was doing on behalf of native talent; it was significant that Vaughan Williams sent his *London Symphony* to Fritz Busch in Dresden for possible performance. Individual programmes contained more items than is now customary, but not all were inordinately long by present-day standards. In December 1904, Fritz Steinbach conducted a concert comprising *Leonore No. 2*, the Third Brandenburg Concerto, Beethoven's Violin Concerto, and Brahms' Fourth Symphony. Similarly, in March 1906 Edouard Colonne played *Carnaval Romain*, Schumann's *Manfred* music, the Overture and Venusberg music from *Tannhäuser* and Tchaikovsky's Fourth. Other attempts at programme-building had results which now seem rather odd. In March 1906, Richter offered *four* overtures, the Third Brandenburg and *Also sprach Zarathustra*, while Mackenzie's programme on 8th April in the same year would have had a modern audience looking exhaustedly for the exit:

Overture . . . *The Flying Dutchman*	Wagner
Concerto No. 1 in E♭ for Piano and Orchestra	Liszt
Symphony No. 5	Beethoven
Scherzo from Concerto No. 4, for Piano and Orchestra	Litolff
Benedictus	Mackenzie
Suite Venetienne	Reed

The trend to the gargantuan was especially evident at festivals and choral concerts. In October 1912, over four consecutive days, the Orchestra played the whole of *Der Ring des Nibelungen*, plus *Elijah* (with an obbligato of revolving noises from the grave in Haus Wahnfried?), Mendelssohn's uncompleted opera *Die Lorelei* and Saint-Saëns' *Samson and Delilah*; purely orchestral items in the same programmes included Beethoven's Concerto in D, with Kreisler, and Chopin's in F minor, with

Paderewski, Schubert's Unfinished Symphony, and sundry other pieces. The next October, in Leeds, the audience assembled at 11 o'clock in the morning to hear the opening programme of the festival. It included *Leonore No. 3* and *The Dream of Gerontius* before the interval, and afterwards came Parry's *Ode to Music* and Brahms' *Alto Rhapsody* and Third Symphony. The conductor was Elgar. In the same evening, Nikisch took over in a programme of Weber and Tchaikovsky. The highlight of the four-day festival was, perhaps, the Thursday morning, when the concert *opened* with the Verdi *Requiem* and after some less weighty numbers concluded with the Seventh Symphony of Beethoven. Wynn Reeves recalled the Verdi as having been "one of the three greatest musical events" of his life.

In October 1913, the Minutes record the first major discussion about personnel policy, as distinct from assessing the peccadilloes of individuals. The Board agreed unanimously that certain players were to be asked to resign their membership on grounds of incompetence. The Directors also resolved to write to Mr Gomez asking him in the interests of the Orchestra to be more careful of his intonation in future. The horn section was reconstructed, since Borsdorf had suffered from severe pyorrhoea, necessitating the extraction of all his teeth. Tom Busby achieved his ambition of becoming first horn, Borsdorf became second, and Vander Meerschen third. The Directors paid their unfortunate colleague generous, but merited, tribute: "It was the unanimous wish of the Board that the great and valuable services rendered by Mr Borsdorf as Principal Horn since the inception of the Orchestra should as a lasting record be entered upon the Minutes of the Company, at the same time the Board desired to record their personal thanks for his artistic services during the past 10 years, with regret that Nature had deprived him of a position so long and honourably held."

The Directors were jealous of the LSO's position as the elite orchestra in the capital city of a world empire. The claim rested on sheer orchestral quality and on the series of international conductors the LSO secured, season after season. Their concern for this aspect of life became evident when Nikisch announced he was going to conduct the Queen's Hall

Orchestra, to oblige Miss Matilde Verne, "a very old friend". The Directors reminded Nikisch that their relation with him derived from a contract for his services exclusively. Nikisch argued that the contract had never been properly honoured by the Directors—who hastily drafted a new one, at 100 guineas a concert. Fritz Steinbach was also put under exclusive contract.

There were, however, financial limits to the Directors' ambitions. In 1913, Casals was rejected, "because of the exorbitant fee asked"; conversely, they wrangled with the agents Schulz-Curtius and Powell in order to increase the size of the orchestra required at a Hubermann concert, and therefore the return to LSO Ltd. Schulz-Curtius was the representative of Bayreuth in Britain. His partner, Lionel Powell, a former violinist, specialised in organising celebrity tours in which Szigeti, Busoni, Melba and John McCormack performed in the same concert! This is evidence of Powell's Lucullan attitude towards music: if it was good, it was worth a risk—a philosophy easier in the more privately open-handed society of Edwardian Britain. Powell's attitude points also to the practice of the trade at the time. Concert-promotion was much more *ad hoc* than it is now. Facilities could be booked relatively easily and waiting periods were weeks, not years. Concerts and operas were organised in definite seasons and reached their climax in the London season from May to July, when musicians were in demand for every kind of function, from grand opera to debutantes' balls. It was an atmosphere in which risks could be taken and losses recouped relatively easily. It did not last.

In July 1914, the Directors congratulated themselves on the successes of the season just closing, particularly the Harrison Tour, and busied themselves with the minutiae of concert promotion. Safonoff and Henri Verbrugghen from Belgium were engaged for the next season; they were to be joined by Nikisch, Steinbach and Emil Mlynarski, from Warsaw. Artur Rubinstein's request for travelling expenses totalling £15 was accepted. The Board noted with regret the death of Mrs Fales, wife of the sponsor of the LSO tour in 1912, and discussed the possibility of returning to the United States, and a possible tour of Australia, both in 1916. This would have been the first round-the-world tour of the LSO. On domestic matters, the

Directors considered what to do about a violinist "whose condition, through drink" at a lucrative private engagement "had rendered him quite incapable of performing his duties on the violin" (his resignation was called for). The Board also debated the suitability of presenting "a loving cup to Professor Artur Nikisch, in recognition of his valuable artistic services to the Orchestra during the past ten years". The Directors had no inkling that the intended recipient had already conducted his last concert with the LSO—as had his colleague under exclusive contract, Fritz Steinbach—and that their tour plans would be totally frustrated.

At the beginning of the next month, August 1914, old Europe died. The outbreak of war involving Germany and Austria-Hungary against Russia, France, Belgium and the United Kingdom fractured its artistic unity. The natural international sympathies of artists were dammed up within alliances, and compositions began to be judged in terms of non-musical values. In Britain, the Edwardian era came to an end, and with it the economic prosperity of the public which supported concert life. Funds found other, more pressing outlets than music, and although after the war there remained sufficient sources to promote some activity, a return to the status quo was impossible. Privately funded music in Britain never re-established itself on the same scale of prodigality.

The first LSO casualty was Borsdorf. On 4th August 1914 the LSO was returning from Ireland. At their meeting in London, the Directors were handed a "round robin" from the players complaining that the presence of Borsdorf, as a German by birth, was not in the LSO's interest and calling for his resignation. Borsdorf—the outstanding hornist of his generation, a Founder Member whose "great and valuable services" had been so recently minuted by the Board as "a lasting record"—went.

IV

In August 1914, the easy-going cosmopolitanism of musical life broke down. Though Borsdorf was German by origin he was a naturalised British subject. But those of his compatriots by birth who had retained their nationality were obliged to report for military service, failing which they would be posted as "deserters" in Germany and would become "enemy aliens" in Britain. Their departure left vacancies for British players, who remained untouched by any form of conscription until 1916.

The war also affected programmes. The nationalist reaction which suddenly found in Nietzsche the source of all wickedness also traced the origins of the conflict to Wagner. No one enquired why the sinister elements in Wagner should have been hidden from audiences in Covent Garden and elsewhere for so long, any more than the critics paid attention to the fiercely anti-Prussian diatribes of Nietzsche. All manifestations of "German" culture became anathema, temporarily, though a glance at the programmes of concerts actually given at the time confirms that such indisputably German figures as Bach, Beethoven and Brahms were exempt. Performances of their works continued after 4th August, as before. Perhaps promoters were consciously or unconsciously influenced by Sir Henry Coward, the distinguished choral conductor, who merely wanted to bar works composed after 1870! This criterion was reasonable, if the enemy were identified as the spirit of Imperial Germany. It would, however, have admitted *Das Rheingold*, *Die Walküre* and the first version of *Siegfried* and excluded all the symphonies of Brahms and three of his four concerti—presumably not quite the consequence Sir Henry intended. The attempt arbitrarily to divide the dominant European tradition in music in terms of politicised aesthetics was abandoned and Wagner and, to a lesser extent, Strauss resumed their place in concert and opera performances.

The demands of patriotism did, however, create an awareness of native composers and performers, apart from Elgar, on a scale hitherto absent. The promotion of British music began. (Beecham emerged from one such concert, characteristically observing that he had just helped to ensure the continued dominance of German music in Britain.) Additionally, in an atmosphere in which it was widely thought that the war would be over by Christmas or at least could not conceivably be prolonged, because of the unprecedented forces engaged, subscriptions to concerts became a means of identifying the patron with the national effort. In consequence, the *immediate* effect of the war on concert life was to alter some of the personnel and some of the programmes: otherwise it was negligible.

The LSO pressed on with its regular series of concerts. Safonoff and Verbrugghen (both "allies") took over the performances for which Nikisch and Steinbach had been engaged. The rest of the series fell to Mlynarski, from Warsaw, and Beecham. The Directors also considered Toscanini, Harty and Albert Coates. They record nothing further about Toscanini. Coates could not travel from Russia and Harty was serving in the Royal Navy. Beecham's international ventures at Covent Garden and Drury Lane were closed for the duration (nearly twenty years as it happened). He turned his energies to music life in general and underwrote a large proportion of it financially. During the four war years the Royal Philharmonic Society, the Hallé Society and opera all benefited from Beecham's purse and attention. So did the LSO.

The Orchestra's initial impetus could not be sustained. It achieved an outstanding and repeated success in introducing Elgar's *Carillon*—a brilliant *pièce d'occasion*, in the form of a setting of Emile Cammaerts' poem "Chantons! Belges, Chantons", for speaker and orchestra. *Carillon* was very much in vogue during the war years. Afterwards performances disappeared from the programme, with the gradual subsiding of the emotions that ensured its popularity. The Orchestra's own promotions concentrated on Beethoven and Brahms.

For Beecham, the war offered a chance to introduce to audiences his own particular non-Teutonic enthusiasms, demonstrated in his two programmes for the LSO in 1915: Bizet's Overture *Patrie*, Delius' Piano Concerto (with Percy

Grainger as soloist) and Mozart's in C minor, K.491, Lalo's *Symphony in G minor* and works by César Franck.

The association with Beecham burgeoned into his becoming the main influence on the Orchestra. On 6th April 1915 the Directors decided unanimously to offer him the position of Principal Conductor of the Orchestra from next season. The title never appeared on programmes, but for the next two seasons Beecham was as much Principal Conductor as subsequent title-holders of the office, Coates, Harty or Krips. His task was essentially the same as theirs—training and repertoire, but uniquely among LSO Principal Conductors, he also assumed financial responsibility. The Directors' decision was timely. The struggle in Flanders turned into a bitter war of attrition, which could only be won by pitting not army against army but nation against nation. Finance was required for grimmer purposes and the patronage of music began to fade. The effect was sharply felt by the LSO in the autumn of 1915, at the beginning of the season.

On 4th October, the Directors resolved that "if there were no success with the first four concerts, the whole scheme was to be abandoned". It was, in fact, not abandoned, but uncertainty kept the question open. In February 1916 an Extraordinary General Meeting weighed the future. The motion before it comprehensively summed up the situation of the Orchestra and Company, that "owing to the losses sustained by the Company and in view of the fact that such expensive advertisement is no longer necessary owing to there being no private Orchestral engagements and with a view to averting the strain on the Company in the matter of paying for deputies, and in view also of the stringent need for economy, this Meeting is of the opinion that our present series of symphony concerts should be curtailed and the Company's expenses reduced accordingly."

The discussion was "of considerable length". The Secretary disclosed that he had interviewed Sir Thomas Beecham that morning and that Sir Thomas had agreed to accept all responsibility for the expenses of the remaining concerts this season and, moreover, had presented the Orchestra with £100 as a gift. These subventions augmented by funds from Emil Mlynarski and some outside engagements enabled the LSO to keep going.

Apart from necessarily unrepeatable engagements such as playing in the pit of Drury Lane Theatre for the Shakespeare

Tercentenary Celebrations in 1916, the wartime work of the LSO concentrated on engagements for charities or appeals and a series of concerts in London. The series took place at the Palladium on Sunday afternoons under the auspices of the National Sunday League. The League had been set up originally to mitigate the rigours of the Victorian Sabbath. Its early concerts had to be "sacred" but they nevertheless ran into protest! A programme in which Szigeti took part was played against the brazen opposition of a Salvation Army band outside.[1] The League persisted and expanded its patronage into regular symphony concerts. Its connection with the LSO began in September 1915, when the two managements agreed on terms for the LSO to appear at the Palladium: 45 per cent to the League, 55 per cent to the LSO subject to a minimum guarantee. The proposition did not at first attract more than about half the Members but the success of the venture turned the concerts into a full LSO occasion. Harty renewed his connections with the Orchestra, when his services were not required by the Admiralty for minesweeping in the North Sea. Then Julian Clifford took over. The programmes reverted to a style reminiscent of the early Newman–Wood Proms: overtures, selections, single movements from concerti, operatic arias and songs. *Carillon* inevitably appeared, as did, rather more surprisingly, the garden scene from Gounod's *Faust*; "young Solomon, the pianist" played at the opening concert.

The LSO participated in two major festivals, both at the Queen's Hall. In April 1915 the Directors promoted concerts devoted to Bach, Beethoven and Brahms. The programmes indicate an apparent determination to cram as many major works as possible into alternate afternoons and evenings during the week. The main items were the B minor Mass, the *Missa Solemnis*, the Brahms *Requiem* and the Ninth Symphony (these two works in the same programme). One concert was devoted to various aspects of *Fidelio*, the scena "Abscheulicher!", and all four overtures written for the piece. The Fifth Concerto and the Fifth Symphony completed the programme.

During the next month, Beecham and Mlynarski engaged the Orchestra and the London Choral Society to present "the best and most characteristic music" of the preceding decade.

Under this rubric, Delius' *Sea Drift* and Piano Concerto, Elgar's *Falstaff*, Vaughan Williams' *In the Fen Country*, Bantock's *Fifine at the Fair* and Harty's *With the Wild Geese* were played, all works which are now somewhat tangential to the main repertoire but which still can be heard. Cyril Scott played in the première of his own Piano Concerto. Stanford, Ethel Smythe, Holbrooke and Percy Grainger contributed works which have disappeared from public concerts.

Touring continued in wartime. Percy Harrison decided in August 1914 to go on with his usual tours "as he considered the wholesale cancelling of engagements a great hardship to the musical profession". He did, however, cut the fees offered by half. The Board bargained, reminding Harrison that at that rate, he could only have a smaller orchestra. Both sides compromised on a fee for seventy-two players—a number considered adequate to perform the *Pathétique* Symphony which was much in demand among Harrison's subscribers. The spring tours took place in 1915 and 1916.

Overseas tours were also mooted. Safonoff invited the Orchestra to tour Norway and Russia—but the high wartime rates of shipping insurance ruled out the enterprise. Verbrugghen, who had just been introduced to London by the LSO, wanted in return to introduce the LSO to Australia. The scheme, apparently, was backed by the Australian Government, but it disappears from the record. A second, more extensive visit to Canada than was possible in 1912 appeared likely for 1916, but the enthusiasm of subscribers in Toronto and Montreal was not matched by that of other cities which would have been necessary to make the tour financially secure. The LSO could do nothing for British prestige abroad or for its own *esprit de corps*.

The 1914–15 season was the last in which the Orchestra could follow the patterns of activity established since the beginning. From 1915 onwards, its way of life succumbed to the circumstances of the war; subscriptions dried up; the Company acquired an overdraft. The national demands on manpower began to affect the ensemble and increase the calls on deputies, for whose fees the Company, as a wartime measure, assumed responsibility. In February 1916 another Extraordinary General Meeting decided that the current season

Above: Artur Nikisch

Left: Hans Richter

The four originating members: (*l. to r.*) Henri Vander Meerschen, Adolf Borsdorf, Tom Busby, John Solomon

The LSO at rehearsal under Weingartner
in the Queen's Hall, 1922

Sir Hamilton Harty

EXIT

Elgar, Albert Coates, Henri Vander Meerschen at the Three Choirs Festival in the 1920s

should be completed but reserved judgement as to the future. The Board tried to raise a guarantee fund but met with no success. The Directors' decision to continue assumed Beecham's support—but he was also responsible financially for the Hallé Society, the Royal Philharmonic Society and his own opera company, and the strain began to tell. In October 1916, his father died; this dragged in tangled problems of the Covent Garden estate and called in question Beecham's own financial resources. He spent most of the next years battling with claimants and creditors and ill health. The immediate consequence was, however, that he could not continue to support the LSO. By that time the season was under way but it comprised only six LSO promotions, divided between Beecham, Safonoff and Harty, in place of Mlynarski who could not get to London. The programmes included an all-Beethoven concert (with Moiseiwitsch in the "Emperor" Concerto), the Elgar Violin Concerto, with Albert Sammons, the closing scene from *Götterdämmerung* and Bantock's *Hebridean Symphony*. The last piece was played on 19th March 1917; it was the first London performance of the work and the last appearance of the LSO. At this stage over half the Orchestra were deputies, and audience attendances were "deplorable". The combination suggested to the Directors that they abandon promoting concerts altogether. In September 1917, they resolved unanimously "that no Symphony Concerts be given until the termination of the War". The Board's decision marked the end of thirteen years' artistic enterprise. It did not mean that the Orchestra would have to disband; there were adequate calls on its services, even when awash with deputies, to provide it with an income. But the series of concerts under internationally renowned conductors of its own choosing, on which its prestige and *amour propre* and therefore its character rested, disappeared from the concert scene. For Britain the darkest days of the war were still to come and the strategists were thinking in terms of campaigning into 1919.

After September 1917, the LSO Board still met to transact business but it was only to consider engagements. The Sunday League concerts went on—their success allowed the Directors to renegotiate terms: the LSO was to receive 65 per cent of the gross receipts up to £130 and divide the rest equally with the Sunday League. In November a second series of concerts was put to the Directors by "a Mr A. C. Boult, who was anxious to give some Sunday concerts either at Queen's Hall or at the Alhambra Theatre; . . . as his abilities were unknown he gave as referees the Liverpool Philharmonic Society." The "Sunday concerts" were in the event given on Mondays, with rehearsals the day before. Four programmes introduced Boult to the LSO and to London. They comprised twenty-eight items of which the most important from the standpoint of posterity was, perhaps, Vaughan Williams' *A London Symphony*, which was given twice. Holst, Bax, Butterworth, John Ireland and Hamilton Harty also represented the unestablished British composers. Elgar's *In the South* and Parry's *Symphonic Variations* stood for those who had achieved respectability. The rest of the programmes included Beethoven's Fifth Symphony, Mozart's then seldom-performed Concerto for Flute and Harp, the Third Brandenburg Concerto and Chausson's *Chanson Perpétuelle*. After attending all four concerts, no one could remain unacquainted with the conductor's range, but air raids and alerts kept audiences small, and it was touch-and-go whether the stage or the auditorium would contain the more people.

The Orchestra was highly impressed with Boult, so much so that, although he was a newcomer to London, the Directors considered him to conduct "at least the first six concerts" of the next Palladium season. Harty, however, thought otherwise. He also raised difficulties for the Directors by stipulating that he be consulted on programmes. After some haggling, the Board admitted him to its monthly programme discussions and persuaded Harty to drop his opposition to sharing the concerts with another conductor. Accordingly, Boult was invited to conduct some of the later concerts in the 1918–19 season. He recalls that "the rehearsal . . . consisted of three minutes' discussion on repeats just before the curtain rose. . . . We gave the first post-war performances of the three early Strauss tone poems, which owing to the reluctance to collect performing fees for enemies, had been totally neglected during the war. The nature of the performance, after five years of neglect, will be better imagined than described." Nevertheless, the Palladium concerts enabled the LSO to survive in some shape, and to make enough money to start its postwar career without an overdraft.

V

THE END OF the war was widely thought to allow a return to "business as usual". In the national context, the thought was illusory and was soon proved so. The economic damage of the First World War had scarcely been repaired when Britain was hit by the slump. In the arts, the notion that nothing essentially had changed since 1914 could, for a while, be more plausibly held. There were still private funds available for music, and opera ventures and concert societies started up again.

The LSO had a position to regain. The ensemble of Richter and Nikisch had broken up, even though a core of pre-war personnel was reassembled. The immediate task was to train the players back to their former standards as an orchestra and thereby attract public attention and support. But who was to take the task in hand? It was thought that the residual passions from the war years ruled out a conductor from former enemy states, who might well train the Orchestra but would be unacceptable to the public. Safonoff had died, in 1918. Mengelberg was firmly committed to the Concertgebouw and to New York. There was no obvious available figure from France. At home, Harty, on Beecham's recommendation, had gone to the Hallé. Beecham himself had temporarily retired from public music, caught up in prolonged legal proceedings occasioned by the liquidation of the Covent Garden estate. At the end of 1919, however, politics made available a man of the right qualities in the person of Albert Coates.

Coates, born in St Petersburg of British parents, had studied in Leipzig with Nikisch—an important recommendation to the Directors. After his student days, he had begun a career as opera conductor in Germany, becoming principal assistant to Ernst von Schuch in Dresden. From Saxony, he moved in 1910 to St Petersburg, to the Imperial Opera, where he worked as first conductor under the Czech, Nepravnik, who had then served about forty years as chief conductor.

At the Revolution, Coates became director of music to the new regime, conducting concerts and opera performances throughout Russia during the Civil War and the famine. In 1919, he took advantage of official permission to leave for Finland (for an operation) to move to London after his convalescence. He conducted some opera performances for Beecham at Covent Garden and looked for an opening in the concert hall. The LSO provided him with one. In return the Orchestra acquired a conductor of known capability and international background, fully conversant with the Russo-German repertoire which formed the staple of its programmes, and a famed advocate of contemporary Russian composers. His rehearsal methods have been analysed by Bernard Shore in his classic study *The Orchestra Speaks*[1] (he joined the LSO violas in October 1921), but Albert Coates' impact on the LSO is, perhaps, most conveniently summed up by another former Member, in conversation with the author: "Coates had a lot to give—and he gave it all."

Coates became Principal Conductor in a profounder sense than his predecessors. Richter conferred massive authority on a mettlesome, brilliant band; Elgar was evidence of an identification with England and of personal friendships, but by the time Elgar took over, the LSO had established itself. Coates' task was, simply, to reconstruct the Orchestra, to restore its ensemble, its morale and its prestige. His appointment illustrates other considerations: not only did the title have a wholly different connotation—repeated in the LSO's history only by Josef Krips after the Second World War—but it sprang from a convergence of interest. The LSO needed a conductor: Coates needed a job. He also had an established connection with a recording company: this was not a negligible factor, though by no means as important as it was to become. Additionally, he was in a position to interest possible patrons.

The prospect of working with Coates determined the Directors on re-establishing the LSO's own promotions. The first season demonstrated the range and the imagination of the new Principal Conductor, who took charge of all the concerts. That there would be a large Russian element went without saying:

the first "Coates" concert included a Borodin symphony and Scriabin's *Poème de l'Extase*. The length of time demanded by Coates to rehearse that work has been blamed for the indifferent reception given to the Elgar Cello Concerto which received its première in the same programme, though it appears equally, if not more, likely that the apparently drastic change in idiom puzzled the audience and muted its response.[2] Elgar himself wrote to the Directors thanking them for the magnificent presentation of the concerto.

Coates experimented with programmes built round a theme, respectively "Fairy Tales" and "Faust". The first included Ravel's *Mother Goose*, Holbrooke's *Queen Mab* and two Russian works, *Kikimora* by Liadov and *The Firebird* of Stravinsky. The second combined orchestral works by Berlioz and Liszt with an excerpt from Boito's *Mefistofele*.

The LSO's newly acquired authority enabled the Orchestra to survive increases in its operating costs by stipulating higher fees and attracting regular subsidies from private subscribers. Coates was important here. He approached, among others, Lord Berners and Baron Frederic d'Erlanger to become patrons and Vice-Presidents of the LSO. Both were authors and composers of some standing; Lord Berners wrote a ballet for Diaghilev, but was mainly a miniaturist, while d'Erlanger had had a violin concerto performed by Kreisler. He also composed several operas and choral works and wrote libretti for Holbrooke. He became one of three main subscribers to the LSO during the twenties. The others were Cyril Jenkins, another amateur composer and Lord Howard de Walden. These two, in association, agreed in December 1920 to support the Orchestra on condition that the LSO included in the rest of the season specified works by Bantock, Elgar and Cyril Jenkins and that "a generous amount of time be allowed all British works at rehearsals. In fact, these works to receive preference over all foreign works at rehearsal."

This was a tall order for an international orchestra such as the LSO and reflected not only the patrons' enthusiasm for British music but also their reaction to the première of the Elgar Cello Concerto—one of the works specified for inclusion in the remainder of the season. Their last stipulation was a public apology from Albert Coates, who they considered had insulted them at a rehearsal. The Board pointed out that the Orchestra was not to blame but otherwise temporised: Coates would be consulted on his return from America. The upshot is obscure but the Minutes record on 2nd May 1921 that the efforts of Busby and Coates "to secure £1,000 from Lord Howard de Walden towards paying the expenses of the symphony concerts had been successful". At the same meeting, however, it was reported that Cyril Jenkins was most displeased with the LSO (whose programmes showed no performances of his works) and that his support was unlikely. Nevertheless through Jenkins' good offices, the LSO received engagements at the Eisteddfod. It is impossible at this stage to unravel the politics of patronage; the account given here merely demonstrates some of the problems raised for the Directors. Lord Howard de Walden became Honorary President of the LSO. Baron d'Erlanger and Cyril Jenkins also helped financially and encouraged other subscribers. Their efforts were essential in assisting the Orchestra to regain its position in the post-war years.

The immediate outcome of their patronage can be seen in the quality and variety of the LSO promotions for 1920–21: the *B Minor Mass* and Mozart's *Requiem*—neither works automatically associated with Coates—the first complete performance of *The Planets*, Vaughan Williams' *A London Symphony*, the Brahms Double Concerto, as well as the more frequently heard Violin Concerto and Second Piano Concerto, and a range of Russian compositions, including the finale from *A Life for the Tsar* by Glinka, the Third Concerto of Rachmaninov (with Cortot) and major works of Scriabin. The patrons were represented by Jenkins' tone poem *The Magic Cauldron* and the Prelude to the third act of d'Erlanger's opera *Tess of the d'Urbervilles*. The season went so well artistically that the Board decided that Coates had fulfilled what was required of him and reverted to the traditional guest conductor arrangement. Coates was—and remained—a prominent and welcome guest.

In dispensing with Coates, the Directors were not only, as it were, falling back on their LSO reflexes, they were seeking to broaden the experience of the re-trained Orchestra by exposing it to conductors from different schools and traditions. Arguably, the most important step in this respect was re-establishing the LSO's connections with the "Central European" insights and disciplines which had formed its original character. The obvious conductor was Artur Nikisch: the Board's decision to invite him back preceded by twelve days Nikisch's death, in January 1922. So the role passed to Felix Weingartner who in May the following year, conducted the LSO in Mozart, Schubert, Beethoven, Liszt, Berlioz and Wagner, with compositions by Holbrooke and himself. Nikisch's successor in Leipzig, Wilhelm Furtwängler, appeared, as did Eugene Goossens, Koussevitsky, Bruno Walter, and George Schneevoigt from Finland. Prokofiev played his Third Piano Concerto and Carl Nielsen made his only London visit to conduct the LSO in his own works. These pieces, Goossens' *Sinfonietta*, Holbrooke's *The Birds of Rhianon* and Ravel's orchestration of Moussorgsky's *Pictures at an Exhibition* are the limits of the LSO's contribution to contemporary work in its own promotions, at this stage. A policy of visiting conductors tends to reinforce the conservative disposition of the audience.

In 1923, Beecham emerged from Chancery and on to the stage of the Albert Hall. In April he directed the LSO and Albert Hall Orchestra combined in a programme which concluded with *Ein Heldenleben* and *Der Walkürenritt*. The occasion demonstrated to the Directors that Beecham was again looking for orchestras for performances. In addition, through the April concert, they were introduced to Lionel Powell and Harold Holt (successors to Schulz-Curtius and Powell). The Board decided that the partnership had more to offer in the way of engagements and ceased to employ L. G. Sharpe exclusively as agent. The Minutes suggest that the fact that Powell and Holt also acted for Beecham was not far from the Directors' minds when they took this decision. The Board invited Beecham to conduct in their own promotions, which he did in the 1923–24 season, thus resuming a connection broken off six years before. At this time, too, he began to reap the international recognition which the war and his enforced withdrawal from the scene afterwards had delayed. He began to conduct abroad, particularly in Berlin and New York. Beecham's experience in these cities was ultimately to implicate the LSO.

The LSO regarded itself as a "concert-hall" orchestra. It

was, indeed, axiomatic that this was where the Orchestra should be, but after the First World War, other centres emerged which have progressively diminished the force of the axiom—recording and broadcasting studios.

The Orchestra recorded Beethoven and Mozart Symphonies under Weingartner, Brahms under Bruno Walter, Holst's *The Planets* under Holst, and Strauss' tone-poems under Strauss. Eugene Goossens conducted recordings of lighter pieces by Chabrier, Delibes and Sibelius. Coates' name does not appear, apart from the initial session, since in July 1921 he severed his connection with Columbia. The LSO's contract was unaffected: in fact, the Orchestra picked up more work, since Coates transferred himself to the rival Gramophone Company (whose records appeared under the trademark "HMV") for whom he recorded Beethoven's Ninth Symphony, the *Enigma Variations*, and a range of Russians and Richard Strauss with "The Symphony Orchestra" which was predominantly the LSO in unaccustomed but profitable anonymity.

In 1920, Coates' gramophone connections resulted in a contract for the LSO with the Columbia Gramophone Company. Their recordings were made by the acoustic process, which had reached the limit of technical development. The players and singers were forced into the gyrations vividly recaptured by Wynn Reeves:

> We had immense difficulties to contend with in the early days of record making, especially of the larger works. Most of the recording took place in a small room, the orchestra being reduced to its lowest possible limit, and we were crowded together in the endeavour to propel whatever we had to play into one or two recording bells. Occasionally we did excerpts from the "Ring"—this was sheer murder.
>
> I remember a series we undertook in midsummer one year, the strings were reduced to: 2 1sts, 2 2nds, 1 va., 1 cello, 1 bass, the minimum of woodwind, brass and percussion; Billy Reed and I were playing into No. 1 bell (or horn), our bows being not more than 2 inches from the rim. The music being away back under the bell necessitated stooping down to see what we had to play; it was my job to turn the pages; woe betide me if the music rustled or if

> my bow touched the bell. Standing behind us with their music-stands leaning on our shoulders, were the woodwind blowing into our ears as loudly as possible; behind them again were the brass.
>
> High up on my left was Albert Coates conducting. Immediately below him stood Florence Austral, as Brünnhilde. Coates quickly discovered that some of her notes jarred the bell, so he grabbed her hair, pulling her forward into the bell for some notes, and pushing her back for the dangerous ones. Try to imagine interpreting Brünnhilde under these circumstances!
>
> On my right was another bell for the male chorus of six and two principals, Robert Parker as Wotan and Robert Radford as Hagen, the routine being that the principals ducked when the chorus had to sing and vice versa. There was a constant pushing and shoving to make way, all of this causing a repercussion on my bow arm. High up was an electric fan perched on a block of ice but perfectly useless as the temperature registered 95° Fahrenheit!

In the early twenties, however, experiments in electrical recording techniques by the Western Electric Company suddenly allowed a far wider range of recorded sounds and a vast improvement in its quality. It also changed conditions for the players. "Imagine our surprise and delight," writes Reeves, "when the LSO were called for a session at Kingsway Hall to find the platform arranged for full orchestra, everyone in his proper position, no bells or horns, but instead a MICROPHONE! This was the first tryout and the excitement was tense. We played something, I think a Weber Overture, which was immediately played back to us from the recording room. To us it was a sheer miracle."

From then on, the record market boomed and contracts became correspondingly more important to orchestras, not only as a source of income and advertisement but also because the new technique required a full orchestra to be used. But it also demanded frequent repetition. Fred Gaisberg highlights the effect for the players. "The instrumentalists composing an orchestra and the conductor controlling it now began to engage my close attention. I often marvelled at the patience of men when drill sergeants like Mengelberg, Klemperer, Karl Muck, Koussevitzky, Furtwängler and Toscanini put them through their paces for a steady three hours on end.... Observe that the names are those of men noted for their intolerance—the men who demanded one hundred per cent every minute of the hours."[3] The LSO at this stage were perhaps more fortunate in having a conductor who was professionally more humane, with no observable difference in artistic results. Their work with Coates, especially in Wagner, eloquently substantiates this proposition.

At this time the technology of sound provided another focus for musicians in the form of radio broadcasts. The transmissions of the British Broadcasting Company began in 1922 and the LSO's first corporate appearance "on the air" took place on 9th February 1924, in a broadcast of Vaughan Williams' *Pastoral Symphony* conducted by the composer, and sacred music with the Cathedral Choir, under E. T. Cook. In the two months following, the LSO was heard, by those with the necessary earphones, from the Central Hall, Westminster, under Eugene Goossens, and under Stanton Jeffries, the British Broadcasting Company's first Director of Music.

Broadcasting and the gramophone both extended the range of work open to musicians, but they had different effects. A gramophone record could provide a stimulus to attending a concert—which accounted for the careful advertising of conductors' and soloists' recording connections in LSO programmes. But, as was soon evident, a broadcast *replaced* attending a concert. Throughout the country, engagements for small orchestras for soirées or quartets for chamber music fell off; subscriptions to concert societies declined sufficiently to induce nervousness among Treasurers. The LSO Directors' initial reaction was optimistic: "the public would always prefer the atmosphere and the live element of the concert room . . . broadcasting would create a keener desire on the part of the public to hear music at first hand." They were more fortunately placed than some, in that they primarily sought to attract a metropolitan public and could engage artists for whom London was their only port of call. Even so, it was not to be too long before the Board felt sufficiently strongly about the Broadcasting Company's policies to forbid

Members from playing in the "British Symphony Orchestra" which the BBC assembled for a series of Albert Hall concerts. The prohibition did not last, since it could not be properly enforced. One Member forced the issue by sending in his resignation "as he was not prepared to be dictated to by the Board as to what engagements he should accept". Twenty-three others exercised their statutory right of demanding an Extraordinary General Meeting on the issue. It was held on 31st March 1922 and the Board's initiative was quashed.

Gramophone records and broadcasting offered new techniques in conveying music to the public in which sound was "internal" to the technique. The other contemporary innovation in the technology of culture, the film, still relied on the provision of sound extraneously to the technique. The film remained "silent" and, in consequence, musicians were in demand in cinemas to create the appropriate mood for the sequences shown on the screen. The virtues noted by Mendelssohn and Wagner—adaptability and skill in sight-reading—flourished. The conductor's job was to select the music and synchronise each piece with the episode or emotion of the drama. Wynn Reeves did so for a number of films produced by the legendary D. W. Griffith, beginning with *The Orphans of the Storm*. He made a practice of seeing two screenings, the second with a notebook and stopwatch, then repairing to his music library in search of suitable music to be "cued in" by him at the run-through, immediately prior to the performance. This whole cycle of operations took one evening and the following day. The orchestra Reeves recruited from among his colleagues in the LSO.

The apogee of this activity was reached by the LSO under its own name, when in 1922 it was engaged for a season of "super films" at Covent Garden by Walter Wanger, then head of United Artists. The conductor was Eugene Goossens, who was obliged

> to devise a continuous eighty-minute accompaniment to the exploits of Mr Fairbanks and his dashing companions. This led to the discovery of much little-known, and, in some cases, undeservedly neglected music. My happiest and most useful discovery was one August Enna, a prolific—and soporific—

> nineteenth-century composer whose music provided an inexhaustible reservoir of tedious but varied symphonic accompaniments. It fitted anything and also conveyed a spurious impression of great emotional depth, making it very suitable for my purpose. It also proved completely anonymous and unidentifiable in performance. My sixty-five players, the flower of the LSO, produced a noble well-rehearsed sound from the pit. . . . The deputy system flourished untrammelled and Covent Garden became the Mecca of those musicians periodically at liberty for an occasional afternoon's or evening's engagement. It is safe to assume that by the end of the run very few orchestral players in London had not seen Douglas Fairbanks in *The Three Musketeers*.[4]

Subsequently the LSO went on to work in the Royal Albert Hall for Herbert Wilcox and to provide a musical accompaniment to the famous German film *Die Nibelungen*.

Gramophone and film work were, it must be stressed, still regarded as slightly bizarre forms of activity for "serious" musicians, whose primary interests and loyalties were in the concert hall and the "live" theatre. It was to be another ten years or so until progress in electrical recording and the technique of sound films consistently shifted any appreciable amount of work into the studios. The challenge of broadcasting came sooner.

Meanwhile, the LSO picked up the threads of its pre-war connections. In 1922 the Orchestra returned to Leeds for the first post-war Festival. Again, the programmes were of prodigious length and slightly curious construction by the standards of fifty years later. Consider the closing programme:

Choruses from *Israel in Egypt*	Handel
Scheherazade	Rimsky-Korsakov
Orchestral work: *The Lincoln Imp*	W. H. Reed
Prelude and Finale: *Tristan und Isolde*	Wagner
Rhapsody	John Ireland
Francesca da Rimini	Tchaikovsky

Elsewhere, the programmes displayed the big pieces: Verdi's *Requiem* opened the first concert, the complete *The Planets* closed the second, and the Ninth Symphony the fourth (after Strauss' *Don Juan*, Respighi's *Fountains of Rome* and Delius' *Appalachia*). Coates' other enthusiasms, Scriabin and Wagner, completed his contributions. Hugh Allen took over extensive programmes of Parry and Bach. The LSO returned in 1925 and 1928.

Wholly different in character from Leeds and moreover an annual event was the Three Choirs Festival, revived in 1920. Members, individually, had played in the orchestras before the war—among them W. H. Reed, through whom the LSO corporately was now engaged—after a certain amount of haggling over the precise influence of inflation on fees—for the postwar festivals. It was the beginning of a long association. In essence, a celebration of Elgar in the country of his origin, the Festival came to be a highlight of the LSO year. Sir Ivor Atkins recollected that "in these years, there grew up a complete understanding between both forces, the LSO delighting in the variety that choral works bring; the chorus showing ever-increasing interest in orchestral music. As the years passed the incomparable qualities of the LSO became clearer and dearer to us all. The players had come to understand the acoustic properties of each cathedral. . . . The LSO could give superb performances of great orchestral works from Mozart to the latest of the moderns. Indeed their playing of Elgar symphonies under the composer himself provided musicians and public alike with spiritual experiences which live unforgettable in the memories of that generation."[5]

For Elgar, as composer and conductor, Sir Ivor's recollection is undoubtedly true. Other composers were not so fortunate. Sir Arthur Bliss vividly recalls the disappointment of the first performance of his *Colour Symphony* at Gloucester in September 1922. "It was a difficult work to play and a very intricate work to conduct. Rehearsals were inevitably very restricted and with wrong notes in new parts to be found and corrected, there was virtually no time for the players to learn the work."[6] Festival conditions are sometimes less than perfect!

The baritone Roy Henderson's opinion is that without the influence of Reed and the LSO's corporate spirit, disaster would have happened more frequently. "Reed was a tremendous help to conductors who seldom had an orchestra to conduct. . . . Billy was the champion up-bobbing leader. For amusement I used to count the number of times he got up to speak to the conductor. His record was twenty-seven times at one rehearsal at Worcester."[7] But the corporate spirit could work against the conductor. Sir Ivor Atkins offended the Orchestra on one occasion and paid the penalty. Wynn Reeves was present:

> We were assembled for a rehearsal when Atkins said—"I have decided to introduce a new gesture when I conduct from now onwards. Whenever I raise my left hand to the level of my head, with my thumb pointed inwards—please understand that I am not satisfied." Heavens! thought I, you've put a rod in pickle for yourself my lad. The rehearsal proceeded without the anticipated signal and we dispersed. In the evening Tschaikowsky's *Capriccio Italien* was to be performed, the last movement of which is in 6/8 starting very steadily and gradually accelerating to a presto; Sir Ivor started much too fast and the work began to gain impetus much too soon. There was some back pedalling on the part of a few who recognised the danger, when up came the left hand and the word flew round "HE IS NOT SATISFIED. All right you blighter, you want it faster you shall have it." When an Orchestra gets out of hand, it's the devil to pay: they are a thousand times worse than run-away horses. Soon it became nearly impossible to play 6 notes in a bar, presently —quite impossible. Still everyone was pressing on and our worthy conductor's hand was pumping up and down like a piston rod, turning over the score pages and gesticulating wildly. Still the Orchestra surged on: notes became 4, 5, 3, 2, until the bars flew by like names of stations from an express train. Nobody knew where they were, I couldn't see the music for tears of concealed laughter, and I think most were in the same boat when Henderson, our stalwart tympanist, thought it about time he took a hand, so he suddenly started a fierce fanfare on all three drums at once and we dashed to the last bar and bashed away at that until our worthy conductor decided to stop.
>
> The audience applauded mightily and thought it marvellous, but the best of the whole thing was that Hobday

> met Atkins in the Cloisters the next day and Atkins said "I fancy I took the Capriccio a little faster than usual didn't I?" "I didn't notice anything" said Hobday. A.: "I'm a little worried about what Henderson played at the end, I have looked it up in the score and can't see anything like it." H.: "Perhaps he was playing from a different edition."

But at the Three Choirs, it was Elgar who mattered most. During the twenties his compositions had already fallen into neglect and he himself into a degree of professional disdain, as a composer representative of a bygone—and despicable—era. This was never true at Worcester, Hereford or Gloucester and it was never true for the LSO.

One of the most enterprising, but shortlived "out-of-town" engagements for the LSO was two concerts in Brighton in the spring of 1924. They were intended as the first of a series by the organiser, Dr Chasty Hector, organist of Brighton Parish Church and music master at Brighton and Hove Grammar School. Hector was typical of those individuals on whose drive and enthusiasm so much of local music-making depends. He organised concerts, engaged soloists such as Marcel Dupré to give recitals, and composed light operas. He was interested in British music and persuaded his guarantors to cover two concerts including works of Holst and Holbrooke, conducted by the composers, and with one of his own orchestral works—a *Concert Overture*—in the programme. The *Perfect Fool* ballet music and Holbrooke's *Variations on Three Blind Mice* and *Birds of Rhianon* were sandwiched in between more conventional items such as Beethoven's Fifth Symphony, Liszt's First Hungarian Rhapsody, and Grieg's *Peer Gynt* music, but the venture failed to command continued support. The Holst visit was memorable, in the Hector household, where he stayed, in that before the concert he "insisted on complete quietude, even to the extent of lying underneath the dining-room table with a dark cloth to shut out the light".[8]

Elgar, Holbrooke, Holst, together with Vaughan Williams and Arnold Bax (whose works also featured in LSO programmes but to a lesser extent) were held to represent a specifically "English" voice in music. Eugene Goossens had more obvious affiliations with his continental contemporaries. But they were all part of the resurgence of the LSO.

Except for a trip to Paris in 1924 for two concerts with Elgar and one at the Casino in Dieppe on the return journey, touring overseas did not assist the LSO in recovering its identity. The Paris trip arose purely from an invitation to Elgar to take an orchestra to France to conduct some of his own works. It was memorable for the performers but it led nowhere in the sense that the Orchestra was not on tour long enough to be welded together, which would undoubtedly have been the effect of another tour planned for the same year—to South America for fifty concerts, with Albert Coates. The sea passage alone was reckoned at six weeks! The effect would have been comparable with that of the North American tour with Nikisch twelve years previously—and possibly slightly more exotic. The scheme fell through—a fate which it shared with the plan for a tour of Australia in 1925 put up by Powell and Holt.

Post-war reconstruction of the LSO both as Orchestra and as concert-promoters had no effect on the organisation. Vander Meerschen became Chairman, Busby resigned his offices and membership in consequence of a dispute with his co-Directors and was succeeded by Bertram Jones. Busby's departure eliminated the protagonist of Founders' rights, and from 1924 onwards the Board became fully elective. The Directors created an Endowment Fund, to provide for the future development of the LSO, funded by an annual concert and sundry other income. Discipline was a recurrent problem, and in March 1925, the Board agreed "That there should be a thorough review of the positions of the different departments of the Orchestra at an early date with a view to obtaining the greatest efficiency in every branch of the Orchestra." This is the first of recurring references to fits of intermittent introspection which have afflicted Boards of the LSO throughout its history. They invariably succeed in embroiling the Board with the Members, or with some of them, and allow the built-in capacity for politics to have full play. In 1925, however, the impulse appears to have been resisted. Less potentially disruptive activities such as the LSO's twenty-first birthday celebrations occupied a prior place on the agenda.

The occasion was to be marked by a concert and a dinner. The concert, at 3 p.m. on Wednesday, 9th June 1925, repeated the inaugural programme, with Elgar conducting his *Enigma Variations* and Beecham the rest. Beecham could not appear—though he presided over the dinner. Coates was approached, but he was engaged to the Paris Opera: so Koussevitsky led the celebrations. A special block of seats was made available to LCC schoolchildren at reduced prices—a gesture towards both London and the future. The dinner, at the Hotel Cecil, was an assembly of musical London. Elgar, Coates, Goossens, Cowan, Landon Ronald, Harty, Sir Hugh Allen, Arthur Fagge of the London Choral Society, Arnold Bax, Frederick Austin, and Edward German were all at the top table. With 150 Members and their guests, among whom was a newcomer to London, named Malcolm Sargent, they surmounted an eight-course menu and a riot of speeches, "conducted" by Sir Thomas.

The Orchestra's view of itself at this juncture is presented in the Souvenir Programme of the concert:

> The London Symphony Orchestra is unique in that it is an orchestral society run on co-operative lines and its general policy is largely conditioned by that fact. It cannot afford risky experiments, although this is not to say that its outlook is unduly conservative, nor that it has not often adopted a policy which did not promise an immediate or adequate financial return. Many of its members have played without a fee at over two hundred concerts. The artistic aims of the orchestra are as high as the quality of its performances which at this time of day need not be insisted upon. . . .

This is the language of self-confidence, of the knowledge that the LSO was nearing the end of the best financial season in its history and that the enterprise was being prudently managed. To contemporaries, the anniversary was likened to a milestone on a journey, but with hindsight it appears, rather, as a watershed. From the middle of the 1920s the conditions which had sustained the LSO since its Edwardian foundation began to melt away. The preferential position built on orchestral brilliance and associations with exciting conductors collapsed. The early expansiveness and casual discipline floundered under sharpened competition and the decline in patronage. The LSO shared the London orchestral scene with others, and on inferior terms.

The process was not instantaneous—and for two seasons or so, the order-book was as full as ever. Coates, Casals, Weingartner, Bruno Walter, Hermann Abendroth and Leo Blech were engaged for LSO promotions. Elgar conducted *Falstaff* and his Cello Concerto—and Beecham began to loom larger in LSO planning. When in England, he appeared most frequently with the LSO, either by invitation as one of the conductors in their annual series, or as an entrepreneur, when he was looking for an orchestra to engage for a specific function or festival. In 1927, Beecham negotiated with the Directors about a visit to Paris, and in the following year, to Berlin. Neither engagement took place, to the mutual regret of both parties. In 1926–27, he conducted three concerts—two at his own expense—notable for Delius' *Sea Drift* and Berlioz' *Te Deum*. He opened the next season, but fell ill on the eve of the next concert, and this provided an opportunity for the LSO to introduce as a replacement a new figure who was to achieve world recognition, John Barbirolli. The circumstances are discussed by Michael Kennedy in the authorised biography.[9] The initiative for the invitation came from the ubiquitous Fred Gaisberg—who was also responsible for suggesting Barbirolli to the Philharmonic-Symphony Orchestra of New York nine years later, as successor to Toscanini. Barbirolli's success with the LSO on 12th December 1927 prompted a re-engagement in the following season.

The Eisteddfod, Leeds and the Three Choirs Festivals furnished the fixed points in provincial appearances. Recording schedules with HMV, to whom the LSO formally transferred on the expiry of their Columbia contract, occupied the Orchestra and its distinguished roster of conductors. Richard Strauss conducted his *Till Eulenspiegel*, Siegfried Wagner, excerpts from his father's music dramas, Casals directed Beethoven and Brahms, Geoffrey Toye, Delius; Leo Blech, Schubert's Great C major, and Albert Coates, Wagner, Prokofiev and Respighi. During this period, too, Elgar recorded his Second Symphony and *The Music Makers*. The LSO seemed a permanent and prosperous fixture in British music.

There were, however, serious problems. Discipline and standards of playing were alike variable. The late Gerald Jackson, who played regularly with the LSO at this time, suggests that the Orchestra's brilliance had degenerated into sourness and that "few, if any, of the players seemed to have heard of the word *vibrato*".[10] The Minutes confirm that Jackson's worry was shared by the Directors, who were beginning to perceive that the deputy system and the highest technical standards were incompatible. From a practical point of view, the LSO's standards were being lowered in response to the increasing calls on Members for the BBC Orchestra. Furthermore, gramophone companies were beginning to insist that the personnel should be the same at each session under the same conductor, and that the LSO's regular principals should be present whenever possible. This was a particular problem for the strings and as early as April 1926 caused complaints to the Board. The new technologies of conveying sound made the deputy system a source of weakness. The Directors' dilemma was that rectifying the weakness would deny the *raison d'être* of the LSO.

VI

IF THE DIRECTORS of the LSO were troubled by the deputy system and its effect on standards, so was Sir Thomas Beecham. He brought the lessons of his Continental and American experiences to bear on the current levels of achievement in Britain. He thought them profoundly unsatisfactory, fixing responsibility on the insecurity of orchestral personnel and the deputy system. He did not deny the merits of the players in general—indeed, he was consistently and emphatically patriotic about their qualities—nor did he ignore the fact that such players could on specific occasions produce results which were excellent. His concern was with the standards usually achieved, which in his view fluctuated around a rather low level. That the difference in standards was not just a Beechamesque fancy was underlined by the first post-war visit of the Berlin Philharmonic Orchestra, under Furtwängler in 1927. The effect on musicians and public alike was revelatory. The Berliners were followed in June 1928 by the Budapest Philharmonic Orchestra, whose playing, under Dohnányi, evoked the comment that such excellence and finish could not be obtained in London until there was at least one orchestra rehearsing assiduously and performing regularly under one conductor. Beecham could not have put the point better himself. It was the remedy he advocated, but he realised that a permanent orchestra in which a player would be relieved from the necessity to scramble for jobs in order to make a living, would necessarily require a permanent subsidy, from either public or private sources.

The BBC appeared to provide the answer. The Corporation had also drawn the necessary conclusions from the overseas visitors whose lessons for London audiences were underlined by the Hallé under Harty in January 1928. There was, clearly, no need to go abroad in search of excellence.

The BBC (by now the British Broadcasting Corporation) decided to form a permanent orchestra to replace its existing body, got together by *ad hoc* engagements to musicians, including members of the LSO. This opened up an alarming prospect, in that the new orchestra would be removed from the market place of concert-giving where even Beecham's subsidised orchestra would have to earn its living. Sir Thomas himself appreciated this point and involved himself in discussion with BBC officials and the Royal Philharmonic Society for a joint "first rate permanent orchestra", to be styled the "Royal Philharmonic Orchestra". It was to be funded equally by the Corporation and by Beecham: basic rates would be £500 a year for rank and file players, rising to £1,200 a year for principals: its work would consist of 100 concerts a year, seasons at Covent Garden and broadcasts; deputies were not to be tolerated.

In July 1928, Beecham privately disclosed his thinking for a permanent orchestra to Bertram Jones, Secretary of the LSO Board. The Directors did not welcome the prospect of a rival on the London scene, which could only undermine the position the LSO had tried hard to re-establish since the war, the more so since the terms which Beecham wanted to offer might well attract away its principal players. This deduction was confirmed by Wynn Reeves, reporting a conversation between Colonel Blois and Beecham, in which the latter expressly stated that the nucleus of the new orchestra would be assembled from "about two-thirds" of the players appearing in the pit at Covent Garden (i.e. the LSO).

The Directors sought a meeting with Beecham, from which they gained, according to their Minutes, "the promise to endeavour to formulate a means whereby the members of the London Symphony Orchestra should be at liberty to perform at the usual series of symphony concerts so that the London Symphony Orchestra as such should be thus enabled to continue in existence and carry on their policy, business and traditions". This was reasonably satisfactory, but the basic situation remained unclear. The Directors quickly evolved an alternative of their own, which would make them invulnerable to Beecham's proposals, whether on the BBC's behalf or his own. In October 1928 they approached the Gramophone

Company, asking for its co-operation with the Royal Opera Syndicate in respect of the employment by the latter of the LSO for the opera season, in order "to prevent the disintegration of the LSO which the proposed scheme of Sir Thomas Beecham's permanent orchestra threatened". This initiative developed, over the next four months, into comprehensive proposals for a programme of work for the Orchestra guaranteed by the Royal Opera Syndicate, the Gramophone Company and the agent Lionel Powell. The syndicate guaranteed the 1930 international opera season and subsequent seasons; and the Gramophone Company, 50 three-hour sessions. Powell undertook to promote tours and concerts amounting to 41 concerts. These arrangements were to yield the equivalent of 151 concerts a year. In return the LSO bound itself to form a permanent orchestra of 75 players, "to be selected from their present members or, if necessary, with additions from outside musicians who would become members of the LSO". The members of the permanent orchestra were individually to receive contracts from the LSO Ltd guaranteeing the definite number of performances over a period of three years. Such contracts were to contain clauses stipulating the right to exclude players considered unsatisfactory, and forbidding deputies, except for proven medical reasons, at either rehearsals or performances. The management of these arrangements was vested in a Control Committee of four, one representative from each of the parties, which was specifically charged with the task of vetting the final selection of players from the list submitted by the LSO. Lionel Powell became the Permanent Manager of the project, through whom all bookings and arrangements had to be made.

On 24th May 1929, Bertram Jones and Wynn Reeves signed the contracts on behalf of the LSO. This scheme provided the LSO with as realistic and secure a basis for the future as could be devised. There was, however, an "internal" aspect to the arrangements. They provided the Directors with a way out of one of their most pressing problems, namely what to do about Members who had ceased "to evince the high standard of proficiency necessary to maintain the reputation of the Orchestra". For this reason, the Directors realised that the terms implied trouble within the Orchestra. They explained, to an Extraordinary General Meeting on 25th April, that the permanent Orchestra would only function in relation to the schedule of work arising through the other parties to the contract: for other bookings, the LSO would continue as before. This disposed of some of the objections and resentments of players who feared they might be left out (thus being clearly shown as "the weaker brethren"), but not all. In this respect, the scheme did nothing to promote morale or *esprit de corps* in the rank and file. "The Three Year Contract," Wynn Reeves reports, "came into being with much misgiving among the players, who resented bitterly giving up their freedom for which they had fought for so many years." The individual contracts were despatched to those players who had been selected by the Directors and approved by the Control Committee. (It subsequently became an item of acrimonious debate within the LSO that the Directors had not waited to sign the main contract until the Members had accepted the conditions offered them.) In the event, some Members refused the offer. Rumours spread that non-Members had been offered contracts with the permanent Orchestra. These reactions prompted a second Extraordinary General Meeting, on 1st July 1929, at the instigation of Members. The rumours were denied by Bertram Jones, who said that "no one outside the Orchestra had received a contract unless there was no member of the Department concerned available" (it is not clear whether "available" was to be construed literally or simply implied that the member had been turned down by the Control Committee). The Chairman, Vander Meerschen, fell back on authority. He reminded the meeting that "the Directors had carried on the activities of the Orchestra since its inception, he felt he could safely say with highly satisfactory results, and the Members could trust their Directors to continue to safeguard the Company's interests in every way". The current implications of this comment were elaborated by the Secretary, who stressed that the Directors "had a very difficult task to carry out, for it was their duty to see that the Orchestra was maintained at the highest possible artistic level and in carrying out this duty they were confronted with the necessity of dispensing with the services of certain Members. This was a very painful business for the Directors who, having been aware of certain weaknesses in the Orchestra for some considerable time, had acted in the spirit of leniency which had always been shown by the Directors. The permanent Orchestra scheme had, however, brought matters to a crisis. . . ." The Board, threatening resignation if it were defeated, got its desired majority by 64 to 11 from the Members and fought off this challenge to its authority.

This they then attempted to consolidate by asking the non-proficient Members, two of whom had caused the EGM to be convened and had led the attack on the Board, to resign. Procuring the resignations and enforcing the transfers of shares occupied the Directors until 1933. It did not help that while this process was in train, one of the "victims" was proposed for a vacancy on the Board of Directors, was declared inadmissable (on the grounds that his resignation had been requested) and promptly went to his solicitor. The Directors put the whole matter before Counsel. His Opinion was that the Member's name had been improperly withheld from the AGM as a candidate but that his rights in the matter were "somewhat vague and speculative". Counsel had no doubt, however, that the Directors had acted *ultra vires* in entering into the contracts with "Lionel Powell, the Covent Garden Syndicate and HMV" in the first instance. The Directors had to go to the Members for formal clearance—which was given but not without additional recrimination.

In the same month as the LSO entered on their new regime, Beecham retired from the scheme for a "Royal Philharmonic Orchestra". His relations with the BBC had not been felicitous: the Directors of the Royal Philharmonic Society complained that they could get no satisfactory evidence that Beecham and the BBC were agreed between themselves. The RPS and the BBC continued to explore possibilities, but a jointly run or promoted orchestra ceased to be practical when, at the end of the month, the Corporation broke off negotiations, deciding to act entirely independently. Thenceforward, recruiting began in earnest; the BBC approached established players, sometimes having advised their existing employers, frequently not—but in neither case did its action promote harmony within the established orchestras. The LSO was a sitting target.

By the end of the year (1929), the Orchestra was not in a

very happy state—the more so as resignations began to be submitted from those who wished to accept offers from the new BBC Orchestra. The Board consented at the beginning but then adopted a policy of holding players to their contracts with LSO Ltd. The consequent friction caused the Board to turn to their solicitors once again. They advised that Members were fully entitled to resign from the LSO; their rights to do so from the permanent Orchestra were still ambiguous; they recommended further discussion with the applicants, but the Directors, according to the Minutes, "came to the conclusion that Members who could act in a manner so disloyal to the true spirit of the Orchestra were not worthy to remain Members any longer and that their resignations should be accepted". They further decided to inform Members of the requests to resign already received "emphasising its disloyal nature and pressing the Members to help the Board by carrying through the Contract for the Permanent Orchestra in a loyal manner, both in the letter and in the spirit". From the autumn of 1929, "loyalty" became an issue within the LSO; it arose in the first place over the LSO's own scheme for a permanent Orchestra and then from the emergence of the BBC as an alternative and better-endowed employer. It had nothing directly to do with Beecham, who continued to appear among the Orchestra's conductors in London and the provinces.

During the year a new figure appeared on the scene: in April, Bertram Jones had an interview with Dr Malcolm Sargent "who desired to engage an orchestra for a series of concerts". Sargent, at this time, was thirty-four and, encouraged by Wood, had appeared on the London musical scene with great *éclat* and was much in demand as a conductor of opera and choral music. But behind the public appearance, there were already professional problems. Sargent went through most of his career exciting the adoration of patrons and the public and the hostility of orchestras in roughly equal intensities. The latter abated only towards the end. One distinguished player, who was a friend and who considers that he knew how Sargent's mind worked, commented to the author: "He arrived on the scene very young, was very assertive and thought he knew everything! The trouble was, he very nearly did. He was an extremely nice man when he was not conducting."

But players, who could know him only professionally, could not be expected to take such a generous view. They resented his attempts to teach them how to play their instruments. They realised, moreover, that Sargent had a number of engagements in his gift, in virtue of which both they and he knew he had a whip hand and, unfortunately, as his biographer makes clear, he could not refrain from showing it.[1] In 1929 he could offer a series of interesting, better-rehearsed programmes in a series financed by Mrs Samuel Courtauld and the subscriptions of a concert club. These became known to history as the Courtauld-Sargent concerts. The idea was Artur Schnabel's.[2] It was aimed at the impecunious music lover who might work in a department store, a bank or a shop. The firm took out the subscription on behalf of the employees. There were six concerts a season, each given twice; all were sold out. From the orchestral point of view, this arrangement allowed for more rehearsals—five or six were the rule—and for unusual works. The LSO accepted Sargent's offer to play and the first series opened in Queen's Hall on 22nd October 1929—just two days before the stock market crash in New York ushered in unprecedented industrial and commercial depression on a world scale. The effects took some while to reach Britain, but the slump struck at the basis of *all* privately supported ventures and sharpened competition for those sources which did remain. It also enhanced the attractions of the BBC for orchestral players in London.

The vulnerability of the LSO revealed during these months rubbed in Richter's dictum that its security lay in artistic discipline. In October 1929, one concert in particular demonstrated that the Orchestra might well be able to recapture the standards of Richter's day. The conductor on this occasion was Willem Mengelberg, making his first appearance in London since his pre-war concerts with the LSO. The programme: *Sinfonia in B flat* by J. C. Bach—a Mengelberg favourite which was condescendingly treated by the critics—*Don Juan* of Strauss and Tchaikovsky's Fifth Symphony. But if the programme evoked little enthusiasm from the professional concert-goers, the performance was universally regarded as outstanding: sonorous, colourful, vital—all attributes which the LSO was condemned for lacking. Quite obviously, the LSO was far from a spent force, provided a trainer with Mengelberg's gifts was at hand—and who better than Mengelberg himself?

Born in Utrecht in 1871, Mengelberg had begun in Lucerne, at the age of twenty, what was to be his life's work, training symphony orchestras, through involving the players themselves in his own passion for orchestral qualities of balance, sound, the minutiae of accentuation, precision; all of which became the hallmarks of a Mengelberg performance. After three years in Lucerne, Mengelberg was offered the post of Director of the Concertgebouw Orchestra in Amsterdam—with which he remained associated for over fifty years. From 1921 onwards he divided his time between Amsterdam and New York. In New York, however, his tenure gave way to Toscanini, fortunately for the LSO. The Board asked Lionel Powell to ensure that as many concerts as possible were conducted by Mengelberg and Beecham in the following season.

During the remainder of the 1929–30 season, the LSO failed to reach the same standards and ran foul of the critics, whose judgements reflected performances given by a continuing procession through London of illustrious visiting orchestras—the Vienna Philharmonic under Furtwängler, the Concertgebouw under Mengelberg, the Colonne Orchestra under Gabriel Pierné and, lastly, the newly amalgamated Philharmonic-Symphony Orchestra of New York under Toscanini. Orchestral musicians tend to be ambivalent about critics in the daily or weekly press, holding them "outsiders" and therefore necessarily debarred from judging the trade they criticise. As assessors of aesthetic experience, critics may be interesting and even relevant, but if they are any good they must raise issues which cannot be disposed of in the space allowed—which is sometimes misleading and always unsatisfactory. On the other hand, musicians, like all performers, are happy if a notice provides evidence that someone has got the point of the performance, and they are aware, as professionals, that favourable notices sell tickets. On the whole, critics arouse friendly curiosity rather than hostility except when, like Ernest Newman, they publicly admit to enjoying the sensation that performers are afraid of them.*

* Singers, conductors and soloists tend to be more sensitive because they are more vulnerable to the professional consequences of bad notices: an orchestra confers a certain collective resilience.

In the spring of 1930, however, some London press comments on the LSO were sufficiently virulent to prompt the thought that they had caused one or two engagements to be lost, particularly a Leeds Festival booking. The Board considered various means of fighting back, including barring the offenders from LSO promotions, notably the critics of the *Daily Express* and the *Sunday Times*. Ernest Newman appeared to some Directors to be "obviously a paid servant of the BBC". The idea of a ban was agreed but eventually the minority view on the Board, viz. that implementing it would be a confession of weakness, prevailed, and nothing was done. The Directors were not seeking to bar all critics, merely to get rid of those they thought intolerably prejudiced; their intentions, fortunately unfulfilled, reflect their disquiet at the stresses within the Orchestra and their awareness of how vulnerable it was to the initiatives being taken by the BBC. Their concern in this respect was shared by the Members, 45 of whom at the end of the year requested a meeting to discuss the possibility of strengthening the second violin and cello departments which in their opinion were "lamentably weak". The Board was divided on the issue: Gordon Walker descanted on the disloyalty implied in Members' presuming to sit in judgement on their colleagues, while Anthony Collins opposed to this view the necessities of the Orchestra. The hard fact was that the formation of the "permanent" LSO split the Orchestra: bickering between groups damaged morale. Furthermore, the threat posed by the BBC increased tensions. Confidence ebbed.

It returned in full flood when Mengelberg arrived to open the 1930–31 season. Forty-five years later, his first rehearsal is still vividly remembered by those who were present. The conductor spent the best part of an hour on the opening bars of Mendelssohn's Overture *A Midsummer Night's Dream* . . . and this without antagonising the players! Wynn Reeves summarised Mengelberg's methods and their effects:

> Mengelberg was an eye-opener: among other things he definitely improved the general intonation of the woodwind by making them listen to each other instead of the prevalent attitude of the time that "I am right". He was also merciless to the strings, insisting that they should not only use the

> same up or down bow but the same part of the bow; this was rather hard on some of us who rather prided ourselves that practically anything was possible at any part of the bow; though such an idea is laudable, there is no doubt there is a proper place of the bow for everything, that is to say, the easiest place, therefore the general result was much better when we adopted it. As to the woodwind, he insisted that no wind instrument was perfectly in tune throughout, therefore it was the duty of all wind players to know which were the slight imperfections of the other instruments, apart from their own, so that when they were playing in combination they were prepared to make the slight adjustment necessary. He also insisted that the wind players should get together in the band room and settle the pitch.
>
> As to the strings, brass and percussion, he was tremendously exacting in all detail and kept us on our toes throughout the performance; at one time he was a percussion player himself and had a lot to tell them, amongst other things that it was necessary for the side drum to tune up to the pitch of the orchestra at all times, and especially in such works as Ravel's *Bolero* to tune to the actual note. This influence spread to all orchestral players.

In case the critics and the public were slow to notice the difference, the LSO took the unusual course of pointing it out to them, in the programmes for the initial concerts under Mengelberg.

> Throughout his career . . . Dr Mengelberg has imbued orchestras with that mysterious quality of coherence which makes them as sentient as a single musician. . . . It has needed no more than the first two [concerts] to convince the leaders of musical opinion in London that the most representative orchestra of the metropolis has entered upon a new chapter of its history. The despondency concerning our orchestral position which was so prevalent in the spring has vanished at the coming of a leader. . . . The result has been remarkable, electrifying.

This message was conveyed not only to metropolitan audiences but to those in the provinces, since Mengelberg conducted the

Orchestra on its spring tour in February 1931: it was at one concert on this tour that he cut the interval to five minutes, because "we are so splendidly in tune".

At this juncture, advertising the LSO's virtues was the more necessary since in October 1930 the newly-founded BBC Symphony Orchestra gave its inaugural concert in the Queen's Hall. As long as the LSO's confidence and artistic merit persisted, its future was reasonably secure, and the damage inflicted by the BBC could be minimised; success in the concert hall could offset the appeal of the BBC's "musical civil service".

In the following season, Mengelberg was not available and the main share of the work devolved on Beecham, with whom the LSO appeared at the Leeds Festival. He also paid for extra rehearsals for the première of Walton's *Belshazzar's Feast*, under Sargent, which was a brilliant highlight of the Festival. The Directors invited Beecham to submit programmes for the various series of concerts in which the LSO was engaged, its own promotions at Queen's Hall, Lionel Powell's enterprises at the Albert Hall and provincial appearances. Beecham did so, and was formally thanked by the Board.

The effect of regular rehearsals and performances under two such conductors as Mengelberg and Beecham over successive seasons was remarkable—so much so that the Board thought it worthwhile to extend its advertising policy beyond LSO programmes to the musical community at large. Press notices were reprinted as broadsheets. The first was devoted to one concert, in November 1931. Ironically, in view of the past, the critic was Ernest Newman and, in view of the future, the conductor was Beecham.

> . . . What the public is now being privileged to hear at LSO concerts is really a new chapter in the art of conducting. The orchestral singing is not only a sheer delight in the melodies that are obvious to even the most casual listener or conductor because they lie on top of the music, but extends to all the melodies that are tucked away in this fold and that of the inner orchestral tissue. For proof of this we had only to listen last Sunday afternoon to the performances of the *Meistersinger* overture and the "Enigma" Variations: in no

> other performances of these works that I have ever heard has the orchestra as a whole given such an impression of being a nest of singing birds.
>
> The second Brahms symphony also acquired an extraordinary sensitiveness without losing anything of its essential strength. . . . In this country, in particular, we have grown too accustomed to hearing Brahms played, and hearing him discussed, as if Hubert Parry had written him. The only trouble with performances such as those of last Sunday is that they will make it difficult for some of us to listen with much pleasure again to performances of the other and less sensitive type.[3]

Beecham was not the only conductor who could get excellent results from the LSO. At this time, the Orchestra was playing splendidly under Coates and Harty—but only to half-empty houses. As Lionel Powell pointed out, the only native conductor who came anywhere near competing in drawing power with such eminent visitors as Weingartner (who wrote privately to a friend that the LSO "has perfected itself and played very beautifully") was Beecham. Even he did not infallibly secure a full house. But he cost the LSO much less than foreign visitors, not only in terms of fees (which he frequently refused) but also in that he contributed towards exceptional expenses. Thus, during 1931, the Directors were predisposed to regard Beecham as their best bet as successor to Mengelberg. For his part, Beecham, having broken off negotiations with the BBC, began to think that the LSO, suitably reconstructed, might be the "permanent orchestra" he was trying to create. The interests of the LSO and Beecham began to converge. Coincidentally, Malcolm Sargent, who wanted to have at his disposal an orchestra capable of more consistently polished performances, was offered £30,000 by Mrs Courtauld for that purpose, together with a subsidy thereafter. Sargent approached the Directors, who were very interested.

The offer was itself an acknowledgement of their efforts over the past two years. The BBC Symphony Orchestra was a *fait accompli*, which could not be shrugged off, but they seemed to have hit on the formula to offer it strong competition. The LSO had guaranteed spheres of work for three years; it had regular personnel for rehearsal and performance: revitalised by Mengelberg, it could offer its own distinctive insights into the repertoire; it could be equal to the BBC, though different.

Nevertheless, the Directors sought to improve the Orchestra's position *vis-à-vis* the Corporation by participating in measures organised by all those concert-giving organisations whose livelihood had been threatened by the irruption of the BBC into public music. They banded themselves together in the Conference of Musical Societies, and, with the Royal Philharmonic Society, organised a conference under the chairmanship of Sir Hamilton Harty to consider "the musical activities of the British Broadcasting Corporation outside the studio". Meetings were held from December 1930 to February 1931. The LSO's submissions put the general case against the BBC, viz. that being financed by licence fees and taxation it enjoyed two advantages denied to others: it could give concerts even if it failed to sell a single ticket and, through the salaries and conditions it could offer, could denude the principal British orchestras of their finest players. The remedy would be for the Corporation to confine its orchestra to the studio and rely on existing organisations for outside performances, which would serve the need, particularly of provincial audiences, for "live" concerts.

In March 1931, representatives of the Conference and of the Royal Philharmonic Society met the Governors of the BBC to discuss memoranda submitted by the two parties, outlining their position. The case of the Conference was put by Harty, Sargent and the LSO Secretary, Arthur Maney. They received no sympathy. The chairman of the meeting, Lord Gainford, agreed that the BBC had a dominant position, which it was determined to assert: public concerts were a necessary part of its policy and were essential to strengthen the orchestra. His fellow Governor, Mrs Snowden, put the "quality" argument: it was unreasonable that the BBC should be expected, having formed their magnificent orchestra, to keep it cloistered and secluded within the walls of a studio. The subsequent formal reply of the BBC echoed this theme: "the Board definitely consider it unreasonable to suggest that the Corporation's new orchestra would be barred from public performance. Apart from the contribution which the orchestra is making to the prestige of British music, and the acclamation with which it has been received, when it is playing as a full unit a public hall must, as a matter of fact, be used, as no studio is large enough to hold it." The letter concluded that if the parties represented had cause for apprehension or grievance, the BBC would be willing to consider any recommendations. The "quality" argument was especially galling in that the excellence of the Corporation's orchestra derived from its having poached players from the others. Furthermore, the arguments about the size of the new orchestra admitted that the BBC had deliberately recruited a number in excess of its available space—which the Conference took as signifying an intention to dominate, *ab initio*. Retrospective evidence of the Corporation's intentions was revealed four years later, in the evidence of Adrian Boult to the Ullswater Committee (on the renewal of the BBC's charter): "Five years ago, the reputation of British music and British musicians abroad was extremely low. *Our capital city contained but one orchestra and that an inferior one*."*[4] By 1935, the damage had been done, from the point of view of the Conference members. But even in 1930, the exchanges with the BBC made it unequivocally clear that the Corporation aimed at dominance, using its public subsidies, and had absolutely no intention of modifying its policies. The other concert-promoters would have to adapt to the Corporation.

The LSO prudently decided that this called for negotiation rather than opposition.

* Author's italics. *M.P.*

VII

THE DIRECTORS MIGHT legitimately have congratulated themselves that the Orchestra had emerged from a period of considerable tension, consolidated, free of deputies and with increased public esteem. All that remained was to clinch the matter of the principal conductor—Beecham preferably, Sargent possibly.

In July 1931, Lionel Powell proposed a visit to Paris in the following December, "the conditions being that the LSO would take the entire receipts for the two concerts—Sir Thomas Beecham being willing to conduct without fee, and to be responsible for expenses". In September, the Board approached Beecham with the idea that he should become a member and shareholder in the LSO, but they kept in mind options of securing support from other sources—"notably Dr Sargent". Anthony Collins pointed out that "before any definite offer of financial support could be secured, it would probably be necessary to reorganise the personnel of the Orchestra". This the Directors had already started on their own account. Anthony Collins sounded Sargent accordingly, and by November, the possibility of his joining the Board, with or without Beecham, was being aired.

By the end of the year, Beecham's thinking had crystallised. The Minutes for 25th November 1931 record a fateful proposal: "A letter was read from Sir Thomas Beecham in which he stated that he had been asked to form an orchestra of the first rank, expressing the wish that the London Symphony Orchestra should be the orchestra to be approached but, before doing so, he wished to know if the Directors would be willing to consider changes in the personnel of the Orchestra, should that be found necessary." The Board rightly asked for further details. Then, immediately afterwards, the LSO suffered two successive setbacks: the Paris visit was cancelled at the last minute, due to difficulties there, and unexpectedly Lionel Powell died.

Powell had been central to the Orchestra's position in public music. He had constructed the arrangements with the Gramophone Company and the Royal Opera Syndicate in 1929, and in consequence had become very involved in the day-to-day running of the LSO. Indeed one Director had publicly aired his disagreement with his colleagues over Powell and urged that, at the conclusion of the contract, the Company should once more take control of the concerts. Powell's death may have freed the LSO from his interventions in the management of its affairs, but, by the same token, it destroyed its financial basis. Early in January 1932 the Receiver to Powell's estate informed the Board that it would not be possible for the estate to carry out Powell's liabilities under his contract with the LSO. An imminent tour and the rest of the season's concerts were in jeopardy. Beecham subscribed and persuaded Lord Howard de Walden to do likewise. Their subventions enabled the tour to go through, but no more. Meanwhile, artists under contract with Lionel Powell to appear with the LSO had had their arrangements cancelled by the Receiver. So, the problem for the Board was to salvage what they could and improvise the rest of the season from conductors and soloists who were available and could be persuaded to accept lower fees. (Weingartner, Harty, Oda Slobodskaya and Walter Widdop all accepted lower terms or forewent payment.) The LSO also negotiated a reduced rate for the hire of the Queen's Hall. On 12th February 1932 Beecham procured a guarantee of £2,000 from the Gramophone Company, and undertook with his friends to bear any deficit remaining at the end of the season, in excess of that sum. The Board recorded its satisfaction with this outcome to Beecham's "untiring efforts" on behalf of the Orchestra. The combination of guarantees, reductions in fees and charges and rapid collection of outstanding debts shored up the LSO. The immediate consequences of Powell's death had been satisfactorily overcome: the long-term problem remained.

Before the Directors could begin to consider policies beyond the immediate season, two decisions deprived them of any reasonable basis for forecasts, or hopes of success.

In March, financial stringency compelled the Royal Opera Syndicate to abandon its projected International Season at Covent Garden.[1] With that, another essential element in the scheme of 1929 disappeared from the scene. Then, the Gramophone Company, in negotiation with the Board, showed itself prepared to do far less than it had promised in February. Now there would be no opera and no large guarantee—and the Orchestra could not survive on fees from recordings (even though Beecham had introduced it to the Columbia Gramophone Company). The arrangements whereby the LSO had intended to secure its own future collapsed. It became correspondingly more vulnerable to initiatives from others.

The arrangements with Beecham were still outstanding—he being abroad. In his absence, his solicitor sent to the Directors a memorandum of his proposals including his suggested criticism of personnel. At much the same time, the Board received a letter addressed to Beecham by the Columbia Record Company, which intimated that in its opinion the LSO needed "a certain measure of reorganisation", which owing to the constitution of LSO Ltd might be a difficult matter for the management. Columbia suggested that reorganisation could perhaps best be effected by outside agency, mentioning Beecham and themselves as competent and willing to undertake the job. The Board agreed with the premise (in view of its own efforts over the previous eighteen months, it could hardly have done less) but thought it "inadvisable, at this juncture to give too great a measure of control to any outside agency".

In April the Board considered other options: one was an offer from Harty, who had just broken with the Hallé, to work with the LSO; the other was a proposal by Sir Landon Ronald that his New Symphony Orchestra, the LSO and the orchestra chosen for the Royal Philharmonic Society concerts should amalgamate. These suggestions offered the Directors a future which involved them with neither Sargent nor Beecham, but they decided to leave them in abeyance pending Beecham's return. He arrived at the beginning of May, and promptly suggested the following changes: "the first desk of the first violins, a number of changes in the rank and file of the second violins and cellos and preferably one in the double basses. In the wind, the second and third flutes, a reorganisation of the oboe department, a new bass clarinet, if possible, a new second bassoon, second and third horns, first trumpet, if a better were obtainable, third trumpet, first and third trombone."

The Board "felt this criticism to be justified to a large extent, but that it was possible to improve the Orchestra without such comprehensive changes, and that any agreement to effect such changes would be, to a great extent, contingent on the nature of the contract it was proposed to offer the Orchestra." Anthony Collins pressed that the LSO Directors should make up their own minds as to who was to be replaced. They would then be better placed to negotiate for the ninety concerts and ten weeks of opera which were to be the basis of the new Orchestra's existence. The Directors drew up two lists—one of those whose services should be retained or sought from outside, the other of those who were not required. The two lists combined proposed changes in personnel almost as extensive as, but not wholly identical with, those suggested by Beecham. Additionally, the Directors proposed to take the opportunity to rid the LSO of players who had been "guilty of bad conduct on numerous occasions at past engagements . . . and were not worthy of any offer of contract". It was common ground between Beecham and the Board, at this stage, that the LSO was to continue to be autonomous, but its activity was to be co-ordinated by an independent company under Samuel Courtauld.

Then Sargent stepped in. At the beginning of July, he informed two of the Directors (Alexandra and Collins) that "the Committee responsible for the series of concerts next season were of the opinion that the Board of Directors of the London Symphony Orchestra was not necessary"; the Committee wanted direct control. Within a week, Harold Holt individually invited three of the Directors (Alexandra, Collins and Gordon Walker) to meet him to discuss the new orchestra. The Board demurred at these unofficial overtures, but agreed that a meeting should take place, so as "to persuade Mr Holt to communicate officially with the Board" in order that "any further discussion should be directed to securing the proposed contract for the LS Orchestra". The three Directors saw Holt on Tuesday 12th July, when he said that "all avenues were open". The next day, the LSO Directors were stupefied and angered by Holt's "official communication"—a letter in which, according to the Minutes "he quite definitely stated that his Board did not propose to enter into any negotiations with the London Symphony Orchestra, nor did they propose to use the title . . . the reason given being that, in the opinion of his Board the LSO had lost most of its former prestige, and that it no longer commanded the confidence of the public." This *volte face* contradicted all the assurances given by Beecham, and the "reason" adduced made nonsense of his negotiations hitherto. On Friday 15th July Collins called on Beecham himself, who admitted to having dictated the letter signed by Harold Holt, but reiterated his personal view that the LSO should be included in the proposed scheme: his own Board of Management, however, did not share his opinion and were opposed to any dealings with the Orchestra. Collins recapitulated the facts of the case, viz. that the LSO Directors had agreed to reorganise the personnel of the Orchestra and were fully prepared for a meeting of the two Boards to decide the final personnel and method of working. The alleged decline in public prestige and confidence could be refuted by press comment and the frequently expressed opinion of Beecham himself, Harty, Weingartner, Sargent and others. Beecham, reported Collins, agreed and even went so far as to outline a form of reply to Holt. With that, Beecham left to keep an engagement in Munich.

The LSO Directors, meeting the next morning, "expressed divergent views . . . as to the reliability to be placed in Sir Thomas' statements". Collins offered to go to Munich, if necessary, to ensure Beecham's support for the inclusion of the LSO in the scheme.

Again Sargent intervened. The Bursar of the Royal College of Music told Arthur Maney that Sargent had tried to secure the cancellation of a proposed LSO engagement for the Patrons' Fund Rehearsal the following October, suggesting that *his* orchestra be engaged and that the LSO would soon cease to exist. After this intelligence, it was hardly surprising that when Collins called on Sargent he was told that Sargent's Board stood by the letter signed by Harold Holt. Sargent did undertake, however, to ask them to meet the LSO Directors.

Holt duly extended the invitation, for 25th July, but wrote separately that his Board could not attend in full. The LSO Directors decided, that, on that basis, "no useful purpose would be served" by their attending. They would accordingly be unable to accept Holt's invitation but were fully prepared to meet his *full* Board at any time. The notion of Collins going to Munich was not proceeded with, as "it was felt that a full [LSO] Board was necessary for a decision on the matter". Instead, the LSO Directors offered Beecham conducting dates for the next season, suggesting that Anthony Collins would be prepared to visit him in Munich. This was their final communication to Beecham.

At much the same time, Sargent was on the telephone to him, announcing the LSO Directors' refusal to attend the meeting of the two Boards in Harold Holt's office on 25th July. Beecham determined to form a new orchestra. The LSO's position collapsed.

What prompted the changes of front during the month of July 1932? The available evidence yields no conclusive answers to this question. At the time, the LSO was inclined to lay the responsibility at Sargent's door, especially as Samuel Courtauld, at the beginning of August, weighed in with a letter upholding the views in Holt's letter of 13th July. This the Board felt especially ungrateful in view of the Orchestra's fine performances at the Courtauld–Sargent concerts. It contemplated a press campaign against Sargent, possibly with support from the Musicians' Union. The LSO certainly boycotted him as a conductor. Harold Holt was not the committed supporter of the LSO his partner had been, but he, equally, was not the vital figure in the transactions which Lionel Powell had been until his death. Beecham was absent from London when the negotiations were in their last, crucial stages; was he privy to the final twist, to the demands to be made and the tactics used, or did he acquiesce *post facto*, knowing that if he wanted a first-class orchestra, whoever paid for it would have the decisive voice? If the latter supposition is true, then responsibility would lie with those who were backing the "permanent orchestra". But Lord Howard de Walden, for one, protested that he had given his support on the understanding that the LSO reconstructed would be the new orchestra.

These speculations are not academic, since assumptions and arguments about what really happened influenced Directors of the LSO for nearly twenty years afterwards. The immediate aftermath emphasised the harm the LSO had suffered when Members were invited to join Beecham's new orchestra. "Loyalty", again, became the dominant characteristic required of musicians in the LSO. The Minutes record an approach to buy the title of the Orchestra—which was derisorily refused. This, however, was all the satisfaction the Directors could salvage from these traumatic weeks. They left the LSO shattered, disrupted in membership, morale and ensemble.

Many of the details are still obscure—a circumstance which has helped to perpetuate a number of myths about it. The most enduring is that the LSO refused to compromise its independence for money. The evidence already discussed shows that the Directors, rightly, had been only too prepared to abridge their scope for autonomous action in order to improve the LSO's financial position and earning power. They had admitted Lionel Powell into questions of management. They had accepted Sargent's suggestions about specific players and even made available to him statements of fees paid to individuals.

Beecham's scheme would therefore have implied no innovations and the Directors were willing to go more than halfway towards his requirements. Much the most intelligent suggestion in the negotiations was to invite him into the LSO as a shareholder, which balanced the risk that Beecham by nature was not a committee man against the advantage of turning him publicly into an "LSO-man".

All these things were overlooked in the aftermath of the *débâcle*. From the side of the LSO, it left a residue of mistrust and hatred of Beecham and all his works. The loss of seventeen players—including a Director who promised to stand by the LSO*—rankled. Some of the Directors indulged in mildly paranoiac language and behaviour, habitually referring to those who had joined the new orchestra in terms of "disloyalty" and "treachery". Cooler reflection would have shown

* "The Board felt this action to be of a most traitorous nature, and worthy of the strongest condemnation."

Beecham greets Mengelberg, 1930

A scene from the Crown Film Unit production *The Instruments of the Orchestra*: the LSO recording Benjamin Britten's music under Sargent, 1946

them that in fact essentially all they had done was to act on the principle which had led to the foundation of the LSO, namely the right of the individual to maximise his professional opportunities. Old revolutionaries are notoriously insensitive to the same initiative in others.

But the Directors had been sorely tried. As recently as two years before, they had enjoyed the strongest position in London music, with the LSO's own promotions and regular engagements by the syndicates running Covent Garden, both of which further advertised their virtues to impresarios elsewhere. Under Mengelberg and Beecham they had recovered from the variable and unsatisfactory standards of playing which had become only too evident. They had tried to establish the LSO's position by initiating the contracts with the Gramophone Company and Covent Garden—only to see their schemes founder through the death of Lionel Powell and the effects of the Slump on patronage.

All their efforts were now brought to nothing. The LSO had to face not one competitor for public attention but two, one of which, the BBC Symphony Orchestra, was subsidised to the point where it could dictate the terms of employment for all other musicians, while the other, the London Philharmonic Orchestra, collected from Colonel Blois seasons of international opera at Covent Garden, and acquired in quick succession Royal Philharmonic Society engagements, a lucrative recording contract, and the Courtauld–Sargent concerts. Moreover, the LPO embarked on a dazzling international career, under a man whom the Directors regarded as primarily or wholly responsible for their plight. The winner took all. Beecham had applied the same formula which the Directors had worked out with the Gramophone Company, the Royal Opera Syndicate and Lionel Powell in 1929! From "the high water mark of financial and artistic success" on which the LSO rightly congratulated itself in that year, the Orchestra had partly disintegrated and its future activity was in question. Beecham's relationship with the LSO dissolved in rancour and feelings of betrayal. After 1932, he conducted the Orchestra only once—at a celebration concert of the Fabian Society, under the presidency of Harold Laski, in 1946.

July 1932 remains one of the most contentious episodes in a

career not noted for conciliation. The public Beecham is a puzzling phenomenon in British life. As a conductor, he could, in the words of one associate, "make any orchestra play 50 per cent better than it knew it could—and nobody knew how he did it". Generations of players and public responded to this quality, and to his sensitivity to orchestral balance and colour. For Beecham, music came first: he was a perfectionist, and other considerations had to give way. The "other considerations", however, invariably forced themselves into the reckoning. They appeared in the politics and administration of music, to which Beecham brought a highly complex nature, often masked by a display of Edwardian flippancy. He was wilful, given to expressing his opinions freely and imperiously—it was a characteristic of his generation—and to rapid changes of front. These were commonly construed as "flexibility" or "unreliability" according to choice. He also showed himself capable of generous behaviour and its opposite alike, except that the first tended to be private and the second, public.

Beecham found it particularly difficult to contemplate the success of others in spheres he considered his own. Thus, Glyndebourne first was ignored and then became "Christie's minstrels". He was emphatically not a committee man, and frequently treated venerated institutions, particularly academies of music, with hostility and contempt. In these spheres, he cultivated to the highest degree "the gentle art of making enemies". So it happened that Beecham was often denied opportunities for which he was on other grounds superbly equipped. He was blackballed by the Hallé in Barbirolli's regime, as well as by the LSO, although he had saved both from the worst effects of the First World War. It was unfortunate that he was not asked to build up the permanent opera at Covent Garden after the Second World War—but it was inevitable, given the mistrust his qualities generated.

Beecham spent his life and his money trying to create a framework for his gifts, but after his father's death, he never personally commanded sufficient funds for that purpose. Hence the succession of boards, syndicates, and *ad hoc* organisations; hence also the disputes and disagreements which made him such a boon to the legal profession. But one framework after another broke in his hands. His international opera ventures were disrupted successively by the outbreak of world war. The Beecham Opera Company and the Imperial League of Opera both foundered over lack of funds. In 1939, the LPO, as Beecham founded it, failed through withdrawal of financial support and was saved by the players who remodelled the orchestra on the self-governing lines of the LSO. While Beecham lived, his postwar Royal Philharmonic Orchestra only narrowly survived some very acute financial shortages. From 1920 onwards, the need for money made him dependent on those who furnished his funds. The world which provided security for his kind of public music making was gravely damaged in 1914 and received its *coup de grâce* in 1939.

VIII

THE DIRECTORS HAD to reconstruct. In short order, they re-established their connection with L. G. Sharpe and took up Harty's offer of the previous April, "to co-operate for the next season". From the negotiations Harty emerged as Conductor in Chief, with the task of re-building the ensemble and maintaining the LSO in the concert world. Financially, the immediate situation was not quite so stringent. Subventions during the 1931/32 season from the Gramophone Company, Beecham and Lord Howard de Walden enabled the Orchestra to declare a dividend of 15 per cent. Getting support for the future, however, was more problematical. At the Director's Meeting on 20th July, when Sargent's *démarche* was considered, an offer had appeared from F. J. Nettlefold, a director of Courtaulds, who wished from his private fortune to guarantee two concerts, provided at one of them Wolfgang Graeser's version of *Die Kunst der Fuge* were given. His proposition was now accepted, and, under Hans Weisbach, from Düsseldorf, Graeser's arrangement became the programme for the opening concert in the LSO's 1932/33 international series. From this beginning Nettlefold emerged as the mainstay of the Orchestra's reconstruction during the thirties, for he became its chief financial support, brought back Albert Coates into the Orchestra's affairs as his Artistic Adviser (from 1935) and provided it with opportunities to perform in public concerts and private engagements, at which frequently appeared Vera de Villiers (in private life, Mrs F. J. Nettlefold). This position inevitably conferred on Nettlefold a role in the management of the LSO: he was, for example, consulted when Erich Kleiber summarily cancelled a concert after his fee lost value when Britain went off the Gold Standard. The relationship between Nettlefold and the LSO was formalised by contract—an arrangement which endured until February 1937.

For the season 1932/33, however, Harty was in charge. A suggestion that he join the Board was not adopted but his position brought him into the problems of orchestral management, not only in programme planning but also in the selection and control of personnel. On 27th September 1932, he attended a Board Meeting (at Pagani's Restaurant!) at which "the complete list of the Orchestra was gone through". He raised the question of strengthening the strings by bringing in players from the Hallé. The Board agreed unanimously. Eventually, seven strings and one tympanist appeared regularly—one being the Hallé leader, Alfred Barker—which immediately posed the problem of what to do about Billy Reed. The Directors had wanted to supersede him for the last two years or so, but had been extremely reluctant to dismiss him because of his services to the Orchestra and of his tremendous prestige with the organisers of the Three Choirs Festival. Harty pushed them towards a decision and provided them with an excuse. Barker became Sub-Principal (though did not stay to become Leader) but his arrival on the front desks brought about the resignation of Wynn Reeves, who refused to be demoted to number three. It was accepted "with very great regret at losing the services of a Member of such long and valuable service". In these matters, the Board and Harty were on the same side. Friction between them resulted when Harty released individual players from appearances, without consulting the Board, therefore upsetting the delicately worked-out system of permissions which it operated. Harty and the Board also haggled about fees, the Board taking the view that as the LSO was helping him to obtain a public in London, after leaving Manchester, he should be content with a nominal fee: Harty thought otherwise. Trouble of a different order ensued when the LSO's Conductor in Chief wanted to record with the LPO. The Board expressed strong disapproval. The Directors were supported by Nettlefold: "I am certainly surprised to hear that Sir Hamilton is going to conduct the London Philharmonic Orchestra. . . . If Sir Hamilton is to conduct any of the London Philharmonic Orchestral concerts, then I think it would be only fair to make an arrangement whereby Sir Thomas Beecham conducted a similar number of LSO concerts." Nettlefold's *quid pro quo* was even less attractive to the Board than Harty's intention! He, for his part, maintained his right to accept other engagements as he saw fit. The two sides compromised on an understanding that Harty would not conduct the LPO *in public*, except at the concert of the Royal Philharmonic Society at which he received the Society's Gold Medal.

Nettlefold turned his mind to strengthening the Orchestra's financial position, to cover deficits and permit some attempt at long-range planning. He headed a Guarantee Fund, consisting of capital contributions from individuals or companies given on the understanding that in any one year, the maximum call would be 20 per cent. By assiduous propaganda, Nettlefold raised £3,300 in the first year, from guarantors who included Lord Justice Scrutton ("As I am over seventy-six, it is not likely to be a five years' guarantee"), Adrian Boult, the Columbia Gramophone Company, and—although their names did not appear in the published list of subscribers—Baron d'Erlanger and, later, Lord Howard de Walden. Both were involved in the LPO, which suggests one possible explanation.

The Guarantee Fund helped to reduce deficits and ensure that the LSO remained credit-worthy, without its having to call on capital. The subscribers larded their annual payments with comments:

> Lord Justice Scrutton encloses cheque for £20, his guarantee for last season. He regrets it was unsuccessful: the programmes did not seem to fill the gallery. A little more Wagner might be desirable.

> I must honestly say that last season's programmes were to me singularly unattractive. Might I suggest that information as to prospective plans should be given to guarantors? They obviously have a very special interest. (A. G. Phean)

> I enclose my cheque for £116. 16. 8, the amount due under my Guarantee. I regret very much that in your prospectus for the forthcoming season, there is only a single work by Elgar to represent native composers. I feel that if this is always to be the policy of the LSO I shall very soon cease to take any real interest in that body. (Lord Howard de Walden)

(The Directors assured his Lordship that they agreed with him entirely, but that concert-goers seemed to prefer the Old Masters, which made it impossible under existing conditions to include the works of native composers.)

One subscriber contributed to the Fund on the condition that Harty remained the permanent conductor or Musical Director of the Orchestra. In fact, the Guarantee Fund enabled the Board to get rid of him.

It became evident during the 1933/34 season that Harty, despite his outstanding merits as a trainer of ensemble and his rewarding insights as an interpreter, did not "draw" the public in London as he had when he visited the metropolis with the Hallé. Restive voices were raised, advocating a return to the former policy of guest-conductors. The Board defended its choice of Harty, pointing to the demonstrable improvement in playing standards. But at the end of the season, in commenting on its results, F. J. Nettlefold drew the same critical conclusion. In consequence, the programme sketched out for the next season omitted Harty. Harty, from America, protested against the breach of his agreement with the Directors, stressing that they could engage whomsoever they wanted for extra concerts, but that the major series belonged to him. The Board, with suspicious rapidity, took this as evidence of Harty's "determination to exercise the most complete domination of the policy of the Orchestra" and, after a number of acrimonious exchanges, Harty's appointment as Conductor in Chief was cancelled. He conducted individual concerts in subsequent seasons, and was responsible for introducing the LSO to the Decca Record Company when the Orchestra stood in great need of such a connection (the LPO recorded for Columbia, now part of Electrical and Musical Industries Ltd and no longer a competitor of HMV). Harty's most significant artistic legacy to the LSO was to interest the Directors in preparing under his guidance a new work by William Walton, his First Symphony. But in the early thirties, immediate income was all-important and reinforced the instinct for independence: Harty had to go.

It was revealing that, in their exchanges with him, the Board had admitted that they "naturally wished to fall in with the views of Mr Nettlefold". During this period, they fell in with his views on a number of matters, agreeing *not* to invite Richard Tauber to conduct, and to replace the Verdi *Requiem* (with Vera de Villiers) by the *St Matthew Passion* in order to avoid competing with the Royal Philharmonic Society. The Board minuted their "feeling that Mr Nettlefold had the right to make this alteration". It was towards the end of Harty's "reign" that Nettlefold proposed to the LSO that Albert Coates should be admitted to its counsels as his Artistic Adviser. For a while, both Harty's and Coates' positions were printed on the programmes. After Harty's dismissal, Coates attended all meetings at which engagements offered to the Orchestra were discussed. His position differed from Harty's in that it rested on a relationship with the man who had first option on the LSO's services. But Coates also had a relationship of a rather more intense nature with Mrs Nettlefold, which ultimately resulted in her becoming the second Mrs Coates. This was known in the profession and the LSO suspected that Coates' interventions in its management problems were perhaps on her behalf, as well as her husband's.[1] In April 1936, Coates raised a scheme whereby Harold Holt would place additional concerts for the LSO provided its playing strengh was improved in certain departments. One infers that, superficially, this formula must have seemed ominously familiar. The Board found the proposed changes unacceptable and took care to discuss the plan with Nettlefold himself, L. G. Sharpe, Coates and Mrs Nettlefold. On the day of the meeting the LSO Secretary contrived to secure "a few minutes alone with Mr Nettlefold, before the arrival of Mrs Nettlefold and Mr Coates". In the course of the protracted interview Nettlefold quashed the proposal and "Mr Coates repudiated all his suggestions made at the previous interview".

Nettlefold's influence, however unwelcome in the management of the LSO's affairs, did secure its livelihood and enable the Directors to consider engaging conductors and soloists who would add to the Orchestra's prestige, increase its drawing power and enable it to compete more effectively with its rivals. Thus the LSO was able to consider Walter, Furtwängler, Kreisler, Rachmaninov and Toscanini for its own promotions. Toscanini, at a fee of £1,000 and *nine* rehearsals, proved too expensive. Rachmaninov agreed to play but insisted that the only British conductors who commanded his confidence were Beecham, Sargent and Wood. The first remained totally unacceptable, the last was unavailable: the LSO hastily scrapped its boycott of Sargent.

Fundamentally, Nettlefold's contribution to the LSO was not only to take the lead in staving off financial disaster but to create the conditions in which it could get along without him. By 1937, the Orchestra was back at full strength and its accounts even showed a credit balance, taking into account the subsidies from the guarantors. This favourable situation proved transitory. It became evident, soon after the 1937/38 season got under way, that losses were to be heavy. The expectation provoked a dispute between the Directors and F. J. Nettlefold as to the grounds and extent of the obligations he had assumed towards the LSO. The Board soon found itself obliged to conduct business with the Orchestra's chief benefactor through their respective solicitors! The available details do not permit any final judgement of the points at issue, but a clue to the Directors' thinking appears in their proposal that Mr Nettlefold's obligations should be reduced against his sharing with them decisions on selecting conductors. The Board's reaction to Nettlefold's withdrawal—technically over questions of subsidy—additionally bears out the notion that the LSO was beginning to feel it was paying too high a price for his support: "The Board accepted this decision [to withdraw support] . . . but agreed that it would be in the best interests of all concerned for the series of symphony concerts to be under the sole control of the Directors." Nettlefold's association with the LSO was, accordingly, wound up at the end of the season, in the summer of 1938. He, more than any other individual outside the LSO enabled it to survive. In this sense he complemented Harty, whose work between 1933 and 1935 kept the Orchestra coherent artistically.

Notwithstanding personal frictions, the main artistic objects of the association with Harty were splendidly achieved. Standards improved, and programmes showed refreshing changes from the usual repertoire, the Overture *Die Meistersinger* being dropped for the more rarely-heard *Euryanthe*, for example. The experiment of playing *Die Kunst der Fuge* was very successful and featured in five successive seasons. That

Nettlefold took a personal interest in the work, doubtless, helped to maintain it in the schedule, but the LSO took it on out-of-town engagements. The two most striking innovations, under Harty, were Walton's Viola Concerto (with Lionel Tertis) and the première of his First Symphony in 1934.

Walton, then thirty-three years old, had already established himself with *Façade*, *Portsmouth Point* and above all *Belshazzar's Feast*, which triumphantly demonstrated his mastery of larger forms, as well as confirming his individual voice in British composition. Walton was recognised internationally: by the time of his First Symphony, he had had four works accepted by the International Society of Contemporary Music (one programme note described him as "the world-famous Wanton"!). He began the symphony at the age of twenty-nine, in 1931, but after composing the first three movements found he had set himself problems he could not solve. Meanwhile, Harty had interested the LSO in the première and the Directors had advertised their intention to perform the piece. They could only apologise to their subscribers and patrons. The piece was re-advertised for the next season, but the composer advised that his problems remained unsolved. So, on 3rd December 1934, the LSO gave the first performance of the first three movements. The completed work was played by the BBC Symphony Orchestra the following November, under Harty. (Why that honour did not fall to the LSO remains unexplained—and is the more odd, since in the very next month (December 1935), Decca issued the first recording of the complete work, with the LSO.) Constant Lambert remarked that "the performance has all the vitality one expects from this orchestra and this conductor in collaboration." Vitality has continued to be the outstanding characteristic of the LSO in regard to Walton's First, which has stayed in the Orchestra's repertoire ever since. Harty began a tradition which in turn has been sustained by Josef Krips, Jascha Horenstein and now, André Previn. But at the time, adopting a new, and first, symphony, even from a composer whose *Belshazzar's Feast* had created a furore at the Leeds Festival as recently as 1931, was to shoulder a considerable risk.

In the same month as the Walton recording appeared, Harty with the LSO introduced to the British public a symphony in a wholly different vein, by Georges Bizet. It was written when Bizet was half Walton's age when he was working on *his* symphony, and was rediscovered by D. C. Parker in the library of the Paris Conservatoire, where it had been since 1869. The LSO gave, according to Lambert, "an admirably piquant and light hearted performance"—to a half-empty hall. The other items in the programme were Mozart's D major Symphony (K.202), played with five first violins and the rest of the Orchestra to scale, and Dvořák's in D minor. These two works were rarely heard. Were the empty seats due to faulty programme-building—through trying too many unfamiliar works, even though by familiar composers? Constant Lambert considered that the basic reason for the empty blocks of seats lay in the public's expectations. "It is one of the unfortunate legacies of the Beethoven Nine that listeners expect a symphony to depict a soul struggle in sound. An even more unfortunate legacy is the fact that every second-rate central European composer since Beethoven has attempted to satisfy this morbid and masochistic desire on the part of the listener." These three works patently did not.

They did, however, require no more than conventional forces. Works which required more, at this time, vanished from LSO promotions. Delius' *Mass of Life* and Strauss' *Schlagobers* have nothing in common except the size of the orchestra demanded: both were proposed by Harty, and both were turned down. Weisbach was allowed to conduct Bruckner's Fifth Symphony "provided it were not too long and did not require toom any extras". Extras, however, were in demand even for conventional programmes, since the Depression encouraged the deputy system. Members, like other musicians, were chasing jobs, and were in fact free to do so. This reassured those who thought that the deputy system was one of the most sacred traditions of the LSO, but was regretted by other Members who saw that deputies and high standards, however compatible in 1904, were definitely not so in 1934. Two other orchestras were demonstrating the truth of that proposition conclusively, in competition with the LSO at the Queen's Hall and elsewhere.

From 1930/32 onwards, the LSO has had a problem it did not have before, namely its place in the competition. Until that time, other orchestras, notably the Queen's Hall Orchestra, under Wood, and the New Symphony Orchestra, under Sir Landon Ronald, competed for the patronage of the public. The LSO could not afford to ignore them, but it enjoyed superior standing, partly in virtue of its "guest-conductor" policy. It was, above all, identified by name with London, and except for the late twenties attempted successfully to live up to that identity. After 1932, the LSO lost its commanding position. It competed for public attention with two far more powerful and dazzling orchestras, with one of which it had to share the claim to "represent" London, both in the United Kingdom and abroad.

Policy towards the LPO was settled by the AGM of 20th September 1932, namely that no Member would be allowed to play for it, either as member, deputy or extra. Those who might be tempted to join it were burning their boats as far as their old associates were concerned. The Board's attitude repeated in sharper terms what they had already expressed about the BBC: leaving to join the LPO deserved censure and was totally lacking in any sense of gratitude to the orchestra which had given players such a splendid opportunity to achieve a first-class position in their profession. The embargo endured and the net was spread wide. Even as late as 1939, a player who wished to accept an engagement with the English Opera Company was refused permission, on the grounds that "the offer had been made by Mr Lionel Tertis . . . who was directly connected with the London Philharmonic Orchestra". This restrictive policy had the merit of clarity, but proved difficult to enforce when the unforeseen appeared: what was to be done, if Members were asked to play in the stage bands at Covent Garden, where from 1933 Beecham was in control and the LPO in the pit? Similarly, what should be the policy about Members playing for *Hiawatha* at the Albert Hall, in an orchestra in which there was a large contingent from the LPO, and under the fell Sargent? The Board discouraged, but could not prevent, the first and reluctantly allowed the second, on the grounds that the performances were under the aegis of The Royal Philharmonic Society. The "loyalty" issue was most acutely raised when the Board eventually displaced Reed as regular Leader. In April 1933, under pressure from Harty, it resolved to ask him to resign.* His most favoured successor, George Stratton, had joined the LPO in the tense and catastrophic summer of 1932. At the Directors' meeting, Gordon Walker vehemently opposed the nomination, on the grounds that Stratton, "a Member and shareholder", had refused to come to the aid of the Orchestra when it was fighting for its life and had preferred to join the LPO. Anthony Collins stressed that the point at issue was finding the most suitable player—a point which the imminent opening of the season underlined. Harty was approached: he bluntly advised hiring the best man for the job, and Stratton was duly appointed, holding the Leadership from 1935 till 1953.

The most serious problem, however, arose from the nature of the LSO itself. After the exodus to the new orchestras, the Directors found that twenty shareholders were now in the LPO and nine in the BBC Orchestra, and these shareholders were still entitled to vote at meetings of the LSO. The Board resolved that such members be asked to resign and yield up their shares, so that they could be transferred to those whom the Directors now had to recruit to the LSO. The absentee shareholders were in no hurry to comply, and the dispute dragged on for four years.

The LPO's success might have been more easily borne if, during the same period, the BBC Symphony Orchestra had not competed as well for public attention and patronage. While the LSO had suffered adverse press comments and the disruption of its personnel, the BBC Orchestra, under Adrian Boult, was establishing itself both inside and outside the studio. The non-subsidised orchestras, having failed to persuade the Governors of the BBC into self-denial, tried to bring pressure to bear through the Musicians' Union—also unsuccessfully. The battered LSO was most unwilling to get into a public fight with the BBC and protested to newspaper editors who

* The Board wanted Reed out of the Leadership but did not want him to sever his connection with the Orchestra. Reed agreed to meet the Board's wishes, provided he remained Leader for those engagements he had brought to the LSO, particularly the Three Choirs Festivals. The Directors also relieved their embarrassment by asking him to become Chairman. Vander Meerschen voluntarily gave up the office to that end.

suggested the contrary. This policy was rewarded when the BBC began to employ LSO players in its studio concerts. In April 1934, the Directors approached Sir John Reith with a direct appeal for help, in the form of support for symphony concerts and broadcasts. Reith, whose attitude throughout seems to have been more flexible than the Governors', agreed, and in consequence the BBC guaranteed an income to the LSO, through paying fees for the right to broadcast LSO concerts: in practice, this aid amounted to some £3,000 a season. It continued till 1938, by which time financial stringency and the fact that the BBC Orchestra was able to cover all the Corporation's requirements, caused the subsidy to be discontinued. By that time, however, the LSO had acquired other sources of income in opera and films.

Opera offered a way back into the theatre pit for the LSO. In 1933, John Christie announced the venture which has since become world-famous as Glyndebourne. Beecham disdained it—otherwise the LPO might have arrived in Sussex earlier than it did. Christie appointed Arthur Maney, the former Secretary of the LSO, to collect the orchestra. Spike Hughes describes the sequel:

> A contingent was recruited from what we later quickly recognised by the familiar faces and sounds in the pit to be the London Symphony Orchestra. For some reason, when the programmes eventually came to be printed, the thirty-three-piece orchestra for the first Glyndebourne season was given no kind of billing! All we were told was "*Leader of the Orchestra:* George Stratton" with underneath, the announcement that—rather like bottles of wine—"Every Member of the Orchestra and the Chorus has been personally selected." Seated at the first desk with George Stratton was Andrew Brown. . . . Also in the first Glyndebourne Orchestra, were Evelyn Rothwell, now Lady Barbirolli . . . George Eskdale, a brilliant trumpet player who died long before his time; Gordon Walker (flute); Anthony Collins . . . was among the violas with Alfred Hobday, who had led the LSO violas at the orchestra's foundation in 1904; the remarkable Draper family of wood-wind players was represented by Mendelssohn Draper as

> second clarinet and Paul Draper as first bassoon. The second bassoon was Cecil James. . . .[2]

The first season opened with *Le Nozze di Figaro* on 28th May 1934. Roy Henderson who sang Count Almaviva recalls that "after a week of rehearsal, Fritz Busch asked us soloists to come and listen to the orchestra, starting with the overture of *Le Nozze di Figaro*. . . . Busch raised his baton, the orchestra was tensed up for the first notes, slowly Busch lowered his baton and said 'It's too loud'. . . ." The Orchestra under Busch played a tremendous part in the great success of Glyndebourne. Not only, it would seem, in the pit. Henderson also remembers that the LSO played the solo artists and chorus, under John Christie's captaincy, at cricket on Ringmer Green. "The Orchestra won, thanks to a fine forcing innings by Jimmy Whitehead who hit us all over the field for 80 odd. It was the first and last game. Busch was frightened lest a member of the Orchestra had a knock on the finger."[3]

Glyndebourne, even with traditional English embellishments, offered in these early days only four to six weeks' work. Less glamorous but more rewarding engagements came from the film business. The advent of "talkies" put an end to orchestras in cinemas and transferred them to the studios, where individual members of the LSO found themselves engaged to make sound tracks. From the industry's infancy, individual film-makers had occasionally interested established composers in writing scores to accompany the action. The first experiment was music for *L'Assassination du Duc de Guise*, composed by Saint-Saëns in 1907. He used strings, piano and harmonium, each part being cued into the film. Recommended and specially composed piano parts for silent films followed, and then, when techniques improved, synchronised records of music. Honegger, Ibert and Hindemith made notable contributions to the genre. The application of sound to film itself, however, allowed the possibility of using music not as an accompaniment to the film but as an integral part of it, along with the pictures and the other sounds. Music thereby became an intended part of the total effect on the audience. Regarded of this way, it could no longer be left to the casual availability in musicians; integration demanded the presence of a full-time music director in the production team. In 1934, Alexander Korda, the leading film-maker of his generation in Britain, engaged a young Music Director, Muir Mathieson. Mathieson was a pupil of W. H. Reed at the Royal College of Music and an aspirant conductor, particularly of opera, but in the nineteen-thirties the touring companies in which he could have gained his experience were collapsing under financial strain and public indifference. "Constant Lambert had the ballet, so for me the film job was a godsend." Mathieson entered an experimental field where he could set his own precedents. He had two basic ideas about film music: that it should be of symphonic proportions, composed by established composers, and that it should be played by established orchestras. Each conviction depended on the other: the better the orchestra, the more established composers would be likely to respond; the better the score, the more attractive to the orchestra. Korda's support over the years gave Mathieson the chance to translate his ideas into actions. In 1934, the project on hand was a film of H. G. Wells' *Things to Come*, with music by Arthur Bliss, whose role in Britain was comparable to that of Hindemith in Germany.

Bliss' problem was to produce music capable of being judged solely as music, i.e. by the ear alone, and at the same time, accommodate his musical individuality to the needs of the film itself. This is now a commonplace situation to which any composer of film scores has to adjust, but at the time, it was novel. Bliss splendidly overcame his problem by composing a score which has become a classic. The orchestra chosen was the LSO, which, augmented by extra percussion, including several experimental instruments, and a large choir, recorded the sound track over fourteen full sessions in the Scala Theatre, London, under Muir Mathieson. Subsequently, the Orchestra recorded the suite, under the composer, for Decca.

In 1935, the LSO corporately entered the film world and stayed there until the Orchestra fractured over film policy in the mid-fifties—but by that time, demand for symphonic scores for films was trailing off. Muir Mathieson recalls that the Orchestra quickly exploited the possibilities which his formula held out: "It soon became a very quick and very impressive recording orchestra because the players were interested in the performance. They also taught me a lot." Featureless general purpose music of the Enna type, which Eugene Goossens had found so useful, disappeared from major films.

The LSO was not bound to Korda. *Things to Come* was followed by *Victoria the Great* for the producer Herbert Wilcox, when it played music composed and conducted by Anthony Collins, who had by now left the LSO for a conducting career. The Orchestra later resumed its collaboration with Mathieson, notably in Vaughan Williams' music for *49th Parallel* (a score whose ultimate origins lay in the composer's desire to write the music for "a film about cowboys and Indians").

The timing was fortunate: the British film industry was beginning to establish itself as a distinctive producer for a mass market—a process speeded up and reinforced by the Second World War: the habit of film-going was still general; the LSO was available and in need of work, and therefore inclined to experiment; above all, the first venture was an immediate and outstanding success. The LSO's pioneering work was paid the compliment of being emulated by its competitors.

Entry into films provoked two important modifications within the Orchestra. Gordon Walker interested himself in this aspect of its work and took a leading part in negotiating engagements from *Things to Come* onwards. His function was formally recognised by the Board in November 1941, when he was officially appointed representative "for all engagements secured in connection with film recording". Film-making also affected demands on the players' technical capabilities. "Good recording quality" became the dominant consideration: aggressive, harsh string tone was not required. Consistency in recording standards and the deputy system did not go together. There was, in addition, the strictly commercial point that if film makers were paying not only for "The London Symphony Orchestra" as such but also for the right to use its name, they felt entitled to demand that the Board should provide the best, i.e. the regular Members. So in February 1937, Gordon Walker introduced the idea of Associate Membership, whereby a panel of selected but non-shareholding players should be created, to provide deputies whose capabilities were known in advance and who, by appearing more regularly with the Orchestra, could help to maintain its ensemble. In the course of time, associate membership became a step to full membership.

In other respects, the deputy system could not be checked. The problem, in essentials, was that unless the full LSO strength were used, the results would not bring further engagements for the Orchestra, but the Board could not offer the Members fees on a scale likely to ensure that the LSO had priority in their personal schedules. The Directors sought to counteract the appeal of outside engagements by giving details of programmes and conductors when making LSO offers to Members, in order to interest them in their work and secure a better attendance. The attempt completely misfired, since the information merely provided players with an opportunity to comment on the Board's policy and to decide well in advance whether they would engage a deputy or not. In consequence, deputies became more rather than less noticeable in the orchestra entitled the "LSO".

Another unsuccessful proposal, but of immense significance for the future, was a suggestion by Frederick Riddle, Principal Viola in succession to Anthony Collins, that the LSO retain an official whose job would be "to secure further business". This is the first hint that the LSO's business could no longer be adequately covered by the Directors and the Company Secretary.

By the end of the thirties, the LSO had recovered from the *débâcle* of 1932, but it was still not a first-class orchestra—in the sense that it could consistently be relied upon to give performances of the highest technical quality and evincing the most penetrating musical insight. But when the ranks were closed, it could assert its vitality and astound its critics. The final flourish of the decade was the London Music Festival from 23rd April to 28th May 1939. It was organised by Owen Mase of the BBC and Keith Douglas of the Royal Philharmonic Society and was the first co-ordinated event of its kind, embracing all aspects of music: symphony concerts, serenade concerts, chamber music, opera, ballet and the customary English choral orgies. Beecham and the LPO opened the Festival with Mozart, Sibelius, Delius and Tchaikovsky; on the following evening, April 24th, the LSO under Bruno Walter contributed Mendelssohn's Overture *A Midsummer*

Night's Dream and two symphonies, Mozart No. 39 and Brahms No. 4. The core of the symphony programmes belonged to the BBC and Beethoven—nine concerts by the BBC Symphony Orchestra, two under Adrian Boult, the rest under Toscanini, including two performances of the *Missa Solemnis*. In this company the LSO, with all Members present and adequately rehearsed, was by no means outclassed.

In May, the Directors discussed plans for the next season. Bruno Walter was engaged for April and possibly May 1940. The services of a range of international conductors, including Fritz Busch, Kleiber, Szell, Ormandy and Stokowski were also to be sought—an indication of the confidence the Board felt in the future. The Board negotiated with the BBC over a possible appearance of Toscanini with the LSO. Soloists contracted included Cortot, Dohnányi, Backhaus, Feuermann and Moiseiwitsch. By the time of their meeting in August the programmes had been settled and the Directors considered the possibilities of making "films of symphonic works" with a Hollywood producer. Additionally, they accepted "with sincere regret" the formal resignation of John Solomon, then eighty-two years of age. He was the last of the founder-members to leave.*

Solomon's resignation was the only item on the agenda which stood: the rest had to be scrapped.

* He lived to contribute his reminiscences to *London Symphony* and died in 1953, aged ninety-six.

IX

ON 3RD SEPTEMBER, 1939, citizens of London, musical and non-musical alike, were introduced to a new sound, the air-raid siren. It betokened, perhaps more vividly than the words of the Prime Minister on the radio, that Britain was at war. Unlike 1914, there had been sufficient preliminary crises and conflicts to give people an idea of what the character of the war was likely to be. It was widely considered that hostilities would begin with devastating air raids, aimed at cities to disrupt the labour force and undermine morale. For this reason, public concerts and theatre activity ceased automatically, while the nation braced itself for the shock. Seasons were discarded, festivals were abandoned. The LSO did not assemble at Hereford for the Three Choirs Festival after its summer break. The expectation of a *Blitzkrieg* proved in 1939 the counterpart of the popular conviction in August 1914 that the war would be over by Christmas. Neither expectation was fulfilled and the lull in the autumn of 1939 allowed artistic life to start—late and in an atmosphere of impermanence, but to get under way nonetheless.

In London, the initiative in music was seized by the LSO. On 7th October, Charles Hambourg conducted a programme at the Queen's Hall, the first item in which was the Overture *Die Meistersinger*. There was to be no repetition of the absurd political aesthetics which marked the opening of the First World War. Myra Hess played the Fourth Beethoven Concerto in the same programme. The Fifth Concerto, the "Emperor" (with Moiseiwitsch), was included in the first LSO promotion, a week later, together with Beethoven's Fifth Symphony and two less familiar items, Elgar's Symphonic Prelude *Polonia*, a fantasia on Polish airs written for Emil Mlynarski during the First World War, and the *Suite for Orchestra* by Dohnányi. The conductor was Sir Henry Wood, who offered his services to the

LSO and who worked closely with the Orchestra till his death in 1944. Both these concerts took place in the afternoon. The first evening venture also belonged to the LSO: on 21st November, under Charles Hambourg, it played a Beethoven–Brahms programme. The LSO was launched into the war.

Impresarios began to draft, very provisionally, series of concerts, as theatres and concert halls were released from restrictions on opening. The LSO got rid of L. G. Sharpe, as agent, since under wartime conditions his work was held to be supererogatory: no arrangements would have to be negotiated with foreign artists and no tours settled. The Board decided to deal directly with domestic promoters and artists.

The Directors ran into personnel problems sooner than had their predecessors in 1914. A form of conscription, introduced before the war, was now rapidly extended to the population of military age. Additionally, the Board learned with surprise and resentment that one of its Members, John Cockerill, the harpist, had some months before signed a secret contract with the BBC, for employment away from London for the duration of hostilities. The requirement of secrecy prevented Cockerill from disclosing the arrangement to his fellow Directors. They had to accept the *fait accompli* but promptly threw him off the Board, though assuring him that his services as a player were most valued. Cockerill was replaced by Marie Goossens, whose tenure of the post, accepted as a wartime measure, was to last nineteen years.

The BBC also seemed to be acting arbitrarily when Owen Mase on being approached for assistance, stipulated in return that he be elected an Honorary Director. The Board pointed out that the Articles of Association recognised no such functionary, and let the matter drop. The BBC nevertheless arranged studio broadcasts for the principal London orchestras and, prodded by Keith Douglas, invited the LSO to play at the "Proms" in the summer of 1940.

Before the Promenade Concerts opened, the German Army overran Western Europe, and thus presented the German Air Force with the bases from which the air attacks expected the previous autumn could be mounted. Practice caught up sharply with theory, and from August onwards air raids occurred regularly. Elisabeth Lutyens, whose *Three Orchestral*

Pieces the Orchestra was due to play, recalled the consequences.

> It was a Saturday night, and Queen's Hall was sold out in advance. We . . . were crossing into Portland Place . . . when I looked up into the blue sky of that early autumn evening to see a row of beautiful silver birds, high up and far away. They looked benign and serene. They were the first bombers of the full-scale Blitz.
>
> We were hustled brusquely into the Langham Hotel basement by a suddenly appearing warden. . . . Warden or no warden, we sneaked out on time for the Queen's Hall Prom. The orchestra arriving early as it had to do, appeared all present and correct, but the usually-packed auditorium held only a scattering of people. The Prom began and ended, no one realising what had happened—what it was all about. I remember meeting Harold Holt, with Parry Jones, during the interval and know that both Moiseiwitsch and Gerald Moore took part in the concert, but beyond this have little memory of the performance of my pieces, or the rest of the programme. I was only aware of the strange atmosphere of hushed expectancy and the odd half-emptiness of the usually packed house.
>
> When the Prom ended the air raid wardens, now in force, refused to let us leave. A brief look outside showed an ominous blood-red sky. We spent the rest of the night in Queen's Hall—all of us, orchestra, soloists and the audience. Gerald Moore played, Moiseiwitsch turned the pages and other performers helped entertain to pass the time.[1]

Elisabeth Lutyens was attending the last of the impromptu entertainments in which Sir Henry Wood and Basil Cameron conducted community singing and competitions, LSO players enjoyed the unaccustomed public luxury of playing chamber music, and one Member, Ralph Nicholson, achieved cabaret status with his impressions of Sir Thomas Beecham. It was the last Prom: after 7th September, the season was abandoned.

Air attacks and the call-up dispersed metropolitan audiences, and created a demand for music away from the traditional city centres—and, as players found to their cost, from the usual concert-hall facilities. The LSO would have been forced to tour, even if the Luftwaffe had not added inducements to do so. In January 1941, Keith Douglas produced the capital for concerts in London and tours outside. For this purpose, he formed the London Symphony Orchestra Concerts Society to engage the Orchestra. The Society, being a registered non-profit-making organisation would be exempt from paying Entertainment Tax and any profits realised would have to be reserved for further concerts. In this way, Douglas' initial capital would generate continuing opportunities for the LSO.

Keith Douglas was followed in his supportive activity by Sir George Dyson, on behalf of the Carnegie Trust, with an offer to sponsor concerts, with direct grants and conditional guarantees, provided the Orchestra numbered not less than thirty-five, and that the concerts were outside Central London but did not conflict with the touring of the established provincial orchestras. The first "Douglas" tour took place in February 1941, and the first "Carnegie" tour, in April. The conductors were Keith Douglas himself, and Basil Cameron. The LSO visited provincial market towns and industrial areas hitherto off the touring schedules of any orchestra, and spas where resident orchestras had been broken up by the war. Beethoven, Dvořák and Tchaikovsky dominated the programmes. These were new types of sponsorship brought about by the war. But traditional metropolitan enterprise continued. Jay Pomeroy engaged the Orchestra in 1940 and 1941 for seasons of opera and ballet at the Savoy Theatre.

Concert-giving became difficult in London, but after the night of 10th May 1941, it lacked what had been its centre since 25th November 1893: Queen's Hall was burnt out in an air raid. Elisabeth Lutyens' Prom had been not only the last in 1940 but the last in their original home. The effect was soon apparent. Concerts migrated to Kensington, but promoters discovered that concerts which would have paid in the Queen's Hall did not do so in a hall with over twice the seating capacity. In the course of time, their calculations were to a degree falsified by the new audiences who revealed themselves during the war and attended the Albert Hall *faute de mieux*. Their preferences, in accordance with what seems to be virtually a "law of initial aesthetic response", ran to Romanticism. Inadequate rehearsal time and irregular playing strength would have restricted the repertoire in any case, but the fact that the main concert centre was the size of the Albert Hall also influenced the choice of programmes: they had to be confined to those composers who would "draw"—in the prevailing circumstances, the mainstream of nineteenth-century composition. The musical reaction to the entry of the Soviet Union into the conflict only slightly altered the proportion of the Slav to the German contribution of popular classics.

London theatres, especially the Cambridge Theatre and the now demolished Stoll Theatre, were pressed into service as concert halls. Jay Pomeroy promoted a series at the Cambridge on Sunday afternoons during the winter from 1943 onwards, with the LSO as "resident" orchestra. The Stoll, originally built as an opera house, provided for the more grandiose "festivals", of Russian music, of "Music for the People", catering for the needs of the mass audience which found its way towards music under conditions of strain and physical danger. The same needs increased the demand for classical gramophone records and accounted for capacity attendances at cinemas. Recordings affected the LSO less than increases in film production.

Work in film studios mitigated the rigours of touring in wartime. The cinema boomed as a form of entertainment and documentary features, and therefore increased job opportunities for musicians. The LSO's pre-war experience and connections stood it in good stead, both as an orchestra in its own right and as a source of players accustomed to the technical requirements of recording sessions. As the LSO, the Orchestra played the scores for such major productions as *49th Parallel* (Vaughan Williams, 1941), *Malta GC* (Bax, 1943) and *Western Approaches* (Clifton Parker, 1945). Films yielded two works which achieved instant and universal popularity, Richard Addinsell's *Warsaw Concerto* for the film *Dangerous Moonlight* (1941) and Hubert Bath's *Cornish Rhapsody* in *Love Story* (1944). These two compositions were pastiche piano concertos, played respectively by Louis Kentner and Harriet Cohen, in concerts which were part of the action of the film. They were designed to convey the impression of being Romantic pieces, without, of course, the length. The *Warsaw Concerto* was embodied in the story, with neither a title of its own nor the identity of the pianist. The screening of the film provoked a rush of enquiries for records and sheet music. There being no time to make a special recording, the sound track was used for a commercial disc. The piece was much in demand at concerts up and down the country, prompted by showings of the film and reinforced by sales of the recording. This is, perhaps, the first large-scale example of an outcome record sales managers, film makers and the advertising industry now labour to create; in 1941, it was accidentally started and thereafter hastily improvised. The *Warsaw Concerto* provoked imitation, but Hubert Bath's piece was the only one which went from film to recording and the concert hall and stayed in the repertoire for any length of time. By 1944, of course, this progression was planned, and recordings from the sound track prepared in advance.

The importance of the film studio to the LSO was reflected in the influence of Gordon Walker within the Orchestra and the fact that it tended to "settle" at a size commensurate with the film studio. For concert appearances, this nucleus was augmented from the free-lance pool, instrumentalists on leave, and, on one hectic occasion, even recruited off the street by a desperate but opportunist Secretary. Bertram Lewis, in need of a French horn for the evening, observed a Welsh Guards bandsman from a bus, promptly alighted and booked him on the spot.

The measures taken by individuals like Keith Douglas or by institutions, such as the Carnegie Trust, essentially adapted peacetime practice to wartime conditions. But, for Britain, the Second World War became "total" in a way for which the First provided no precedents. Many cherished convictions were jettisoned, many ingrained patterns of behaviour broken up. Change was rapid and its effects revolutionary; not the least of these being that *the state began systematically to support the arts.* It was not, of course, inaugurated deliberately and with a portentous flourish, but was the consequence of a piece of inspired improvisation. In January 1940 the Pilgrim Trust and the President of the Board of Education, Lord de la Warr, set up a private committee "to meet an immediate war-time problem: the sudden isolation of country places during the first winter black-out, the concentration of workers in new centres, and the collapse of all ordinary sources of theatre and music". The Pilgrim Trust funded the work of the organisation, styled the Council for the Encouragement of Music and the Arts, but found its contribution matched by the Treasury. "Air raids intensified the need and gave the work a certain glamour in the eyes of the public. . . . CEMA began to be known as a name and as an idea." After two years the Pilgrim Trust, whose intentions and expertise concerned the laying of foundations, withdrew, the Treasury assumed full financial responsibility—and the trick was done! For the specific art of music, CEMA guaranteed concerts and financed tours by artists. Additionally, it helped to create stable audiences by developing or supporting music clubs.

In its promotions of music, CEMA—in contrast to the Carnegie Trust—could be less than entirely helpful to the LSO, since it required the recipient of its aid to be "a properly constructed non-profit-making organisation". This requirement implied constitutional change within the Orchestra, which, with some 70 per cent of Members in the armed services, the Directors considered they could not initiate. Throughout 1944, the conflict remained in abeyance and the LSO was assisted by guarantees for specific concerts. In February 1945, the Council warned the Directors "change your constitution—or else", and the Board elected to forgo further assistance: as the LSO was losing its own money on CEMA tours. The move brought a sense of relief. Its independent status was to prove disadvantageous after the war.

The LSO benefited from the flow of other official funds into music through the Entertainments National Service Association, which engaged the Orchestra for concerts for servicemen. The LSO appeared, therefore, on air stations, in naval and army barracks, and in cinemas taken over for military purposes.

Touring by the London orchestras and by the Hallé and Liverpool Philharmonic outside their own cities led to confusion and duplication of effort. To rationalise schedules, the LSO, LPO, Hallé, Liverpool Philharmonic and the Scottish Orchestras joined together in July 1943 in the National Association of Symphony Orchestras. The BBC was invited to join, but declined—which proved to be a tactical error, since the NASO members found that their association had other uses than sorting out tours. They were soon pressing the BBC for increased fees for broadcasting. The LSO representative, Gordon Walker, supported by his Directors, agreed with this aim but not with the corollary, that NASO members should threaten to enter no commitments with the Corporation until agreement was reached. He could hardly have taken any other position, since the LSO was angling for Prom engagements at the time. NASO was divided on the issue, with the LSO in a minority of one. A letter was sent to the BBC and publicity given to the matter—which left the Directors threatening to withdraw, the more so when they found that the Secretary of NASO had failed to keep minutes of the crucial discussions in the Association. NASO survived these troubles and the LSO collected its Promenade Concerts.

They were to mark Sir Henry Wood's jubilee, and were the culmination of a celebration begun in March 1944 on the conductor's seventy-fifth birthday, when the Sir Henry Wood Jubilee Fund was inaugurated with a concert of the combined LSO, LPO and BBC Symphony Orchestra, conducted in turn by Sir Henry Wood, Sir Adrian Boult, and Basil Cameron. The programme offered a conspectus of Wood's enthusiasms: the Overture to *The Flying Dutchman*, the Third Brandenburg Concerto and Beethoven's Third Piano Concerto (with Solomon), Elgar's *Introduction and Allegro* for Strings, the scherzo and finale from Beethoven's Fifth (shades of the original Proms!) and *The Ride of the Valkyries*. Only an example of the modern works he systematically took on was missing. This was the first in a series of concerts designed to build up a fund in the recipient's honour. Harold Holt asked the LSO to "donate" an evening; a date was agreed and Sir Henry volunteered to conduct. The concert never took place. In July, Sir Henry conveyed through the Secretary the desire that Sir Thomas Beecham should be invited with the LPO to join the Orchestra on this occasion. The Board pointedly replied that they preferred the original suggestion, but that "if this was not entirely agreeable to Sir Henry, then no objection would be raised to association with the LPO, together with Sir Adrian Boult or Mr Basil Cameron." Wood might wish to bury the hatchet with Beecham, but the LSO did not. The Promenade season supervened. Wood opened his Jubilee celebrations, but they were disrupted by flying-bomb attacks and had to be abandoned. In August, he died. The LSO's last tribute to its "negative" founder was to participate in the last season of the concerts through which his name is perpetuated.

The war years witnessed two "domestic" occasions for the LSO; the first was the death at the age of sixty-six of W. H. Reed, one of the formative influences in the LSO for thirty out of its first thirty-eight years. When the Directors had asked him to become Chairman, they were not merely finding a way to save their own faces in an ineluctable but embarrassing situation: they were recognising Reed's stature as a musician and the need for continuity which he, through his identification with the Orchestra, expressed. The LSO strings played at a memorial service in Croydon Parish Church, on 18th July 1942, and George Stratton led his own quartet at the interment of Reed's ashes in Worcester Cathedral, three months later.

The second domestic occasion was more joyous: the fortieth birthday concert, held at the Albert Hall on 9th June 1944. The original programme, of which only the Liszt Rhapsody was unfamiliar to the wartime public, was played under Sir Adrian Boult. The celebration provided a necessary spur to assessing the Orchestra's aims, as well as its achievements. This was highly necessary.

Under the stresses of war, the LSO tended to disintegrate. The call-up disrupted the ensemble, painfully built up during the late thirties. The Orchestra was reduced to a core of players, approximating the requirements of the film studio. The difference between the studio and the concert platform was made up from free-lance musicians. As the Members continued to exercise their constitutional right to send deputies, the artistic results achieved were extremely variable. A combination of an attractive engagement and service leave schedules could yield a strong team. Boult, at one concert, was so impressed by a performance of the *Pathétique* under Albert Coates that he offered to give up *his* concert the next day to Coates, as he was sure the performance would be better—a tribute both to the conductor and to the LSO's power of rising to the occasion. This was exceptional. The uncertainties of accommodation—the floor of a police station is not ideal—and the impression of being condemned for eternity to wait on Didcot station, did not encourage some Members (who, by definition, were the senior component of the Orchestra, as then constituted) to tour or to regard the LSO as their main professional activity. In July 1942 the Board began to investigate those Members who displayed "a great lack of interest in the Orchestra" and to tighten up on the attendance of Members in the violin sections by requiring them to "attend 75 per cent of all concerts and the like percentage of all BBC and any other engagements secured by the Orchestra", and to undertake to go on tour when called on. "In future, certificates would not be accepted whereby Members could be relieved of the obligations of touring . . . unless it was that any Member should be completely confined to his house and totally incapacitated from working." Such drastic measures helped to stabilise the Orchestra, but by December 1943 the Secretary, W. G. Wood, gave his opinion to the AGM that the "discipline of the Orchestra was rapidly deteriorating". His remarks, according to the Minutes, divided opinion and provoked a lively discussion. In the next month (January 1944) Andrew Brown, Sub-Principal violin, submitted a programme of improvement which allows some estimate of the state of the Orchestra. Apart from platform discipline and certain aspects of orchestral administration, Brown singled out faults in string playing, the lack of good quality of tone in the first violins and of "virile leadership" of the seconds and the prevalence of too many "bad" deputies among the violas. He suggested that these problems could be tackled by the leaders of the string departments themselves selecting extra players for engagement when required, that a meeting of Principals and Sub-Principals should ensure correct playing and that all sections, but particularly the strings, "should rehearse in order to become familiar with new music, to secure better ensemble and to further correct faulty intonation", to which woodwind and brass were also prone. Brown's points were emphasised from another quarter, when Gordon Walker learned that Sir Henry Wood did not intend to engage the LSO for the Proms "owing to the extremely poor horn section of the Orchestra". (This report accounted for the LSO's attitude to the BBC in NASO.) It is an eloquent comment on the state of the LSO that the Board endorsed Andrew Brown's strictures, but produced no proposals to put his remedies into effect.

What could be achieved, even under wartime conditions, was demonstrated to the public at the Albert Hall the following October, when Beecham returned to the LPO in a typical programme (Berlioz, Delius, Mozart, Sibelius and Chabrier) which displayed a fire and a vitality notably absent from the generality of concerts in the fifth winter of war. The conductor had at his disposal an orchestra which had suffered under the same conditions as the LSO but which, unlike that Orchestra, had sole claim on the services of its players. The same lesson could be drawn from developments in Manchester, where John Barbirolli was beginning to stake his claim to be the natural successor to Mengelberg, both as trainer and Romantic interpreter.

The Board drew the necessary conclusions: it was essential to re-establish at the earliest possible moment the "LSO Symphony Concerts". Four Monday dates were booked at the Albert Hall and a programme for 1945 drawn up. It did not materialise but indicates the Directors' thoughts as to the kind of challenge the Orchestra needed, and had to meet. The first conductor was to be Bruno Walter, who had directed the LSO's last pre-war triumph in the far-off spring of 1939 and who had on the books an engagement "postponed" from the spring of 1940. Other concerts were to fall to Albert Coates, Freitas Branco, from Spain, and John Barbirolli. In order to meet the demands of such conductors, the Board put Principals and Sub-Principals under contract for the series, and applied the "75 per cent rule" to the rank and file. These measures involved the Board in scrutinising the membership of the Orchestra, to select those whose playing and attitudes merited their receiving contractual terms. Invoking the "75 per cent rule" brought about a number of desired resignations among the "old hands". Younger players who, in the expectation of being released from the forces, applied for membership, accepted the rule as part of the natural and necessary order of things. Thus, eighteen months after, the Board responded to Andrew Brown's scheme for reform, and the artistic prospects of the Orchestra were thereby improved.

Much leeway remained: the Directors' policies implied that they thought the future of the Orchestra could be secured by offering "quality" performances in a market which had not in essentials changed since 1939. Their having deprived themselves of state aid did not seem so very important and they even failed to follow up an offer of large-scale commercial sponsorship! Their task was merely to translate the wartime discovery of music which many people had made into regular attendance at LSO concerts through the traditional means: LSO promotions, engagements by impresarios, gramophone recordings, and films. In the spring of 1945, relations with Jay Pomeroy deteriorated, partly through the absenteeism of several principals at Cambridge Theatre concerts and partly through clashes between these engagements and the Promenade Concerts, during which period the BBC required the exclusive services of the Orchestra. Opportunely, Harold Holt emerged with the offer of a series of engagements at the Albert Hall. The chance "to resume the LSO's established position at London's principal concert hall" encouraged the Directors to terminate their association with Pomeroy and throw in their lot with Holt. This they did, in July 1945, not without threats of injunctions from the impresario, opinions from counsel and general recriminations which dragged on for several months. Discussions with Mr Walter Legge of EMI and with the Decca Record Company for exclusive contracts progressed more pleasantly.

Meanwhile, the Orchestra appeared for the first time under the aegis of the Royal Philharmonic Society and took part in the Henry Wood Promenade Concerts. Ferrucio Bonavia's comment sums up the impact of the LSO at the end of the war: "The London Symphony Orchestra is a good orchestra, if not as good as it used to be before the needs of the Forces depleted its ranks. It played as well as it could be expected to do considering the heavy tasks imposed by daily concerts."[2] At this juncture in its fortunes, the LSO's main assets were money in the bank and considerable experience in recovering from difficult situations.

X

THE END OF six years of war is, in itself, a rather arbitrary demarcation in the history of the LSO but it does permit an assessment of the situation of public music-making in Britain, in which the Orchestra intended to find a more impressive and significant place. In the summer of 1945, concert life in Britain on any scale larger than the chamber orchestra was in a bad state. Musicians were exhausted and over-extended. This was more than the consequence of concert-giving and touring in wartime. The repertoire had contracted, with three symphonies by Tchaikovsky, and concertos by him, Grieg and Rachmaninov as the staple items. Beethoven was better served in that more of his symphonic works got a hearing, but even then Symphonies Five and Seven received a disproportionate degree of attention. There were notable exceptions in programme-building, but the frequency of "All Tchaikovsky" evenings or "Music from the Ballet" or selections from opera kept rehearsals to a minimum and allowed deputies to be accommodated easily, but at the price of endemic artistic fatigue among players.

Orchestras had mushroomed to meet the demand for concerts: in 1946, there were fourteen in London alone, though the personnel were conspicuously interchangeable! Too many orchestras with too many indifferent performers, all concentrating on relatively few works: the result—by 1947 audiences began to fall off. Moreover, the facilities available for concerts offered them no inducement to stay. Gordon Walker in a radio interview instanced only ten halls in England and Scotland which were better than adequate, and none in London, where the Albert Hall, improved acoustically but still unsatisfactory, was the main concert hall.

Cinemas, town halls designed for public meetings rather than concerts, and even Harringay Arena were pressed into service.

John Cruft

Ernest Fleischmann

Harold Lawrence

Stephen Reiss

Josef Krips

The remedy most favoured by public sentiment was to rebuild the Queen's Hall, or a new hall in Regent's Park, as a memorial to Sir Henry Wood, for which public subscriptions were invited. In 1948, a new hall was mooted as part of a scheme to reclaim the derelict area on the south bank of the Thames between Waterloo and the river. As news of the proposal filtered through the profession, various interests took issue with the LCC over the project. Audiences, it was freely alleged, would refuse to cross the river for concerts; the proposed site would merely transfer the disadvantages of Kensington to the South Bank; somewhere more central was needed. The South Bank scheme won, however, partly through administrative confusion about alternatives—the Henry Wood Memorial sank between committees and the funds were eventually handed over to the Treasury.

The years from 1945 to 1950 in the musical arts in Britain were years more of activity than of progress, when the attempt to widen the social basis of concert-going was hamstrung by grossly inadequate facilities, poor economic conditions (hot-water bottles were *de rigueur* at concerts during the fuel crisis in the prolonged winter of 1947) and the muddle which inevitably accompanied the attempt to work out suitable long-term relationships between public and private funding. In 1947, as in 1929, prevailing general standards of orchestral playing were put into perspective by visits from foreign orchestras—the Vienna Philharmonic accompanying the Vienna Opera at Covent Garden and the Concertgebouw under van Beinum. The appearance of the former inspired protests from British players, some of whom paraded outside the opera house wearing placards announcing "we can play as well as they"—a claim swiftly falsified for the audience inside. The resentment was not simply over lost jobs; it was also well known that the Vienna Orchestra had gone wholly and enthusiastically Nazi, and that the conductor under whom the players demonstrated such warmth and involvement, Josef Krips, had himself been banned from conducting and compelled to work in a factory when Austria was a "Mark" of the Third Reich. The Concertgebouw had no such political overtones (or if any, they were favourable), but their playing conclusively proved that wartime deprivations did not in themselves account for inferior standards of performance.

The fact of the matter was that in the heroic age of postwar reconstruction, the arts enjoyed high ideals and low priorities, especially when they needed to be housed in buildings the size of concert halls. The gap between proclaimed intentions and actual achievements yawned wide, not merely through competing claims on resources but because the idea of national policies for the arts met with a muted and sporadically hostile response. Moreover, the Arts Council, successor in title to CEMA, was still groping to find suitable principles and mechanisms for disbursing what funds it did have among the arts. There were, in British experience, effectively no precedents: significantly, all the arguments tended to proceed from Continental models. It was a time of experiment, much of it inevitably inconclusive and wasteful.

In the prevailing atmosphere, the notion of a concert hall on the South Bank, taken by itself, might well have failed. The Royal Festival Hall was successfully carried through because it was an integral part of the Festival of Britain—an event which provided the necessary transfusion of public interest and support which musical life needed in London and throughout the country. The foundation stone of the new hall was laid on 12th October 1949, and the completed building was opened by King George VI on 3rd May 1951. The Hall was designed to be the focus of concert life in much the same way as had the Queen's Hall. That, however, was until the Festival, still only an aspiration; until it was built and its drawing power proved, no purposive pattern of activity could be established, and the Albert Hall acoustics continued to yield uncertain and occasionally eccentric aesthetic results.

All the London orchestras suffered under these general conditions: they created particular problems for the LSO.

The Directors had to rebuild the Orchestra, to restore the repertoire and attract audiences from among former regular attenders at Queen's Hall and from the new audiences whose interest in classical music had been aroused but not extended during the war.

The first priority was reconstructing the Orchestra. The Directors initially thought this involved them in the familiar tasks of reintegrating Members returning from the Forces, getting rid of their more unsatisfactory wartime substitutes and thereby raising the standard of technical proficiency.

In short order, however, reconstruction came to involve changes in the aims and management of the company. The incentives to change were twofold: experience quickly showed that the LSO as a profit-distributing institution was denied the Arts Council grants which enabled its competitors to quote lower terms; by the same token it became liable for Entertainment Duty on its own promotions. These problems demonstrated the other reason for change, namely that in the postwar world, traditional management practice might no longer suffice. The idea of appointing a General Manager re-emerged.

Access to Arts Council funds required altering the Memorandum and Articles of Association of LSO Ltd. The debate over the proposal revealed a strong body of opinion in favour of remaining out, free of any relationship with officialdom on the grounds "that any monetary benefit . . . would result in a loss of independence"; the future could be better secured by drastic overhaul of the playing strength, combined with acceptance of only first-class engagements. The necessary authority to achieve these ends should be vested, not in a general manager, who would necessarily be an executive official of the Board, but in a Managing Director appointed from the Board and subject only to its final jurisdiction. This proved the more immediately attractive proposition and in December 1945 the Chairman, Gordon Walker, became Managing Director. His especial concern was to be the negotiation of contracts for film and recording work, in which respect he assumed complete control of the personnel of the Orchestra subject to the final authority and jurisdiction of the Board. His commission was fixed at half the net income accruing to the LSO Ltd for sessions obtained through his efforts. The appointment was for six months, in the first instance.

The scheme was ratified by the AGM of 28th December 1945—Gordon Walker refusing an offer that his commission be back-dated to the preceding October. In a speech outlining his policy for the LSO, he "emphasised the fact that apart from securing additional work for the Orchestra it would be his firm endeavour to equalise attendances between the Recording Sessions and the Concert engagements, and in assuming complete control of the engaging of the personnel . . . he would maintain as far as was humanly possible the engaging of all Members, with the exception of the Principals, strictly according to rota." This statement pointed to one of the divisive elements in the Orchestra. The strings were based on an establishment of fifty (14, 12, 10, 8, 6), but film work usually required fewer, including the Principals, whereas woodwind and brass could expect to be more regularly employed. Equity as well as the nature of the Orchestra demanded that players have equality of access to film sessions, which logically suggested their being shared out through a rota system. But Gordon Walker's *caveat* "as far as possible" admitted that considerations of equity had not always applied. Rank-and-file players who received less than what they considered their fair share tended to attribute that result to their not being *persona grata* to Gordon Walker, whom they regarded simply as a "fixer" for Muir Mathieson and his *confrères*. Whatever the subjective judgements involved, there was the factual situation that the studios required the best players, irrespective of their status within the LSO. They did not welcome situations when equity considerations left them with a string section full of back-desk players. This is a problem which can only be overcome by the Orchestra's employing virtuosi in all departments (which the LSO did not) and by cutting out replacements (which the LSO could not).

The experiment did not work well, largely because the LSO had to struggle to re-establish itself in the concert world. Gordon Walker, as Managing Director, could not be identified with success, in spite of his negotiating favourable contracts with film and record companies. He could not resolve the problems of the rota principle, which, within the Orchestra, increasingly demonstrated a conflict of interest between the Principals and the rank and file. This was more easily expressed on the Board in that it had a majority of string players. Had LSO business boomed, the conflict could have been contained, but the Orchestra artistically and financially wallowed in the doldrums. The consequence was unavailing appeals to loyalty, a spate of resignations and a series of highly introspective meetings, about policy. The Minutes of the EGM of 20th August 1946 reveal the tensions within the LSO. The Board challenged the Members to define their requirements, pointedly asking whether they wished to continue in the same way, or go over to a weekly salary, as in the LPO; did they want "to engage a more virile management"; were the Members in fact prepared "to give the Board their wholehearted co-operation in any way they might ask"? The subsequent debate revealed the clefts within the Orchestra, particularly over the suggestion that Members guarantee 75 per cent of their time to the LSO. The Secretary's proposal was scouted, one Member giving his opinion that three-quarters of a working life was a sufficient contribution to make to any organisation. The Board was commanded to investigate schemes of reorganisation, but no more explicit conclusion emerged. Gordon Walker suggested, but without positive result, that "the engaging of a keen business man as General Manager would be of advantage". Matters were not improved when Gordon Walker was adjudged at fault when a majority of the Board absented themselves from a concert organised in connection with gramophone recording sessions, in order to take part in a film recording. One Director forced the issue by submitting his resignation: "I am well aware that they had permission to be absent . . . but I consider that they had the strongest moral obligation to attend personally. All the talk at previous Board Meetings about 'loyalty' becomes a farce in view of their action. . . ." The Board temporarily disintegrated. Gordon Walker apologised, though stressing he had acted throughout in the best interest of the Orchestra, and had done what he thought to be right. This was accepted, but his office of Managing Director was abolished, on the grounds that no one person should be responsible for and in complete control of the personnel of the Orchestra. The Board re-assumed collective responsibility but set up three subcommittees "for the better working of the Orchestra" respectively for film recording (of which Gordon Walker was Chairman), personnel policy and rules governing engagements. Directors began to meet regularly, instead of simply as and when required. The notion of a General Manager was quietly dropped.

The LSO suffered at this time not only through intractable

problems of management and personnel but also from the narrowing of the market for its services. The LPO, whose war-time reorganisation and policies have been admirably analysed by its former Secretary, Thomas Russell, emerged from the war years with a more widespread public and, for a while, the services of Sir Thomas Beecham. This association did not endure and Beecham was followed by a series of guest conductors, notably Victor de Sabata, Albert Wolff, Charles Munch and an unknown American named Leonard Bernstein. These provided, if nothing else, excitement and panache, both notably absent from the LSO.

Beecham had meanwhile involved himself in a scheme for an orchestra financed largely by the Gramophone Company for recording purposes, but which would be under his artistic direction for public concerts. He conducted the new organisation, the Philharmonia, in its debut in the lugubrious Kingsway Hall in 1946, but disappeared from the venture, having had substantial differences with the company and Walter Legge. The Philharmonia remained, however, and, through offering higher fees and recording contracts, was able to attract talent emerging from the Continent such as Cantelli and Karajan and also to finance a Brahms Festival for Toscanini in 1952.

Having parted company with the LPO and the Philharmonia, Beecham founded his last orchestra, the Royal Philharmonic, in 1946, and it soon began to demonstrate the musical qualities of its founder. With the RPO, "the four London orchestras" came into existence. They provide the framework in which the postwar resurgence of the LSO must be judged.

In the postwar years, however, the LSO clearly occupied the fourth place. While capable of giving good performances on selected occasions, it could not match its competitors in power to draw the public, or in the training which regular employment under a first-class conductor could provide. Its programmes were distinctly more enterprising: the Directors attempted to make them add up to something more than a number of individual items. The Goossens family, Eugene as composer and conductor, Leon as soloist and Marie as Member, were the core of one memorable concert, and a programme of three piano concertos, with Colin Horsley, comprising not Grieg, Tchaikovsky and Rachmaninov, but Mozart (an unfamiliar work in E flat), Chopin and Lennox Berkeley also demonstrated the Directors' enterprise. They proved in addition a rapid method of running down the Orchestra's funds.

The LSO was, in a word, lacking in consistent quality. George Stratton drew the attention of the Directors to its source of weakness.

> Gentlemen,
>
> No doubt this will not come as a bombshell to you after the painful exhibitions we have all heard lately. I hope you will appreciate the necessity which causes me to write in such a manner.
>
> The fact of the matter is that if we hope to survive as an Orchestra in the face of present-day competition, the whole of the 2nd violin section must be reconstructed, for there are very few of them that are worth their place in a first-class combination. (Stratton went on to identify the shortcomings of individuals.) In fact, I would suggest auditions for the whole lot, or something equally drastic to separate the chaff from the grain.
>
> This must be done very quickly for complaints from Conductors are coming in thick and fast and we must have a good team for the Proms. . . . There are quite a number of excellent players among students of the RCM, RAM, GSM, etc., who although short of experience would instil a new life and enthusiasm into our Orchestra and we might do worse than supplant our poor ones with some of these.
>
> I am sorry to have to write in such a vein, but, believe me, it is only because I have the future of the London Symphony Orchestra at heart.

Stratton, with the directness which marked his playing as Leader, restated the LSO's first principles and uncannily recommended a course of action which was to be followed shortly after his death. How otherwise were "new life and enthusiasm" to be generated?

One immediate answer, failing Stratton's drastic measures, was for the LSO to find a first-class conductor and trainer, who would in short do for the Orchestra after the Second World War what Albert Coates had done after the First, with the significant difference that now the LSO had more rivals. Where were the Directors to look? Both Weingartner and Wood were dead; so were Harty, who would have been the most welcome and obvious choice, and Leslie Heward, who had shown the right quality. Coates, since his return from America, was, in the judgement of musicians, not the force he had been. It was, in any case, known that he was not available, and, accordingly, he was not considered. He left Britain for South Africa, where he died in 1953. For different reasons, which will occur to the reader by now, Beecham was out of the question. Eugene Goossens was in America, Boult was at the BBC. Barbirolli, although offered an inducement of £6,000 a year, refused to leave the Hallé, where he was earning far less.

The effects of the decline in touring opera in Britain between the wars now began to make themselves felt, in the lack of trained conductors of discernible international potential. Nor had six years' war service assisted the careers of those who appeared immediately after demobilisation. It was also crucial that the LSO was not in a position to confer prestige on whomever it appointed (quite the reverse, in fact!). In practical terms, its post-war options were Sargent, Basil Cameron, or someone from abroad. LSO players were reasonably happy to work with Sargent by now, provided he could be kept away from the classics . . . which, as Principal Conductor, he obviously could not. Cameron, a superbly equipped musician and the leading contender for the honour of being the most underrated British conductor of his time, was considered unacceptable in that (unlike Sargent) he had no discernible public following and was thought unlikely to establish the right enduring personal rapport with players. In 1947, gramophone recording sessions introduced to the Orchestra a conductor who seemed likely to meet the Directors' requirements, Josef Krips. Their impressions were confirmed by two public concerts at the Albert Hall in December 1948. The first was devoted to Tchaikovsky and Beethoven, the second to Mozart's Symphony No. 39, Mahler's *Kindertotenlieder*, with Ferrier, and the Second Symphony of Brahms. The choice of works and the way in which they were performed—all traces of routine and fatigue were banished—give a clue to Krips' natural and artistic origins, in Vienna.

The Board thought they had found their man and opened negotiations. In the business of choosing conductors, availability limits the field, whether for isolated performances or for posts which by definition imply that the services of the conductor will be claimed by the Orchestra for some considerable time. Krips was interested, but could not be free from Vienna for another year or two. The LSO decided it could wait.

The Directors' decision was influenced by the arguments of Harry Dugarde, a cellist who became a Board member in 1945. Professionally he was never more than a very competent performer, but none excelled him in devotion to the task of reinstating the LSO in the concert world. Dugarde was elected Chairman, in succession to Gordon Walker, in December 1949 by vote of the whole Playing Membership at a meeting in the Albert Hall. This was an exceptional procedure in LSO terms (the usual practice is for the Board to elect its own Chairman) and ensured that Harry Dugarde was the first rank-and-file player to hold that office—a fact of which he was very proud. This result reflected the deepening division within the Orchestra between principals and rank and file over film engagements. He had, however, his own conception of the role of Chairman, which was not construed in sectional terms. He became the essential link between the Orchestra and its Conductor in Chief.

Another key appointment was that of John Cruft as Secretary. Documents tend to overstate the importance of executive officials, but it is clear—and supported by contemporaries—that his arrival in office was a crucial step. The third member of his family to play in the Orchestra, John Cruft had played in the LPO and Suisse Romande Orchestra, under Ansermet, and had free-lanced in London. He was elected to Membership of the LSO in 1946 and became a Director in the same year. In 1949, he found himself Secretary, following two previous incumbents who had abruptly left the LSO for professional reasons in quick succession. Cruft was to stay ten years. His first task was to restore a degree of continuity to the administration. In discharging his duties, he was considered by some of his colleagues to be too much of an adjutant ("which, curiously enough, in the Army, I had been"), but these were the qualities very much demanded by the situation.

The decision to appoint Josef Krips was fundamental: in him the LSO would acquire a musician of the right quality and experience, whose work it was hoped would bring the artistic success which would make the divisions within the Orchestra less acute. But Krips did not arrive till 1950 and, in the interim, the Orchestra continued to lose business to its competitors, whose state subsidies enabled them to quote lower rates. The assumptions behind the entire postwar policy were in this respect erroneous. In September 1948, the Orchestra, in Extraordinary General Meeting, reconstituted itself into a non-profit-distributing concern (*de facto*, it had been that for some time) to qualify for better treatment from the tax authorities and for support from the Arts Council.

The LSO parted company with its own past, at the behest of a new patron, the state. The residual fears of some Members that the patron's representatives would take over the Orchestra were dispelled. In December 1948, John Denison attended the first Board Meeting as Arts Council Assessor, stressing that his job did not entitle him in any sense to control policy or even to vote. On his advice the LSO submitted a preliminary plan to underpin the Orchestra's sagging finances for the remainder of the season. The change brought a gesture of tangible appreciation from an unexpected quarter:

19th November 1948

Dear Mr Gordon Walker,

I was very honoured and delighted to take part in your first concert under your new regime with the orchestra. Please accept the following little donation from me as a small token of my good will and appreciation of the fine work they have done in the past, are doing in the present and I feel sure will continue to do in the future.

With my best wishes always,

Yours sincerely

Malcolm Sargent

Malcolm Sargent's appreciation of the efforts the LSO was making was not shared by the general public, which absented itself from orthodox and enterprising programmes alike. On Remembrance Day 1949, the LSO offered Butterworth's *Banks of Green Willow*, Vaughan Williams' Sixth Symphony, conducted for the first time by the composer, and Bliss's *Morning Heroes*, also conducted by the composer and with Sir Ralph Richardson as narrator. The public, as John Cruft put it, "stayed away in thousands". The receipts, which under the new regime were tax-free, were adequate to cover the cost of the hall and the expenses of the BBC Choral Society, which sang in the Bliss.

At this stage, the Orchestra, struggling to establish a definite place in the esteem of the concert-going public, was kept going by gramophone recording and film sessions.

It was fortunate for the LSO that it had thrown in its lot with Decca, which till then had lagged behind its rivals in the market, except for certain issues currently prized by connoisseurs. Decca stole a march on the competition first by adopting full frequency range recording for 78 rpm discs, and then going over to long-playing records at 45 and 33 rpm. For these the company had the technique, but no catalogue. The task of building one was entrusted to Victor Olof, a former violinist and conductor, who had recruited and managed for its first year Beecham's Royal Philharmonic Orchestra. Olof's connections with the orchestral world, and the availability of the LSO, ensured the Orchestra of a leading place in the new venture. Its contribution in these pioneering years to Decca's catalogue of basic classics is impressive. Sargent and Krips conducted the bulk of the work but Clemens Krauss and Georg Solti, Enrique Jorda, Warwick Braithwaite and Anatole Fistoulari made significant contributions. Olof himself conducted pieces by Auber and Dvořák.

In February 1950, the Orchestra began a novel undertaking —recording a complete cycle of Sibelius' symphonies. Olof recalls

> The fact that I had engaged an Englishman, Anthony Collins, to conduct his former orchestra, the LSO, of which he had been both a director and principal viola, caused

> some discussion in Decca, but knowing Collins for very many years as a serious musician, I was fully confident, as he was a gifted conductor and, most important of all, a dedicated admirer of Sibelius. . . . During our preliminary discussions, we agreed to contact the composer to elucidate some of his rather ambiguous metronome markings affecting the vitally important matter of tempo. I sent a lengthy telegram to Sibelius at his home in Finland covering all our queries, he immediately replied: "Pleased to hear about recording stop metronome marks difficult to follow strictly stop conductor must have liberty to get performance living greetings Jean Sibelius."

Conductor and Orchestra did get their performances "living", as evidenced by the immediate success of the cycle and its subsequent reissue.

The Orchestra went on to make outstanding recordings of Delius, Elgar, and Vaughan Williams, including all the latter's symphonies. The composer was present at the sessions for the Sixth. He commiserated with the Orchestra: "It must be hell to play it for three hours: I know, it's been hell to listen to it." Recording commitments began to influence programme-building in that a public concert of a particular work under a well-known conductor could form part of the preparation for a recording, or could follow the completed sessions, but in either case the concert could be used to advertise the sale. This arrangement was not unreasonable, especially since it helped build up the Orchestra's repertoire, but for the LSO it could mean that the public concert, for which it was responsible, lost more money if the work was unfamiliar. Bartók's *Concerto for Orchestra* was played in 1950 because the Directors judged that the income from extra recording sessions would outweigh the loss on the public concert attributable to its being in the programme. The decision created incidental trouble for them because some of the players who, under the LSO rules, had a right to the concert were not required for the recording.

This episode illustrates the nice judgements involved in what was a mere matter of routine. The extent to which record companies could influence the decisions of orchestral managements, in the extreme case, was demonstrated in 1952 when the LSO recorded *Swan Lake* for Decca. The commercial management complained about the quality of the violin solos, which had to be re-recorded. The sequel appears in the Minutes for 25th March.

> The three Directors who attended the special playing of *Swan Lake* reported fully on it to the Board, and the action which had subsequently been taken to re-record certain sections, discussed. A letter from Mr Stratton was read, in which he expressed his wish to retire from the position of Leader of the Orchestra. . . .

George Stratton continued as Assistant Conductor and was unanimously elected an Honorary Member of the Orchestra, at an Extraordinary General Meeting convened *ad hoc*. He accepted the honour but declined a benefit concert. A few months later, he died. In nearly fifty years, the LSO had had only three Leaders, Payne, Reed and Stratton. Stratton had graduated from café bands to the Queen's Hall Orchestra, and then, in 1925, to the LSO, which, with one interval, he had served ever since. He ran his own string quartet for seventeen years, and was Professor at the RCM. But by the 1950s the pressures of orchestral life were already beginning to rule out this type of career. Stratton was a good Leader, a forthright, direct player of the score which was before him, though his rather harsh tone was a drawback in the studio. Continuity in the Leadership was vitally important to the LSO in the depressed thirties and disrupted forties. Stratton provided it.

In terms of immediate impact the most important assignment in the years after the war was a film designed to show a symphony orchestra in action, demonstrating the colour and range of instruments and the role of soloists within the orchestra, as well as the teamwork of the whole. The film *Instruments of the Orchestra* was made by the Crown Film Unit for the Ministry of Education in 1946 and directed by Muir Mathieson. The music was specially written—being a set of variations on a theme of Purcell by Benjamin Britten. The work was played by the LSO and conducted by Sir Malcolm Sargent. The film itself has been one of the most successful experiments in education through the cinema undertaken in Britain, and the music has a permanent place in the concert repertoire.

Mathieson involved the Orchestra in another educational venture, the Harrow Children's Concerts. These were, and are, designed to introduce children to classical music and to concert-going, not as a break in routine but as part of their musical education, reinforcing what they learn at school. The scheme as finally practised was the residue of vast postwar plans for the musical education of children in the county of Middlesex, which proved financially impossible. The idea proved more realistic when applied to Harrow and district and a beginning was made in January 1947, with the LSO under Mathieson, playing Mendelssohn, Tchaikovsky, the new Britten variations, and Elgar to an audience of enthusiastic, and curious, children in a local cinema. The response was encouraging, but the organisers soon found they had to grade concerts to junior and senior age-groups, and to support the concerts with lecture-recitals in schools by instrumentalists from the Orchestra, either solo or in small ensembles. In this way, LSO Members became as familiar to the school children as football players. The Directors were drawn in to the planning of the series.

The LSO's "constitutional" problem emerged even here. Muir Mathieson wrote to Gordon Walker: "I was both disturbed and disappointed by the quality of the orchestra which appeared under the title of the LSO at Harrow and Barnet recently. As those members of the Board of Directors who were present will, I am sure, agree, too many principals and even rank and file were missing to call the orchestra more than 'scratch'. . . ."

Within the Orchestra, the situation which Mathieson identified was still regarded by a majority as evidence of a fundamental virtue of the LSO; they were simply not interested in playing for a more regimented orchestra. From the Directors' point of view, some action, short of wholesale constitutional reform, had to be taken. In March 1947, "for the maintenance of the high standard and efficiency and excellence of the performances of the Orchestra," the Directors amended the rules of the Company to give them the right "to direct the personal attendance of all playing Members at certain of the Orchestra's engagements should they deem it advisable to do so". Such "special engagements" would not exceed 75 per cent of those accepted in any one year, absence would only be permitted "in exceptional [undefined] circumstances", any Member in breach of the rule was liable to dismissal by resolution of two-thirds of the Board. Having armed themselves with these powers, the Directors re-examined the strings, experimenting with various seating arrangements in order to improve their efficiency.

There were, however, external constraints on the revival of the LSO, especially the lack of suitable and convenient premises for rehearsal. In consequence, Members customarily travelled about London, frequently using three different buildings in the morning, afternoon and evening, which added to both strain on players and the expenses of the Orchestra. It also meant that conductors had no guarantee that the balance found "right" at rehearsal would be equally acceptable at the performance. This problem still (1974) plagues the LSO, but a solution is in sight.

The concert hall problem was largely solved for the Orchestra by the opening of the Royal Festival Hall. The public controversy over sites was paralleled within the profession by a dispute over its use. The LPO campaigned for prior rights of access to give it in London a role comparable with that of the Concertgebouw in Amsterdam. Thomas Russell, the LPO's Secretary, developed this theme in private and in public through his book *Philharmonic Project*. Russell based the LPO's claim on its permanent character as a contract orchestra, and the wider conception of its duty to the community which its activities had shown since 1939. The argument had merit but it was not tactfully deployed. That unforgettable concerts were presented (by the LPO) "for their cultural value, while film sessions and other remunerative engagements were not sought"[1] was undeniable, but the assumption of superior virtue by an orchestra enjoying a public subsidy of £25,000 per annum implicitly denigrated the LSO as the pioneer film orchestra and did not smooth the passage of Russell's argument within the profession. Nor did his demonstration of the inequity of an egalitarian policy for LCC promotions in the new hall. Russell argued that offering the main London orchestras an identical number of engagements would not promote equality. "The basis of any reward must bear some relation to the contribution of the recipient, and when one orchestra organises at its own risk a series of symphony concerts over a wide area, and watches over the proper interests of its own members, while another sits around and waits to be engaged, leaving its members meanwhile to earn their living as best they can, it is no justice to treat both organisations alike."[2] This aspersion of the LSO was in no way mitigated by Mr Russell's later ascription to them of a definite but junior role in the new undertaking.

To some older hands in the LSO, Russell was merely arguing for a monopoly in order to be able to dictate the terms on which his rivals should continue to exist. In this sense his arguments were dismissed as a piece of special pleading. Within the LCC, the responsible committee sounded eminent personalities in the musical profession, including Sir Thomas Beecham and Sir Malcolm Sargent. Both were individualists: neither had any particular reason to favour the LPO. Beecham's postwar association had terminated in the usual controversy while the LPO had not only dropped Sargent as a conductor but allowed the reasons to be known in public. It may legitimately be inferred that neither conductor was in favour of the LPO as resident orchestra. At any rate, the LCC decided not to proceed with the idea. From the LSO's point of view, the decision meant that it could compete for access with the other orchestras and concert organisations, rather than as sub-tenant of a competitor on the orchestral scene. In March 1950, the Directors decided to try to promote a series of Sunday concerts from October 1951 onwards.

The Orchestra first entered the Hall on 14th March 1951 to take part in a series of acoustic tests. The programme consisted of orchestral pieces, piano works and pistol shots. The Orchestra, under Basil Cameron, contributed *Coriolan* and *La Mer*. Twenty Members took part in the composite orchestra for the opening night on 3rd May, but the LSO's first corporate appearance was six days later, at the end of the initial series of concerts, sponsored by the LCC. Clarence Raybould conducted Haydn's *Overture to an English Opera*, Handel's *Fireworks Music*, *Cockaigne*, Walton's Viola Concerto, with William Primrose, and Sibelius' Second Symphony. The LSO subsequently promoted a series of six concerts as part of the opening season. The programmes covered two of Haydn's Symphonies and a series of works by British composers, William Alwyn, Bax, Ireland, Delius and Elgar (to whom a whole evening was dedicated), and Rawsthorne, whose Second Concerto received its première, with Clifford Curzon as soloist. All these works were conducted by Sargent. The Orchestra's other contributions, two concerts of Viennese classics, enabled it to demonstrate its response to its new Conductor in Chief, Josef Krips.

Other centres were also enjoying festivals in 1951: from the South Bank the LSO moved to Norwich in July; September found it in Worcester for the Three Choirs.

The LSO had contributed notably to the opening season of the new hall. Its experience confirmed the Directors in their decision to transfer the activities of the LSO to the South Bank. The value of the Festival Hall to the Orchestra was twofold: the appearances in May and June advertised within a restricted period of time the renovated LSO; in the longer term, the Hall provided the Orchestra with a London "home" comparable with the Queen's Hall. It seems fanciful to reflect now that in moving to the South Bank the Directors were taking a risk, but in the first years, after the initial excitements, there was no great rush among impresarios or orchestras for the new facilities. The LSO's declaration of faith helped to establish it as a going concern.

However, by this time the Orchestra had not only a regular hall but also a regular conductor. Josef Krips made his debut as Conductor in Chief on 19th November 1950. The programme was all Brahms: the *Academic Festival Overture*, the First Piano Concerto and the First Symphony. The performances entranced a public which had had no continuous access to the Viennese tradition since the pre-war concerts with Bruno Walter.

Krips was born in Vienna, had studied at its Academy of Music and, as chorus master and assistant to Weingartner (older Members were pleased to note) at the Volksoper, had entered upon an "orthodox" conducting career in European terms. This quickly yielded an appointment in Karlsruhe, at the age of twenty-four, and engagements with the main orchestras in Berlin, Frankfurt and Vienna. From 1931 to 1938 he became permanent conductor at the Staatsoper in Vienna. The "Anschluss", however, put an end to permanency. Krips was banned from conducting: he continued to work clandestinely as an opera coach. In 1945, he took up his public career again, and was largely responsible for restoring the musical life of his native city, both in opera and concerts. He reopened the Salzburg festivals and took the Vienna Opera on its first post-war tours. He first appeared in London to conduct the Vienna company at Covent Garden in 1947. The next year he returned with the Vienna Philharmonic Orchestra as co-conductor with Furtwängler. At the time of his appointment to the LSO, Krips' name might have been known only to a relatively restricted public in Britain, but his qualities as a musician and disciplinarian were appreciated in the profession. These qualities the Directors had now engaged to rebuild the Orchestra. Their agreement with Krips provided for his exclusive services in London and stipulated, at Krips' specific insistence, that the control of the personnel of the Orchestra should remain vested in the Directors. Krips' opinion was (and is) that in view of the insecurity of orchestral musicians in Britain, he, as a foreigner, should not be made responsible for engaging or dismissing players.

Over the next four years, Josef Krips consolidated the Orchestra, restoring its morale and ensemble and its standing with the public by basing the seasons on cycles of the main works of Beethoven, Brahms and Mozart. Cycles of Beethoven had been performed before, notably by Toscanini before the war, and de Sabata after, but Krips made them a regular feature of the London concert scene, so that every season both new and old audiences could get a *vue d'ensemble* of these fundamental works in the literature of the symphony. So it was also with Brahms and Mozart. These cycles went on even after Krips had ceased to be Conductor in Chief. He extended the LSO's regular repertoire—notably with symphonies by Schubert, Bruckner and Mahler. The Directors had no reservations now about including a Bruckner symphony "provided it were not too long". Mahler was also adopted with enthusiasm. His *Das Lied von der Erde*, with Ferrier and Richard Lewis, was on one occasion performed four times in a single day—a rehearsal and public concert in the afternoon, a studio rehearsal and broadcast in the evening. These changes in quality and repertoire were not restricted to audiences in the capital. Bruckner's Second was played to acclamation in Swansea.

The artistic relationship was not designed to be "one-way": the Viennese Krips took on Elgar and Walton's First Symphony—in view of the LSO's traditions he could hardly have done otherwise—but he conducted them *con amore*. In this respect, he could legitimately claim that he was continuing the tradition of Richter and Nikisch.

The LSO continued to make a feature of British music in the concert hall—on occasions playing a new work twice in the same programme in order to allow listeners to become more familiar with the composer's idiom. Additionally, the Orchestra played neglected works by established composers such as Bax, or neglected works by neglected composers such as Dyson. The essentially international obligations of music prompted the inclusion of works by Hindemith, Bloch, Martinů, and items of contemporary Spanish and Finnish music. They all helped to create deficits but the Directors persisted. In January 1953, even a season of "Winter Proms" of unimpeachably orthodox character failed to draw, and precipitated a financial crisis within the Orchestra. (On learning of this result, Sir Adrian Boult, who had conducted, generously returned his fee.) A contract with Decca hung fire, and the BBC indicated that they would require the services of the LSO for only eight of the summer Promenade Concerts. The Principals took the occasion jointly to present a demand for improved terms, which had been mooted for some time. Discussions with the bank about overdraft facilities evoked the helpful regret that the LSO had not seen fit to acquire its own office building, the deeds of which could be used as security. The Secretary retorted that the overdraft was needed because concert societies were not always punctual in settling accounts—but, evidently, the bank had no high opinion of the Orchestra's earning power.

John Cruft investigated the financial situation and found it "worse than expected". The problem for policy was whether to make the Orchestra available for engagements at a comparatively low cost by keeping down fees, or to risk losing engagements by raising them. The answer implied more than a preference as to the better method of securing business. If fees were raised, then the Orchestra would have to bind itself to give "star" performances—in which case, a number of

Principals would have to be replaced by more distinguished players from outside. The move would be unpopular and expensive. Alternatively, if terms were not improved, the LSO stood to risk losing the Principals it had. The Board sounded Members, by questionnaire:

1. Are you in favour of the suggestion of an increase in certain Principals' fees to X per concert and Y per extra rehearsal?

2. If you have answered YES to Question 1 please vote by a cross against the names of those whom you think should receive the increased fees.

3. If you have answered YES to Question 1, are you in favour of the increased fees being paid to anyone who may on any occasion replace any of the above-named players in those positions?

4. Are you in favour of retaining the present rate of payment to Members?

The majority for the first question was only two—and there were two abstentions. The names suggested in answer to the second question yielded a list of priorities. Questions 3 and 4 were emphatically rejected and sustained respectively. In the event, all Principals receiving over fifteen votes received an increase in their fees. So the proximate cause of the enquiry was resolved. The corollary was that, in future, the LSO would cost more to hire. But in proceeding by questionnaire the Board was attempting to involve the Membership collectively in an incomes policy which freed its hands for the immediate future.

The most important event artistically, and in the longer term financially, was the Orchestra's fiftieth anniversary. This was to be not a single concert at which the original programme was played, as in 1925 and 1944, but was to be a series of four concerts spread over a week and designed to show the LSO's affiliations with composers and conductors over the years. The original programme was to be given on 9th June, but with a number of conductors associated with the Orchestra. Thus, it happened that on Sunday 6th June Krips directed the

Orchestra in Vaughan Williams' *Tallis Fantasia*, the Second Piano Concerto of Alan Rawsthorne, with Clifford Curzon as soloist, and Walton's First Symphony; the following Wednesday, 9th June, the original LSO concert was given in the same order, but with five conductors, Muir Mathieson, George Weldon, Basil Cameron, Sir Malcolm Sargent and Anthony Collins; on the Friday the Orchestra accompanied the Croydon Philharmonic Choir (with whom its connections went back to Billy Reed) in Elgar's *The Dream of Gerontius*; on Sunday, 13th June, the LSO wound up its celebration in a programme of Handel, his *Polonaise, Arietta and Passacaglia* in Harty's arrangement, the Elgar Violin Concerto with Campoli, a new Concerto for Bass Tuba by Vaughan Williams specially composed for Philip Catelinet of the LSO, and Bliss' *A Colour Symphony*, the conductors being Sir John Barbirolli and Sir Arthur Bliss.

The conspicuous absentee from the actual birthday celebration on 9th June was Josef Krips, who, in consequence of a dispute with the Directors at the beginning of the series, resigned his position as Conductor in Chief. This was the greater pity, since Krips, as much as any one individual, was responsible for there being something to celebrate, other than the remembrance of things past. Krips returned to the LSO in subsequent seasons, but its continuous development under his guidance abruptly terminated. His achievement was to take over an orchestra of inferior quality and no prestige, and leave it with an identity and its artistic morale restored, fit to compete with the other three London orchestras. The LSO could still not legitimately be described as "first class", that is, capable of consistently achieving standards of excellence in a wide range of compositions and styles: there were too many rifts within the membership and too many professional alternatives for *that* to result. But its playing was interesting and effective, and in the Viennese repertoire, under Krips, it could give exciting and splendid performances.

By December of the same year, the question of a successor to Krips was being raised, not only to maintain standards but to create an atmosphere in which the discipline of the Orchestra could be improved. Without that, the LSO would not make any further progress, regardless of its policy over conductors. The Board took the view that it was necessary for the LSO to be indisputably first class and that progress made towards that goal since the abysmal days of 1947–48 justified them in demanding certain restrictions on Members' liberty of action as regards other engagements. It certainly demanded the end of "unofficial arrangements with conductors and others", whereby Members acted as "fixers" of engagements for LSO colleagues. The Directors unanimously agreed to amend the Rules, to give themselves a prior right to the services of Members and Probationary Members at all engagements for which the title of the Orchestra was used; on which occasions, even if, exceptional leave of absence were given, Members could not appear with organisations similar to the LSO.

The changes heralded a revolution in policy: "liberty of action" was the crux. Chamber ensemble work provided stimulus and income for Principals; the film studio gave opportunities to a somewhat greater number but by no means the whole orchestra. At this time ideas were canvassed among the Members which would, if followed, have turned the LSO into a recording orchestra for film sound tracks. The reference to "unofficial engagements" shows the Directors' awareness of that aspect of the LSO, and the amendments their determination to stop the rot, as they saw it. The rifts were ominous. In February 1955, a suggestion to re-engage Josef Krips for concerts in the following May and June was received with less than wholehearted enthusiasm—which turned into positive sourness when the Directors made attendance compulsory. The issue was not the return of Josef Krips but the attempt to enforce discipline. Meanwhile, the film studio beckoned.

The winter of discontent turned into a bleak spring. The Board adopted a tough policy towards those who absented themselves without good reason and dismissed one such, Sidney Fell, Principal Clarinet. Thirty Members exercised their right to demand an Extraordinary General Meeting to discuss his case, and the possibility of amending the rules. The meeting took place on 31st March. The sequel was the resignation of the Principals *en masse*.

> It is with very deep regret that we, the undersigned, find it necessary to write and ask you to accept our resignations from the London Symphony Orchestra. . . .

The reasons which have made this move necessary are that we can no longer continue to work under the present administration of the orchestra. It is an indisputable fact that the orchestra is suffering a serious decline—in number of engagements, standard of performance and *esprit de corps*, and it is our opinion that this is due to the faulty administration.

Unless the principals could be given the opportunity of taking a full part in the administration, with a reconstituted organisation, we feel that the decline will continue. We deplore this situation, but it has been made quite clear at meetings that no such co-operation is encouraged by the existing Board of Directors, which is elected by an unfair representation of the string-playing majority. There was even an organised "Rank and File" pre-election meeting from which the principals were excluded. Later it was stated that the company is not interested in personalities but in the enforcement of rules and discipline. Making music to the best of our ability, individually and collectively, which should be the administration's chief concern, is not possible under the existing frustrating conditions.

Moreover, by the recent dismissal of Mr Fell, the Board have quite nonchalantly lost the orchestra one of the finest artists in the country. Furthermore, they have approached his successor without taking into consideration the opinion of the members of the wood-wind section and others.

It is our earnest desire that this orchestra, which bears the great name of "The London Symphony Orchestra" and for which we have gladly made many sacrifices, should regain a status worthy of its early traditions. We would like to help to achieve this but feel it will only be possible with a drastic change of administration.

The letter correctly identified the sources of strain. "Principals versus Rank and File" had come to a head. Personalities exacerbated professional relationships, but *au fond* the dispute was about the nature of the LSO. Was it to continue on its traditional basis or not? In 1929, the creation of a permanent orchestra had caused intense bitterness, which had only been eased with the collapse of permanency, and the provision of external opposition in the form of the BBC and LPO. A quarter of a century later, the issue was raised again, but by this time the LSO had more competitors and it had been demonstrated that habitual reliance on deputies was no longer compatible with the highest standards of performance: the practice would only tend to confirm the LSO's existing position *vis-à-vis* its main competitors. It would undo the work accomplished under Josef Krips.

The Directors met one of the signatories of the letter, Roger Lord, whose motives seemed to them more strictly to do with artistic standards, and persuaded him to re-apply for membership. He did so. The resignations of the others were simply accepted: their association with the LSO terminated as from 11th May. They, for the most part, based their careers on the film studio, as the Sinfonia of London. Meanwhile, the Board began urgently to search for replacements. One crucial figure, Gervase de Peyer, had, fortuitously, just been recruited in the normal way. Another, Barry Tuckwell, arrived from the Bournemouth Orchestra. Neville Marriner became Principal Second Violin. The damage was rapidly made good and, in consequence, the LSO suddenly became a "young" orchestra—the average age was cut to about thirty.

This in itself affected the tone quality, the *esprit de corps* and the dedication to work. For most of the newcomers, this was their chance of rapid and public personal achievement. Tuckwell made this the crucial consideration in his discussions with the Directors and in his decision to join the LSO rather than another orchestra which was interested in his services. Energy, ambition and the need to close ranks combined to create the modern LSO. George Stratton was posthumously justified. Fortunately, the film industry provided the "new" Orchestra with an opportunity to work. Paramount were remaking *The Man Who Knew Too Much*, for which an orchestra was needed for the sound track and in a concert scene. The BBC offered some timely broadcasts, including the Second Symphony of Charles Ives, and Bernard Herrmann reintroduced the LSO to Leopold Stokowski, after a gap of forty-three years. To make sure of Stokowski's services Herrmann and John Cruft travelled overnight to Paris to be on the platform to meet Stokowski on his arrival there at 8 a.m. before his agent could interfere! They promptly informed the General Manager of the RFH of the outcome. Josef Krips was booked for a Beethoven cycle, both as a "draw" and as an exercise in consolidation. Bliss was asked to conduct his *Morning Heroes* on 11th November, with Sir Ralph Richardson. Rudolph Kempe, Hans Schmidt-Isserstedt, Sargent and Cameron were engaged for the rest of the series. A spur to further achievement was the offer to appear at the Johannesburg Festival from mid-September to late October 1956.

The city celebrated its seventieth birthday with a six-week festival of the arts, in which the LSO gave five concerts. The programmes were built round the development of the symphony: Haydn's *Oxford*, Mozart's No. 40 and *Jupiter*, Schubert's *Unfinished*, the *Eroica*, Schumann's Fourth, Brahms' First and Mahler's Second. Britain's contribution to the literature of the symphony was—inevitably—Walton's First, which was given twice. Programmes also included such works as Strauss' *Don Juan* and Brahms' Haydn Variations. The series was designed to be conducted by Josef Krips, but he had to cry off through illness, and his place was taken at the last minute by Jascha Horenstein. Horenstein was shown the programmes and asked which items he desired to alter. "I know them all, except the Walton. I will learn that on the plane"; which he did. The journey, by piston-engined aircraft, lasted thirty hours, with an unexpected delay at Cairo. The conditions proved admirable for work on a new score, to judge by the resultant performances, but the payload of the aircraft did compel the LSO to leave behind its tympani and double basses. These were hired in Johannesburg.

The LSO's five concerts were acclaimed by packed houses, though one or two critics dissented on points of interpretation. After the final concert, the conductor and Leader of the Orchestra, Hugh Maguire, were presented with laurel wreaths by the Festival musical director, Ernest Fleischmann. Johannesburg effectively marked the re-appearance of the LSO internationally, and alerted the British public to the fact that the reconstruction of the LSO merited such recognition. Within the Orchestra, it helped to consolidate morale and ensemble.

On Krips' departure, the LSO had reverted to its usual practice of engaging the best available conductor, though it tended to work more with some conductors than others, largely through relationships brought about by recordings. Antal Dorati gradually built up a regular connection with the LSO in this way. But the need for a Conductor in Chief to replace Josef Krips continued to be canvassed within the Orchestra.

The case *for* a Conductor in Chief was, in essence, that he was necessary to turn the LSO into a great orchestra. The candidate would either have achieved such eminence as to be uninterested in any aspect except the purely artistic satisfactions of the job in hand, or alternatively would have an interest in enlarging his own reputation through the LSO—in which circumstance he was likely to be younger. In either case, it would be preferable that he brought with him a recording contract.

The case *against* was basically economic: the LSO could not afford the time-lag between the conductor's arrival and his establishing himself with the public. One Member pointed to the dangers, from previous experience: "When I was a member at the LPO, we appointed Mr Van Beinum as our permanent conductor. Within six weeks he turned the LPO into a first class orchestra—but we continued to play to half-empty halls." Only the grants then enjoyed by the orchestra enabled the experiment to survive long enough for it to succeed with the public. Another drawback, peculiar to the LSO, was that a permanent appointment would cut across the guest-conductor tradition. The LSO had previously jettisoned it when the Orchestra was in trouble artistically and needed to be re-trained. Coates, Harty and Josef Krips had fulfilled this role admirably, but, in the minds of Members, it was finite: Coates and Harty were dismissed, Krips resigned. Now, however, the Orchestra was not in an artistic abyss: it only wanted to improve; could this not be achieved without committing the LSO to the degree of exclusivity which any suitable candidate would naturally require and which would tend to increase?

For the time being, these arguments proved decisive, though not without misgivings as the Philharmonia, at this stage, was taking on a new character under Otto Klemperer, and holding Beethoven cycles of its own. The Directors acknowledged the situation by dropping their own, by now traditional, series, and concentrating on Mozart and Brahms.

As a more positive remedy the LSO Board attempted to engage conductors for batches of concerts, over three weeks or a month. This scheme would allow better communication between orchestra and conductor, as well as permitting broadcasts and recordings to be grouped round their joint public concerts. The latter intention was hardly realised, since the BBC and record companies showed little practical interest. It was, however, very successful in regard to a guest conductor new to the LSO—Pierre Monteux, with whom the Orchestra prepared and gave and subsequently recorded three public concerts in the summer of 1958. These made a tremendous impact on Orchestra and audience alike. Monteux, then eighty-three, had begun his career playing in the orchestra at the Folies-Bergère in the *belle époque* of the 1890s (to which experience he attributed his sharp sense of rhythm) and subsequently took charge of the famous Casino summer concerts at Dieppe. He acquired European renown as conductor for Diaghilev, in particular of Stravinsky's scores. After the First World War his career took him to Boston, Amsterdam (where he shared seasons with Mengelberg), Paris and San Francisco, so that by the time he began to appear with the LSO in the late 1950s, Monteux's was a name which, except for the few survivors of the Diaghilev era, conjured up a legend rather than an experience.

The Directors also considered conductors who were showing promise of international stature. In the late fifties, the LSO began to work with Colin Davis, who unmistakably "arrived" after standing in at the last moment for Otto Klemperer in a concert performance of *Don Giovanni*. Davis' impact on the Orchestra awaited the next decade. At this juncture, the most regular conducting influence over the LSO was Antal Dorati. It was exercised through a long series of recordings made for the American "Mercury" Company and a parallel series of concerts. Dorati recalls that he had the luck to arrive at the psychological moment: the Orchestra had good players but weak ensemble; it knew it could be much better. This awareness was vital. The Orchestra plunged into an appalling schedule of work—three sessions a day seven days a week during one summer—tackling new repertoire such as Schoenberg's *Kammersymphonie* and Berg's music from *Wozzeck* and *Lulu* as well as works which had disappeared from LSO programmes like *The Firebird*. Orchestra and conductor fought their way through. The LSO emerged tougher and technically a better orchestra, highly aware of its potentialities and in a mood to take on anything. In the evolution of the LSO from competence to virtuosity, not the least important factor were these concentrated and exhausting sessions under Antal Dorati for the Mercury Company and its manager for classical recordings, Harold Lawrence.

In August 1959 John Cruft expressed his intention to resign, in order to join the British Council. To fill the vacancy, the Board considered eight candidates, one of whom was the man whose work had so impressed the LSO at the Johannesburg Festival, Ernest Fleischmann, who, in fact, had not formally applied.

Cruft approached Fleischmann who sent him a copy of an application to the municipality of Cape Town, where he lived, to become the official Director of Music. This document showed that Fleischmann had studied music under Erik Chisholm at the University, had acted as repetiteur in an opera company started by Albert Coates, had qualified in accountancy and written music criticism for the *Cape Times*. The enquiry from the LSO as to whether he would be interested in submitting an application arrived in Cape Town at a point when Fleischmann had been offered the position of both Director and Conductor of that orchestra, but the offer had not been ratified. He was not especially anxious to stay in South Africa, but a conducting career had to start somewhere.

The LSO's initiative disrupted this whole framework of ideas, and forced Fleischmann to consider whether he "could *really* discipline himself to learn the conductor's trade on a world level". He had enjoyed running festivals and the opportunity to build something in the world of music was very attractive. While Fleischmann was turning over these questions, the Directors concluded that if he could "sell" the LSO with as much panache as he "sold" himself, Fleischmann was their man. Accordingly, they offered him the job, by cable. He began working for the LSO in November 1959.

Of necessity, his relationship with the Directors differed from that of his predecessor. John Cruft had been a Performing

Member and Director, although he had abandoned both to concentrate on his job as Secretary. Fleischmann had no such background, either in the LSO or in the London concert world, the characteristic and often curious working rules of which he had to learn, whereas they were, metaphorically, part of John Cruft's genetic inheritance! Equally, however, Cruft freely concedes that he was not good at "chromium plating" the Orchestra: he was a good salesman to the knowledgeable, but not to the ignorant. In that sphere, Fleischmann excelled. He exemplified the qualities of the "keen businessman" whom Gordon Walker thirteen years before had suggested as necessary in a general manager for the LSO. He was tough minded, aggressive and hard driving; he erupted into the world of committees, memoranda, enthusiastic but amateur organisers, shrewd agents and highly individualist soloists. The files of these years reflect Fleischmann's unfamiliarity with, and perhaps, contempt for, the subjunctival niceties of English official correspondence ("I would be grateful if you could, perhaps, kindly see your way. . . ."). Such dynamism was divisive, both inside and outside the LSO, but it propelled the Orchestra, whose standards had improved out of all recognition since 1950, on to the world stage.

XI

IN THE LSO, impending major changes in policy or administration customarily encourage Members to forsake their usual informal representations to Board Members, and contribute their diagnoses and remedies in writing. ("The changes taking place/envisaged/discussed at the present time make it opportune for me to express my own personal views. . . .")

The impending departure of John Cruft provoked wide-ranging interventions from Members on questions of principle and detail. They did not mince matters.

> I consider the administrative mechanism of the LSO creaky, old fashioned and periodically ineffectual . . . [it] could be streamlined, time-and-motioned into a more efficient body.

> One of the greatest drawbacks the LSO suffers is that we appear to have no musical policy. . . . Our programmes fall between two stools: they are not for the musical public nor for the general public.

> The Beethoven cycle has become distinguished only by its longevity. . . . The Proms are lucrative handouts, performed under difficult conditions with an indifferent conductor. . . . The Press are half-hearted and the audience is merely a seasonal phenomenon.

> In our endeavours to place the orchestra before the public and the press with programmes of artistic imagination conducted by mentors of the great traditions or firebrands of the personality brigade, we appear to fall heavily between at least three stools. Taking Monteux and Stokowski as our mentor quota, we find ourselves stuck with as big a collection of indifferent international giants as the agents can pass us off with.

> An orchestra of stature should promote new ideas: we must be more venturesome and lead the way.
>
> The secretary as we have known him has gone. The job should be much more potent with regard to the business of acquiring work and polishing our professional and public relations.

Such comments, it must be remembered, express not only attitudes of players towards the artistic management but of shareholders towards the Board of Directors. "Please accept this brief letter as an indication of my wishes 'for the good of the orchestra', not entirely unmitigated by the anxieties of an investor in your company."

Evidently, the LSO was ripe for change. This realisation stemmed from the progress achieved during the late fifties and from the attitudes of younger players who, at this time, had completed four or five years' service. They formed a particular and identifiable group whose views, broadly, were expressed on the Board by Barry Tuckwell, who became Chairman in 1962. In November 1959, Fleischmann arrived, and in July 1960, Harry Dugarde resigned as Chairman, to spend the rest of his career as a back-desk cellist. He had steered the Orchestra through drastic postwar changes, aiming "to restore to the LSO its original function of serving the art of music, rather than that of the film studio." Dugarde's resignation marked, as one says, the end of an era—and was felt as such by his contemporaries in the Orchestra.

A collective feeling that the old order is changing tends to accelerate the rate of change. The appearance of new personalities provokes new constellations of attitudes. Old questions are dusted off and re-examined and new policies result. The LSO underwent this process in 1960.

Within months, a whole series of innovations was made.* Printed programmes were improved in quality and style, members began to be paid through their banks, the administration

* It is perhaps, symptomatic that 1960 was the last year in which the LSO played cricket. Colin Davis captained the side, against the press critics. The game was memorable for Osian Ellis' appearing on the field in shorts! The result of the match is lost in the mists of time.

of the Orchestra was improved by scrapping the part-time posts of Orchestral Manager and Librarian (held by Playing Members) and replacing them with full-time officials, the Directors debated the acquisition of permanent offices for the administration and the library (they regretfully concluded that this project was over-ambitious).

The Board's thinking necessarily ranged over the content of LSO promotions, and the approval of conductors. They decided to give the season more coherence by running an "International Series" instead of a "Beethoven Series", and to try to attract subscribers. The discussion threw up one idea which was to have momentous artistic consequences nine years later, namely a "Beethoven to Berg Cycle", tracing the development of tonality in the Viennese composers of the nineteenth and twentieth centuries. At the same time, the Directors aimed to cut down the number of conductors engaged for LSO promotions, allowing three to four weeks with each, so that the players would benefit from longer contact and the conductor could build radio, television and gramophone recording sessions round his work with the Orchestra—all of which could be co-ordinated by the LSO. It was also decided that the LSO should have its own chorus.

The Directors were not alone in thinking that a more co-ordinated approach to the business of music-making was desirable. T. E. Bean, then General Manager of the Royal Festival Hall, put it to Ernest Fleischmann that formal and regular discussion among the four London orchestras would promote a more rational distribution of dates at the Hall. That would have the added benefit of allowing more appearances, possibly with better financial support from the London County Council. The result would be that more control of the Hall's artistic policy would rest in professional hands.

The Board stifled its doubts about co-operation, in favour of increased bookings and subsidies. Eventually, a committee was set up to co-ordinate programmes: forward bookings were secured through a system of ticket vouchers, entitling the subscriber to a chance of booking seats well in advance, at reduced rates. By the end of 1961, the LSO and LPO were beginning to co-operate in representations to the Arts Council on adequate working conditions for musicians in London.

Above: Antal Dorati

Right: Istvan Kertesz

Below: Sir Georg Solti

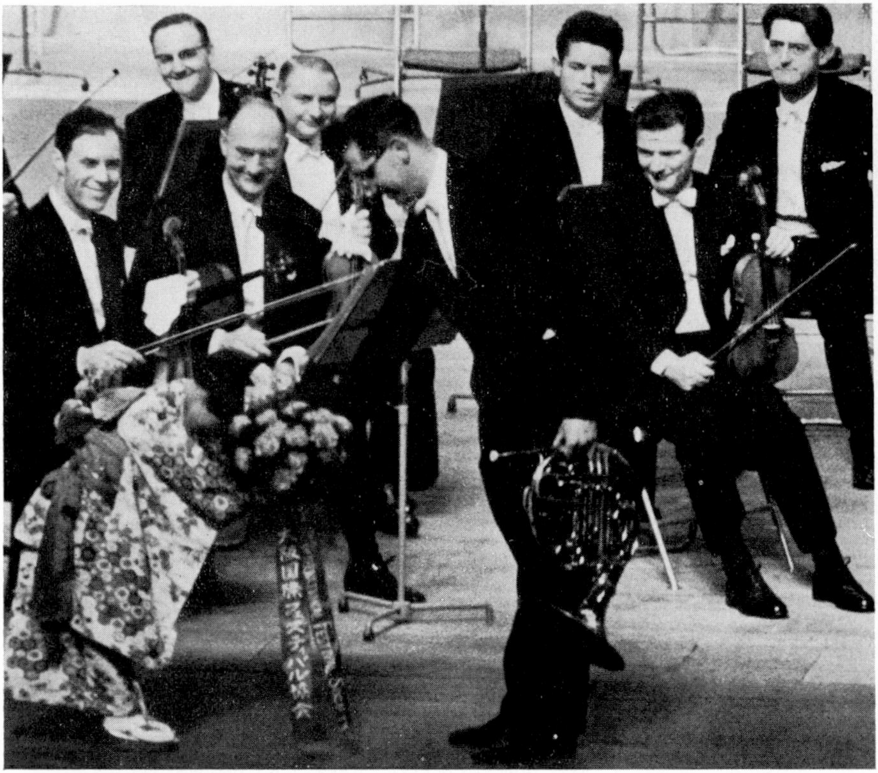

Barry Tuckwell receives a bouquet from a young girl in Osaka during the World Tour, 1964

Sir Arthur Bliss, Jack Lyons and Sir Robert Mayer greet Sir Malcolm Sargent, Ernest Fleischmann and the Orchestra on its return from the World Tour, 1964

All these were changes whose effects would be confined to the Orchestra or would be observable by the public only after a period of time. The most immediately dramatic change in policy concerned touring. The Johannesburg visit pointed to the advantages for an orchestra constituted like the LSO. For the duration of the tour, the personnel were unchanged, and they were put on their mettle by playing before critical audiences in new environments. Further, success overseas improved the Orchestra's standing at home. Harry Dugarde raised the possibilities of further tours during the late fifties, but finance was an insoluble problem. In the spring of 1960, the British Council suddenly offered to underwrite a short tour of the Netherlands.

The psychological effect on the Orchestra was profound. The reception of audiences on tour, particularly in the Concertgebouw, demonstrated to the players just how good they had become—which was reassuring—and how good they could become—which was challenging. From that time onward, the LSO energetically pursued touring as a deliberate policy.*

As Ernest Fleischmann explains, in the early sixties "the fantasy place" was Vienna. He contacted the Director of the Festwochen; "If I produce for 1961 Monteux, Solti and Stokowski, will you take us?" There could only be one answer, and the LSO was scheduled for Vienna.

The Vienna visit enabled the Orchestra to demonstrate its new-found quality to critical audiences in one of Europe's historic centres of music. The LSO returned buoyed up with their acclaim—and with a new Principal Conductor. While President Kennedy and Mr Khruschev were engaged in their historic meetings at the Imperial Hotel, the LSO Secretary and Pierre Monteux discussed in the same place a possibility which in a more limited context was equally epoch-making, i.e. that Monteux should become Principal Conductor. This was to be purely honorary. Monteux was happy to advise but not interfere with the running of the LSO but, at eighty-six, insisted on a twenty-five-year contract, with an option of renewal! Members were delighted at the prospect, which the Directors soon translated into fact. The artistic consequences

* Appendix I, pp. 223–7, shows the extent of the Orchestra's odysseys since 1960.

were tremendous. Pierre Monteux conferred on the LSO the benefit of about sixty years' experience as a conductor whose credo was "to communicate with the Orchestra and bring out the composer's conception". By 1961, his early modernism had become traditional: the scores of Stravinsky, Debussy and Ravel no longer had the power to shock, but, under Monteux, the LSO's performances conveyed a sense of their immediate impact. By this time, too, Monteux had long dispelled the notion that Brahms and Beethoven were inaccessible to "Latin" musicians. He ignored the contemporary, disliking "abstract" music as much as abstract painting. While he was Principal Conductor, modern works had to be confided to other guest conductors.

There were, from the Orchestra's point of view, other drawbacks. Monteux was not a trainer—and orchestras, if they aspire to the first class, have to be kept in trim. His age had two contrasting effects: in public, the Orchestra played as if every concert were likely to be the last, but studio sessions with him could not be planned at more than one a day. It was, in practice, difficult to fit sessions with other conductors round Monteux's personal schedule. This evoked no more than regret: the players held Monteux in professional admiration and personal affection—and it showed in their playing.

Touring brought artistic success and helped the Orchestra to establish its identity, but the costs were heavy, even with British Council subventions. The Council is charged with showing Britain's artistic and intellectual achievements abroad but it is not bound to deal equitably between candidates for patronage, in order to promote understanding of the country's cultural achievements. Its activity does not extend to the United States where the LSO had most interest in going. These were two severe drawbacks, and a constraint on the LSO's progress. In 1963 two separate sources of funds emerged, which materially assisted the LSO to progress from being a good London orchestra to being accepted in the world class.

Chronologically, the first source of funds appeared unexpectedly from the tobacco business. At this time, the directors of Peter Stuyvesant of London were considering the nature and extent of their obligations to the community, apart from meeting a demand for cigarettes. They decided to support the arts and social causes, and took advice as to how these generalised aims were to be most suitably translated into specific projects. The answers took Peter Stuyvesant to Whitechapel Art Gallery (and to the seminal "New Generations" exhibitions) and to the LSO. Ernest Fleischmann did not need to be asked twice. With Michael Kaye, from Peter Stuyvesant (whose activities in this sphere were subsequently entrusted to an eponymous Foundation), he quickly worked out some "ground rules" for subventions. First and foremost, there was to be no infringement of artistic policy or the Orchestra's management of its affairs. Equally, however, the LSO recognised that Peter Stuyvesant had a legitimate interest in how its money was spent, since the aim of subvention was not simply to contribute towards the LSO's operating expenses but "to change the musical scene in some way". So it was agreed that Stuyvesant money should assist the Orchestra to plan and perform unfamiliar music, commission new compositions, or give concerts with unusual items in places off the traditional LSO circuit. Accordingly, in 1963–64, the LSO began to include in some of its programmes an "item to be announced" which was introduced to the audience by a well-known specialist. In this way, the LSO presented Satie's *Parade* and Alun Hoddinot's Harp Concerto to audiences attracted to the concert by Beethoven and Tchaikovsky; compositions were commissioned from Richard Rodney Bennett and Don Banks, and the Orchestra appeared in new, or neglected, centres.

This relationship was an influential development in industrial sponsorship and it still continues. It began at a critical time in the LSO's fortunes, before public funds became available through the London Orchestral Concert Board,* and enabled the Directors, who were conscious of the need to experiment and expand, to do so in the confidence that the funds would be forthcoming. The relationship thus begun has extended to other commissions and projects, and to the financing of tours. It also provides the Directors with a source of friendly external advice on financial or commercial matters, if they wish to use it. The contrast with the 1930s could not be more striking: *then* F. J. Nettlefold's support took him directly into the

* See below, pp. 170 and 176.

management of the LSO and its promotional policies; *now* the success of the arrangement depends on the patron's staying out of management, but nevertheless helping the Directors to form a view of what they ought to be doing. On these terms for the last ten years, the relationship with Peter Stuyvesant has underwritten the independence of the LSO and enlarged its artistic options.*

The LSO was financially vulnerable in more than related to its artistic policies. The problems of providing for a permanent home for the Orchestra and security for Members in the form of sickness benefits, pensions, and holiday pay were as great an incubus as financing sufficient rehearsals and covering the costs of foreign tours. Barry Tuckwell and Ernest Fleischmann devised a scheme for a Trust which could receive and administer moneys to provide a reserve for these purposes, and thus help to stabilise the environment in which the Orchestra now worked *and* offer better conditions to Members. To translate these aims into practice, Fleischmann turned to the Rt Hon Edward Heath, whose acquaintance he had made when Heath, then President of the Board of Trade, had "dropped in" on part of a Mozart concert and shared Fleischmann's box in the Festival Hall. Heath agreed to act, and, with John Spencer Wills and Edward Pollitzer, comprised the first Board of Trustees, in December 1963. The management of any funds was, by the Trust Deed, assigned to a Committee, which included Pollitzer, Benjamin Britten, Sir Robert Mayer, Jack Lyons and five Members of the LSO Board.

In law, the Trust was purely a passive instrument and the building-up of Trust funds depended largely on the generosity of a small number of individual benefactors including notably Jack Lyons. He was a former Chairman of the Leeds Festival, whose interest in the LSO was solicited by Fleischmann when he (Lyons) moved to London. He became a personal patron of the Orchestra on condition that he was not allowed to have anything to do with its management! The personnel of the Trust has changed: Spencer Wills resigned in 1968, as did

* The LSO received similar patronage from 1964 to 1966 from Rediffusion Television, and currently, is also being helped by annual grants from British Airways. The Rupert Foundation, of Switzerland, supports the LSO's annual Conductors' Competition.

Edward Heath, in 1970, on becoming Prime Minister. His connection with the LSO was sufficiently enduring to allow him to conduct the Orchestra in Elgar's *Cockaigne* Overture in a Trust Fund concert in 1972. The present Trustees are Ronald Plumley, Sir Jack Lyons, Sir Gilbert Inglefield, Sir Richard Powell, Bernard Clarke and Edward Pollitzer.

After Vienna, and with the possibilities held out by the new sources of finance, planning was more ambitious: suddenly the whole world seemed available. It was decided that the Orchestra's sixtieth anniversary could be best celebrated with a world tour. During 1964, from 27th September until 11th December, the LSO travelled from London to London via the United States, Japan, Korea, Hong Kong, India, Iran, Israel and Turkey. One single occasion stands out in the minds of the Members, the United Nations Day Concert in the UN Headquarters in New York, which presented the Orchestra through radio and television throughout the United States from coast to coast, and also through satellite transmissions to member states of the UN. It was *the* Diamond Jubilee occasion. The American part of the tour revealed one different aspect of the LSO's life. The Orchestra was invited to play in New York regularly, each spring. This was the first such invitation to any foreign orchestra, but the LSO's legitimate pride in this recognition of its achievement had to stop at that point. The visits could not be economic, the British Council could not help and the LSO's own resources from the LSO Trust and Peter Stuyvesant were exhausted by the World Tour. The invitation had to be declined. Nevertheless, in consequence of the World Tour, regular touring became an indispensable part of the LSO's working life.

During the early sixties, the LSO developed its present strong corporate personality. Monteux demanded dedication and, in the nature of things, urgency; Colin Davis conjured up an inner fire; Dorati and Solti, both exacting taskmasters, drove the Orchestra towards collective technical virtuosity. Yet another Hungarian (the LSO was returning to its origins!), Istvan Kertesz brought out a sheer delight in making music, evident in the Orchestra's refreshing performances of such familiar works as Dvořák's symphonies. The common factor with which all these conductors and their colleagues had to work was not just the musicianship of the players but their collective willingness to find out what their artistic limits were. The secret of the resurgence of the LSO lay in the collective psychology of the Members at that time.

The LSO promptly founded its chorus—by employing the Ambrosian singers under a new alias ("we perform under any name suitable either to the Conductor or Promoter"). But from the outset, the Directors had in mind a chorus which would be more strictly related to the LSO and soon reverted to the formula which had worked so handsomely with the Philharmonia, namely amateurs selected by exacting auditions, with age restrictions to promote a "bright" tone, and with a cadre of professionals. The amateurs were recruited mostly from the music colleges, especially the Guildhall School of Music. John Alldis was appointed chorus master. In this form, the LSO Chorus made its debut in 1966, in a performance of Mahler's Second Symphony under Solti.

The idea did not work out smoothly in practice. The professionals could not be phased out as quickly as the Board had planned, and remained an increasing financial burden. The students from the Guildhall tended to feel that they were semi-professional singers being exploited by the LSO—a feeling to which an apparent indifference on the part of the Directors contributed. Performances which fell outside the Guildhall terms or which coincided with examinations inevitably broke continuity of appearances and forced the LSO to rely either on other choruses or on professionals. In October 1966 the recruitment, structure and training of the Chorus was investigated and liaison between it and the Orchestra improved.

One of the casualties of the LSO's entry on to the world stage was the concerts for the Harrow schools. Members had come to find the lecture recitals more rewarding than the concerts themselves, which could no longer be easily fitted into the Orchestra's schedule of engagements and gradually came to enjoy less and less priority in its planning. In May 1965 it was unable to comply with requests for dates: the Harrow authorities, quite reasonably, queried the apparent lack of interest, after eighteen years' association. It soon appeared that the LSO was unable to give any firm forward bookings, in view of which the relationship with Harrow terminated.

This episode highlights an intractable problem for orchestras in a competitive world. The rates paid for education are lower than those for other engagements and far lower than those current at gramophone sessions. The social concerns of musicians, to say nothing of their shrewd appreciation of the need to build up interested and informed future audiences, lead them to take part in educational schemes, particularly when, as at Harrow, concerts are integrated into a syllabus. In 1948 these two factors were not far apart, and the LSO's diary was not so crammed with other engagements. By 1965 this had ceased to be true and the Orchestra had become more self-consciously competitive. The interests of Harrow and the LSO necessarily diverged. The issue was forced because the Harrow scheme was intelligently devised and did not allow an orchestra to be engaged at a moment's notice.

It is easily and widely assumed that artistic success commands its own reward at the box office. There is, of course, a relationship—sometimes, an inverse one—but time is all-important to it. So, although in the early sixties the news filtered through that something exciting and worthwhile had transformed the LSO, it was some time before curiosity translated itself into attendances, and then they were by no means unvarying. The year 1963 conveniently illustrates what was happening. The "new" LSO was in its third season: sufficient time had elapsed for the Orchestra to have made an impact. Yet attendances fluctuated considerably, as the table on the next page shows. The concert on 9th January was the first performance in London of Britten's *War Requiem*, which, virtually without advance publicity, sold out the Albert Hall. Yet, at the end of the year, the same work played to some 300 empty seats in the Festival Hall. On 29th May, Monteux conducted the fiftieth anniversary performance of *The Rite of Spring*, with the composer present. The first performance under the young Monteux had caused a riot celebrated in the history of the lyric theatre; the anniversary, even under a conductor whose association with the work was also being celebrated and who was loved by the public, failed to pack the Albert Hall. A casual visitor could have dropped into Monteux's own eighty-eighth birthday concert, on 6th April, which included the Ninth Symphony, while ticket sales on 21st November seem to show that the LSO was

Date		*Hall*	*Seating Max.*	*Sold*	*Conductor*	*Composer(s)*
Jan.	9	RAH	4792	4684	Britten	Britten (*War Requiem*)
	24	RFH	2982	745	Solti	Britten, Mahler, Brahms
	28	RFH	2982	1428	Solti	Beethoven, Mozart, Bartók
Feb.	3	RFH	2982	2207	Hurst	Beethoven, Tchaikovksy
	12	RFH	2982	593	Kertesz	Mozart, Bartók, Dvořák
	21	RFH	2982	1782	Kertesz	Brahms, Mozart, Strauss (R.)
Mar.	3	RFH	2982	1683	Celibidache	Brahms, Hindemith, Stravinsky
	5	RFH	2982	1136	Celibidache	Mendelssohn, Wagner, Shostakovich
	28	RFH	2982	2571	Hurst	Hindemith, Prokofiev, Dvořák
	30	RFH	2982	2878	Davis (C.)	Schubert, Tchaikovsky, Rachmaninov, Beethoven
April	6	RFH	2982	2610	Monteux	Beethoven
	9	RFH	not available		Schuricht	Weber, Mozart, Brahms
May	5	RFH	2982	2611	Menuhin	Mozart, Enescu, Beethoven
	7	RFH	2982	2295	Monteux	Berlioz, Franck, Brahms
	14	RFH	2982	1269	Davis (C.)	Schütz, Britten, Tippett, Mozart
	29	RAH	4923	4057	Monteux	Wagner, Brahms, Stravinsky
June	24	RFH	2982	1640	Dorati	Stravinsky, Bartók, Prokofiev
July	3	RFH	2982	2813	Dorati	Schubert, Schumann, Brahms
Sept.	24	RFH	2982	1757	Monteux	Sibelius, Vaughan Williams
	26	RFH	2982	2498	Monteux	Brahms, Strauss (R.)

Oct.	4	RFH	2982	1860	Monteux	Weber, Berlioz, Beethoven
	13	RFH	2982	1331	Hurst	Debussy, Bruch, Walton
	15	RFH	2982	1039	Markevitch	Busoni, Bartók, Berlioz
	25	RFH	2982	1128	Rozhdestvensky	Shostakovich, Tchaikovsky
	29	RFH	2982	953	Rozhdestvensky	Walton, Bartók, Prokofiev
Nov.	7	RFH	2982	1522	del Mar	Schoenberg (*Gurrelieder*)
	10	RFH	2982	1553	Rozhdestvensky	Mussorgsky, Rachmaninov
	11	RFH	2982	1413	Markevitch	Rossini, Strauss (R.), Tchaikovsky
	21	RFH	2982	883	Davis (C.)	Purcell, Tippett, Elgar
	28	RFH	2982	1428	Davis (C.)	Berlioz (*Beatrice and Benedict*)
Dec.	8	RFH	2982	2982	Monteux	Berlioz, Rimsky-Korsakov, Ravel
	12	RFH	2982	2620	Britten	Britten (*War Requiem*)

losing money on Elgar in the sixties, as it had done in the late twenties. These results suggest that even an orchestra which was demonstrating a new and dazzling quality, and which enjoyed an enthusiastic "press", nevertheless failed to draw a consistent public. The available evidence suggests that the LSO was not the worst-placed of the London orchestras, whose collective future was jeopardised by persistently empty seats. By the end of 1964 the forecasts showed the situation to be critical, and the LSO, LPO, and New Philharmonia Orchestra jointly approached the Arts Council. During the same seasons, 1963 and 1964, the Royal Philharmonic Orchestra nearly broke up altogether, through lack of engagements. In December 1963 its players took over the management and survived only by virtue of an emergency grant from the Arts Council. Clearly, during the following year, the RPO's long-term future was seriously in doubt.

In December 1964, the Arts Council, in consultation with the London County Council, appointed a committee, under Mr Arnold Goodman, to consider the situation of the four London orchestras in relation to (i) the demand for their services, (ii) whether they should or could be regrouped, and (iii) stabilising conditions of employment for their members, having regard to the need to maintain the highest standards of programmes and performance and the continued provision of employment. These terms of reference would have justified a comprehensive tome, but the financial situation of the RPO and, to a lesser extent, the NPO determined that the enquiry had to be completed in a hurry. The Arts Council made £10,000 available to keep the orchestras going for the duration of the enquiry. The Committee first met on 23rd December, and completed its report by the end of March. The report was discussed by the Arts Council in April and published in June.

Arnold Goodman and his colleagues considered that fluctuating attendances derived principally from the chaotic manner in which concerts were promoted, and proposed the formation of a concert board to rationalise dates and programmes, allocate subsidies, approve budgets and negotiate, on the orchestras' behalf, for additional subsidies with local authorities and other bodies. The Committee also recommended that each orchestra receive a basic annual grant of £40,000 as a major contribution towards administration costs, holiday and sick pay for the players, and eventually the establishment of a pension scheme, plus a subsidy per concert.

The report concluded that the scale of work justified "the existence of rather more than three but less than four orchestras", but, for lack of conclusive evidence that work available would *not* expand, avoided recommending such an allocation of subsidies as would cause one orchestra to disband. Since the Committee had been at great pains to enquire whether the other orchestras could absorb players from the RPO, this outcome was a temporary vote of confidence in its powers of survival. "Goodman" was confined to London, but has become a basic document in any discussion of the problems of orchestras and the funding of music.

The representations made to the Committee by the LSO give a useful summary of the state of the Orchestra and the environment in which it had to work.

The Committee asked:

> Do you consider that the orchestra would be improved by either decreasing or augmenting its basic membership?

The LSO's reply was:

> We strongly feel that the orchestra would be improved if its basic membership were to be augmented. The following, briefly, are some of our chief reasons for this:
>
> During the financial year ended 31st March 1964, more than £25,000 was paid to extra and deputy string players alone. Our present membership consists of 50 strings (14.12.10.8.6.), whereas for most public concerts and many recording sessions and broadcasts we require 60 strings (16.14.12.10.8.). On most foreign tours a further desk of strings all round (10 players) is advisable for both artistic and practical (health, exhaustion) reasons. It should be pointed out that the major American and Continental orchestras play at most important concerts with 65–70 strings.
>
> *Woodwind:* Our present complement consists of triple woodwind, but this should be increased to at least four players all round and, in the clarinets to five players (principal, co-principal, second, E flat and third, bass and fourth).

The addition of a second, or co-principal, is highly desirable not only to give the orchestra's distinguished principals more time for solo and chamber music work, but to relieve the physical and mental strain to which the orchestra's very heavy work schedule subjects such principals. In any event, a considerable portion of the late nineteenth- and twentieth-century repertoire calls for at least quadruple woodwind, and many conductors demand "doubled" woodwind (four players all round) in much of the standard nineteenth-century repertoire (Beethoven, Brahms, Schumann, etc.).

Brass: Present complement, 5.3.3.1.; desired complement, 6.4.4.1., i.e. 3 additional players. A permanent sixth horn is desirable largely to relieve the 3rd player, and to play in 6th position where required for a particular work, or by a particular conductor (to reinforce the horn section in much of the nineteenth-century repertoire). A co-principal trumpet is urgently required to relieve the strain on our principal player—the trumpet is physically probably the most exhausting of all instruments in the orchestra. An all-purpose 4th trombone player, who can relieve not only on tenor but also on bass trombone, is also highly desirable.

At present we have two permanent percussion players and no permanent keyboard player. A third percussionist and a keyboard player are desirable additions to the orchestra's permanent strength, which should thus at least be 98. This compares with our present total strength of 78. . . . By increasing our permanent complement by 20 musicians, as outlined above, it should be possible to reduce the working hours of our members to more reasonable proportions without materially diminishing the orchestra's present revenue-earning capacity, which, during the last financial year, amounted to approximately £285,000, excluding donations, grants and guarantees. However, it should be stressed that an increase in the orchestra's permanent playing strength can only be contemplated if all present members, as well as the new players, can be offered financial *guarantees* based on the present level of members' earnings from the orchestra.

Ideally, of course, the orchestra's permanent strength should approximate to that of the great Continental and

American orchestras if the working and artistic conditions of our musicians are to be commensurate with their quality and status as the leading members of their profession. An ideal complement could be 115 players.

Question: Does the orchestra consider that present conditions of employment enable proper working and musical standards to be maintained and fair remuneration paid to its members? If not, what improvements does it think desirable in order to achieve these ends?

LSO: The answer to the first question is a most emphatic "no". To the second question the obvious reply is that we need money—and a great deal of it—to achieve the working conditions in which we can maintain, and improve upon, the artistic standards which are expected of what critics everywhere have seen fit to call "one of the world's great orchestras". Our first duty is, of course, to our audiences at home, but on our frequent foreign tours in recent years we have also endeavoured to show that we are capable of acting as cultural ambassadors of whom this country has some reason to be proud. However, a situation is rapidly approaching when, as a result of acute overwork and borderline finance, it will be impossible to maintain standards, let alone (and we consider this essential at all times) improve on them. This would be tragic, because if we have managed to achieve our present artistic position under working conditions which are intolerable by pre-industrial revolution standards, the potential under reasonable working conditions is truly enormous. What, then, do we consider our basic essentials?

Working hours: At present often over 50 per week *excluding travel*, should be reduced to 30–33 per week.

Paid Holidays: At least 4 weeks per year, as against the present "nil".

Guaranteed Salaries: All players should be offered minimum financial guarantees based on their present earnings. One of the reasons for our having to accept far more work than is good for the musicians' health, both physically and artistically, is the insecurity caused by the lack of any guaranteed income, whether for the musicians or the orchestra as a limited company. At present we exist from year to year, or rather from month to month, and one never knows when a "lean period" may occur.

Sick Pay and Pensions: This follows on logically after the question of financial guarantees. Both are essential, neither are available to our musicians at present.

Our Own Home: A great orchestra needs a home. It needs regular acoustic conditions to develop its own style and sound, its personality. Its members should not, as now, be required to rush from one end of London to another—often to three different halls in the course of a single day—in order to carry out their duties. Nor, indeed, should it be necessary to load, transport and unload expensive instruments many times a day. The wear and tear on both musicians and instruments shortens their working lives and lowers artistic standards. How can even one of today's great conductors realise an orchestra's potential, particularly in regard to quality and balance of sound, when every one of four rehearsals for a concert takes place in a different hall? And the audience? How can an orchestra really build up its audience with an intelligent artistic policy when it has to share an anonymous hall with four or more other orchestras? Greater London is large enough to "take" four good concert halls—the Festival Hall as a central venue, a hall to cater for North London, one in the West, and one for those living South of the Thames. There are huge potential audiences everywhere, provided they do not have to spend large amounts in time and money on travelling to a concert, and provided concentrated efforts, in the form of intensive publicity, intelligent artistic policy and consistent musical quality are made to attract them. It is far easier to build up and maintain a "local" audience, than the transient customers one has to attract from a huge area to the Festival Hall.

Freedom: The high technical virtuosity and superb musicianship demanded of the members of an orchestra of international class makes it essential to allow such members a certain flexibility and freedom to pursue at least a limited solo and/or chamber music career. If one expects one's principal oboist, for example, to be an outstanding exponent of his instrument, he must be good enough to play, and be asked to play, concertos and solo recitals. And No. 12 in the first violins should still be able to make a valued member of a first-rate string quartet. Solo and chamber music work is essential for keeping up a player's standards—and no member of a great orchestra is worth a position in that orchestra if he is not capable of performing as a soloist or chamber music player. This must be recognised and the members of the orchestra must be granted a certain amount of free time for this purpose—and also for practising their instruments, for constant practice is essential for a musician to be able to meet the rigorous demands and exacting standards required at all times of a member of an orchestra like the LSO.

In their oral evidence, Barry Tuckwell and Ernest Fleischmann made the point that the fees paid to Members of the LSO were governed by what they could earn outside the Orchestra, that the average player performed 700 to 750 times a year, although only 75 per cent of the sessions required the whole Orchestra. The LSO's more adventurous programmes seemed to attract students and the more impecunious members of the public: it was the expensive seats which remained empty. One exchange touched the most sensitive nerve of the LSO: the Chairman asked whether, if the Orchestra were subsidised, a member of the subsidising body should sit on the Board, but to be concerned only with financial aspects of its deliberations and not exercise artistic control. Barry Tuckwell emphasised that the LSO had always been run by its players and had never had any outside members, but would consider ways and means if a subsidy were found.

Publicly, the LSO welcomed the Goodman Report, with two reservations: firstly, that the subsidy fell short of need (it worked out at about £80,000 to £100,000 a year, against an estimated requirement for the LSO of £175,000); and secondly, that the Concert Board, in the form proposed, would waste £10,000 a year and undermine the artistic and administrative independence which had been the cornerstone of LSO policy. The existing machinery for avoiding programme clashes (i.e. the committee set up in response to T. E. Bean's initiative in 1960) worked well and cost nothing.

Nevertheless, the London Orchestral Concert Board began its work, on the lines proposed by the Goodman Committee, in December 1965. Its Annual Reports provide valuable insights into the working of the subsidy system and developments in public taste, in so far as they are reflected in subsidised concerts. The existence of the Board has not put an end to the competition among the four London orchestras but has merely provided another forum in which their policies can be pursued. Nor has the LSO found its independence seriously infringed.

Concurrently with this public enquiry into its status and activities, the LSO was undergoing one of its intermittent fits of introspection. The formula on which the LSO was founded was that artistic success would bring public success which would in turn induce players to want to perform for the LSO, which—again—would promote harmony and cohesion within the organisation. In the sixties, this logic no longer led to the same soothing conclusion. The LSO's public success, not only in Britain but round the world, did not promote inner cohesion. The Directors were increasingly preoccupied with what to do about players whose contribution to the Orchestra's artistic value was unquestioned, but whose attitudes and behaviour were consistently disruptive. This problem overlapped the time-honoured conflict of interest between the Principals and the rank and file. Endemic indiscipline showed itself in constant reshufflings of individual sections to accommodate personal incompatibilities—complainants were careful to state that their objections were not professional but personal! Finally there was the specific source of conflict that the Leader, rightly or wrongly, did not command the confidence of the entire Orchestra, to the point that, at one international engagement, just before a concert, the strings refused to go on unless he were replaced. Regardless of the specific grievances, and whether they issued from genuine concern for the LSO or

Pierre Boulez and John Georgiardis during a rehearsal for the 20th Century Music Series, 1969

Colin Davis with Sir Michael Tippett at a rehearsal for Tippett's Third Symphony, 1972

Left: André Previn

Below: Leopold Stokowski with Arthur Oldham, 1970

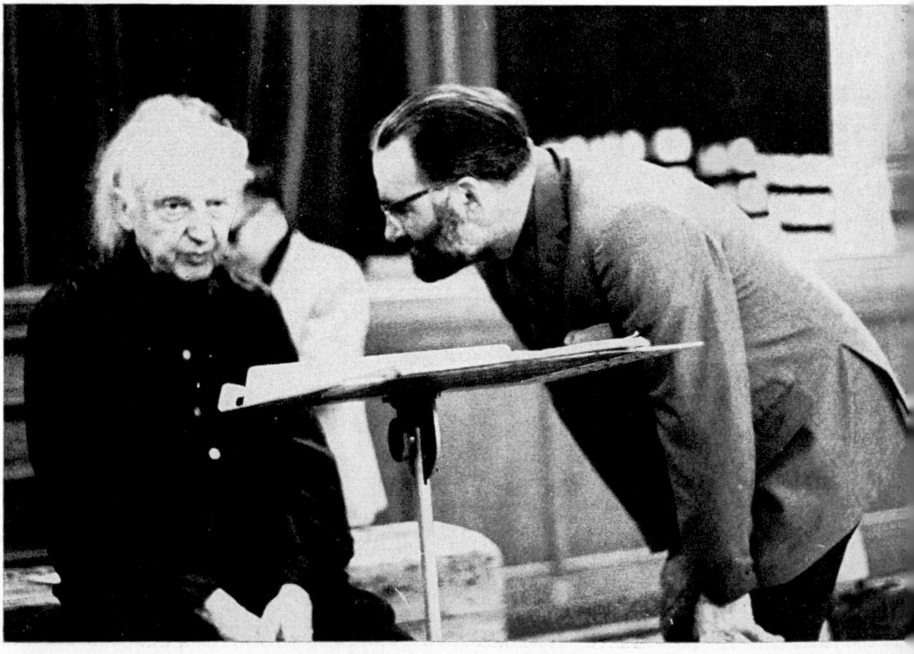

simply from self-interest dressed up in an acceptable guise, the threat dramatically shows the state of the Orchestra at a time when it was receiving enthusiastic public acclaim in Europe, the United States and Asia.

To Barry Tuckwell, the solution lay not in appeals to the players' loyalty or the usual system of fines—the Orchestra was working so hard that these could cheerfully be paid—but in increasing and consolidating its playing strength. He broached his ideas to a Board Meeting in Jerusalem, in December 1964. An improved fee structure made it "possible to consolidate all positions in the orchestra for a fixed period, say five years, but . . . this kind of security of position could not apply to everyone at present in the orchestra". The qualification showed that organisationally, the LSO was back in 1929—professionally there was no comparison. The outcome also differed.

Tuckwell's ideas were elaborated in a series of meetings with Principals in attendance, which constituted a grand enquiry into the state of the LSO. The issues were complex. "Whose playing had deteriorated?" (The answer was "no one's"; it was merely that the failings of players who had never been really satisfactory were now more obvious.) Should those Members by whom the LSO was immediately identified to the profession and the public be given "red carpet" treatment? Could the fees guaranteed to the rank and file at a level which they would accept be squared with requests to the Arts Council for increased financial assistance on a scale necessary to do any good? It did not improve matters when Stuart Knussen, Principal Double Bass (whose personal position was secure), threatened to leave for the New Philharmonia Orchestra on the grounds that it was a better orchestra; its second violins were superior to the LSO's firsts, and the NPO's cello section incomparably superior.

Musicians, like other men, commonly pour their passions into disputes over money. Inevitably, the discussions divided the Board, arousing the obvious range of interests and attitudes from far-sightedness to self-preservation. Their proceedings leaked out to the Members, in the form that the Chairman was planning a drastic "purge" of the LSO. Constitutionally, of course, the Chairman could not dismiss anyone—*that* had to be a Board decision—and, logically, consolidation implied improvement. These propositions became the substance of political controversy within the LSO, and were thrashed out at the Annual General Meeting. There "consolidation" foundered among the Members. All the enquiring and attempts to evaluate jobs resulted only in the resignation on request of one Member, who expected to be asked on grounds of age in any case.

The new tempo of LSO life brought strains and highlighted weaknesses in the string sections, whose performance degenerated not so much in spite of but because of the Orchestra's improved opportunities and prospects. Neville Marriner pinpointed the problem: "The amount of work the orchestra is obliged to undertake not only inhibits personal attention to one's technical ability but is physically and mentally enervating. . . . The second reason is that we seem unable to attract or maintain the standard of player that would be invaluable to an orchestra with internationally competitive aspirations. These players are the young, ambitious and technically well-endowed people of whom we realise there are too few in London to supply five orchestras." Marriner went on to suggest two means to a solution. One was to scrap the rota system devised to ensure equal financial gain for all (which on many occasions led to artistic catastrophe), and replace it with a rota that worked purely on artistic merit so that, for example, at desks two and three of the first violins there would be six players, only four of whom were on call at any given time. The other means was to introduce a system of differentials in order to encourage rank and file players to sit as high up in their sections as possible. This second proposal went to the political roots of the Orchestra. The Board debated both fully and amended the fee structure without reductions in existing rank and file fees. This implied a small reduction in the fees paid to Principals and Sub-Principals. Neville Marriner's first point could not be implemented.

The inquest went on, into other sections of the Orchestra—the clarinet section coming under persistent scrutiny, since the artistic ability of the Principal, Gervase de Peyer, naturally drew him away for concerto engagements and chamber music. His situation could have been the more easily accepted ten years before, when the organisation of the Orchestra was much looser. Now the drive for world fame made other demands and de Peyer's situation became a problem for the management. He was not unique in this respect. Several Principals regularly appeared with other ensembles and their non-availability became a recurrent source of dispute.

In July 1964, the LSO's direct access to nineteenth-century Romanticism snapped. Pierre Monteux, who had planned to retire after conducting his ninetieth birthday concert, died eight months short of that occasion. "We knew it had to happen some time," wrote one friend, "but the time had been so long delayed that somehow we hoped the miracle would go on renewing itself." The Orchestra had shared that hope, in defiance of the dreadful law of mortality. Its performance under Colin Davis of Berlioz' *Grande Messe des Morts* at the opening of the City of London Festival—took on a special and unanticipated significance. The Directors decided not to appoint a successor for twelve months.

When they did decide, the choice fell on Istvan Kertesz, a conductor who had emerged from Hungary after the 1956 uprising and who had established himself in Germany, first at Augsburg then at Cologne, as Director of the Opera. Kertesz was a fine, natural musician, who became a regular guest of the LSO after 1960. In January 1965, largely but not exclusively through Tuckwell's persuasiveness, he emerged as the leading candidate for the post of Principal Conductor, whose task was to be to maintain the Orchestra's artistic standards. The Directors agreed that Kertesz' qualities equipped him for the post in these terms and settled a three-year contract with him in February 1965. Their decision was acclaimed at the Members' quarterly meeting.

Kertesz conducted his first concert as Principal Conductor on 19th October, with two typical works: Dvořák's Cello Concerto, in which the soloist was Leonard Rose, and Bruckner's Fourth Symphony. The playing was idiomatic and glowing, but the promise held out by the relationship was never satisfactorily realised. Kertesz' Continental employments blinded him to the delicate differences between being a General Musical Director and being Principal Conductor of the LSO. He soon became impatient on being excluded from spheres of policy on which he thought he ought to be consulted.

Moreover, being an outward-going and warm personality, he found it difficult to conceal his personal preferences among the players—which did not improve his relations with the Orchestra. His tenure of office was therefore anything but smooth, in spite of his having a stimulating musical relationship with Members.

The Orchestra's main activity in London became the International Series. Beethoven cycles had been abandoned, but ideas of offering music lovers a conspectus of works persisted in the Directors' programme planning. It was only realised in 1965, but then on a grand scale. The LSO promoted a series of concerts in which Rostropovich played 31 concertos, covering the repertoire for cello and orchestra from Vivaldi to Britten. The usually played compositions by Dvořák, Schumann, Elgar and Haydn were buttressed by lesser known pieces by J. C. Bach, Tartini, Respighi and Honegger, contemporary French and Soviet concertos and important repertoire works such as Strauss' *Don Quixote* and Brahms' Double Concerto. Not all the works were of outstanding musical distinction, but the playing of Rostropovich and the Orchestra under Gennadi Rozhdestvensky communicated a heartfelt musical experience. At the conclusion of the series, the LSO presented the soloist with a medal struck in recognition of his unique artistic achievement.

In the summer of 1965, just after the Rostropovich series, the LSO learned of a project which held out the possibility of the Orchestra's gaining a permanent home in London—in the Arts Centre which the City of London announced it wished to build as part of the Barbican development, a complex of residential, educational and cultural buildings. Three London orchestras were asked to submit memoranda on their respective situations and prospects. Within forty-eight hours, Ernest Fleischmann complied. He was not reluctant to advertise the LSO's virtues ("undue reticence about the merits of one's products can be as harmful [in music] as it can in commerce and industry"), stressing its artistic achievements, as evidenced by the Goodman Report, and the international connections established since 1960.

It was important, from the LSO's point of view, that the Royal Shakespeare Company had already been invited to move to the Barbican. The two organisations had already collaborated and were exploring possibilities of working more closely together. Fleischmann sketched out different arrangements for managing the enterprise, with representation from the City, but the essence of his proposals was that the LSO should assume complete financial and artistic responsibility for the Concert Hall, paying a rent related to construction costs.

The Court of Common Council accepted the memorandum as a basis for further discussions, in which the problems could be defined more closely. Fleischmann and Peter Hall (then Director of the RSC) participated in a series of meetings with City officials. On the LSO side, the rental charge became the crucial issue. Fleischmann was careful to point out the premises on which his estimates had been submitted: for example, no significant change in the value of the pound, that alternative uses for the Hall (for conferences) had not been taken into account, and, above all, "that the hall has not yet been designed, and a number of factors—labour relations and legislation, cost of materials, special problems posed by design requirements—may materially affect the estimates".

The negotiations between the LSO and the Court of Common Council issued in Heads of Agreement, which the Court accepted on 3rd March 1966. Now all that remained was to get the hall built. The LSO found itself drawn into detailed discussions with architects and City officers.

For the LSO, a move to the Barbican promised an end to a particular way of life. A permanent hall for rehearsals, concerts and recordings allows a permanent orchestra. The LSO could put its Members under contract, could improve standards and offer more varied programmes. Even day-to-day practice would be changed: the saving in travelling from rehearsal hall to recording studio to concert hall was computed at 4,000 miles a year per musician.

In 1966, the LSO took on a new type of overseas engagement, as resident orchestra for the Florida International Festival at Daytona Beach. The first season was conducted for the most part by Colin Davis, with Aaron Copland and Richard Burgin. The formal orchestral concerts were only part of the schedule: chamber concerts and public rehearsals attracted enthusiastic audiences. The scope and atmosphere of the Festival were vividly portrayed by J. B. Priestley, who accompanied the Orchestra on its return visit in 1967. The players gave master classes to students and concerts as before. The conductors were Kertesz, Szymon Goldberg, Sir Arthur Bliss, Horenstein and a conductor whom the Orchestra had got to know in the recording studio, André Previn.

Previn's origins were formally in Berlin—a fact which is now considered relevant solely in German-language newspapers. Artistically, his background and training reflect Central Europe only as transplanted to California. He established his first professional reputation there as a composer and conductor of film scores and as a leading contributor to the jazz scene. Hence, symphony orchestras commonly invited him to conduct special concerts of Gershwin, and perhaps even Milhaud's *La création du monde*, but were reluctant to let him loose on the standard classical repertoire. The recording studio and, later, an appointment to Houston as associate with, and then successor to, Barbirolli finally helped Previn to make the transition into the kind of professional music-making he wanted. At Daytona, he conducted Rachmaninov and Prokofiev, and played in chamber music concerts. But the outstanding memory of one LSO Member of first contacts with Previn is of hearing him and David Gray (French horn) playing jazz in Patti and Marty's Bar. Perhaps the ambience was superior to that of the Peabody Auditorium.

The success of the Orchestra owed much to the energetic methods and personal panache of its General Secretary. This the Orchestra acknowledged, but with two important qualifications: the first that even Ernest Fleischmann could have achieved little had not the Orchestra itself magnificently responded to the challenges of its situation, and the second that his methods provoked as much antagonism as assent. One, fortunately well-disposed, correspondent wrote that he would win an Oscar for battering at doors which would otherwise open to a gentle push. The short-run effects of abrasiveness could be enjoyed, its long-term consequences were incalculable. For these reasons, the LSO's General Secretary became a divisive figure in the Orchestra. He could be identified with success but that pleasing effect did not, in the event, wholly strengthen his position.

With the Orchestra simply more heavily engaged than ever before, and now explicitly before an international public, the Directors, as practising musicians, would have had to leave far more scope to any executive officer, regardless of his abilities and temperament. But they had to deal with a man who was not at all reluctant to fill any vacuums in policy which circumstances might provide and who additionally came to represent the LSO to the increasingly complex outside world. In the course of handling the Orchestra's business, the General Secretary gave the impression to the Members that he stood for the LSO. They thought *they* did. One trivial incident is symptomatic.

In June 1966 the second half of an end-of-season concert of Viennese music was the occasion for some impromptu clowning between Kertesz and the Orchestra. The conductor tried to catch the players napping by delaying entries before breaking into three-four time in the *Zigeunerbaron*; the Orchestra retaliated by starting the *Radetzsky March* while the conductor was off the platform and by beginning a polka when he (and the audience) was expecting a waltz. Kertesz nonchalantly turned his back on the players and let them get on with it. These antics, if less stylish than the Marx Brothers, nevertheless made for a splendid party atmosphere (or so it seemed to the author), but they moved Fleischmann to a *public* expression of anger. He subsequently argued that the jokes should have been rehearsed and the public warned—in which he was supported by at least one Director—but the rank and file tended to think that their Secretary had over-identified himself with the Orchestra.

The fact of the matter was that the course of the LSO since 1960 had forced open a discrepancy in the terms of the memorandum covering Fleischmann's engagement. "Except where decisions follow an accepted pattern already applied over a period, the Secretary's decisions must be submitted to and be the responsibility of the Directors" proved incompatible with "The Secretary will be required to act as a salesman for the Orchestra. This will call for considerable initiative. . . ." The whole point of exercising salemanship was to break down the accepted patterns of the LSO's way of life.

The Chairman, Barry Tuckwell, took the discrepancy as one

among many pieces of evidence that the organisation of the LSO was cumbersome and unworkable. In December 1966, he proposed to his fellow Directors considering "a new policy and approach in keeping with the Orchestra's enhanced status". The two basic provisions were to reorganise the administration and guarantee incomes to the Members. In this way, Barry Tuckwell opened a debate on the state of the LSO which precipitated upheaval within the Orchestra and his own resignation from the Board. It is a nice point in the annals of the LSO whether 1967 is more traumatic than 1932 or vice versa.

It was relatively easy to agree on proposals for a new committee structure within the Board and to reorganise the functions in the Company office. It took rather longer to reclassify the Playing Members on a scale to which their income could be related. But these things were done. In the process, however, examining the Company's procedures, with a view to assessing the incremental costs of additional personnel, revealed that the Company's accounting systems were somewhat slipshod and its overall control of finance less than adequate. This proved Tuckwell's point. Additional, minor, evidence of the way in which the LSO's administration was sagging appears in the keeping of the Board's Minutes. The accounts of meetings from September 1966 to March 1967 were only written up in March 1967. The Secretary may not have been able to devote time to this matter but, apparently, the Directors had condoned it. In a small management group in daily contact the lack of formal records is not necessarily heinous, but the lapse from good administrative order illustrates the strain on the LSO's structure, imposed by success. Since Ernest Fleischmann was nominally responsible for the good administrative ordering of the Company, the enquiry into the administration did not strengthen his personal position. He quickly became the natural focus of many members' dissatisfaction. At this stage, too, the Secretary and the Directors began to dispute the interpretation of the complicated formula on which his own salary was based.

The atmosphere in the Board was discordant as morale in the Orchestra deteriorated. Rumours spread that work was being lost, the concrete fact being that the long-standing contract with Decca, which had been the sheet-anchor of the

LSO's planning, began to sag. At this juncture, Barry Tuckwell resigned.

The Members promptly called a meeting to discuss the matter, their keenness to exercise their constitutional right sharpened by the memory that, at the previous AGM they had elected Tuckwell to the Board with virtually a 100 per cent vote in his favour—a result almost without precedent. The Secretary sent out the official notice of the meeting, pointing out that no motion could be voted upon. The Members gathered in the Bishopsgate Institute. Tuckwell's letter of resignation was read to them: ". . . in view of the attitude and behaviour of Mr Fleischmann, I consider the affairs of the Orchestra are no longer in the hands of the Board." The meeting indicated to the Board that it considered Ernest Fleischmann's presence no longer necessary. The Board took the point, and by a majority vote resolved to ask Fleischmann to resign. His supporters on the Board tried to intervene with Kertesz, though they presumably realised he, as Principal Conductor, had no standing in the matter.

Fleischmann thought himself, with some validity, the victim of a *coup* engineered by Barry Tuckwell. He certainly had no opportunity to defend himself either to the Board or the Members. But from their point of view, this was neither necessary nor called for: they were merely getting rid of an employee of the LSO who had begun to show too proprietorial an attitude towards the Orchestra, and whose performance had in their view been less than satisfactory.

Personalities clashed, but wholly different men from Tuckwell and Fleischmann might easily have found themselves in the same situation, since the problem is, *au fond*, constitutional.

The LSO Board is responsible through the electoral process only to the Members. It can delegate as much power as it wishes. The willingness to delegate fluctuates with the composition of the Board and particularly with the calibre and temperament of the Chairman. When Fleischmann arrived, the Board was "weak", that is, it was disposed to delegate powers, either formally or informally. This worked to Fleischmann's advantage, since he was demonstrably energetic and ambitious, and put the LSO on the world map. But gradually, the Board was less disposed to delegate, even though the enlarged and more complex sphere of the LSO's operations compelled it to do so. This of itself created difficulties. But once the Board elected a Chairman who also had ambitions, not only was a clash more likely but it could, from the nature of the LSO, have only one outcome. So Fleischmann went.

His abrupt departure sent shockwaves through the concert and recording community. The strength of the position he had achieved was immediately demonstrated by the comment of one recording organisation:

> Dear Mr Tuckwell,
>
> I am in receipt of a letter from you saying that Mr Ernest Fleischmann has "relinquished" his position . . . and that you are dealing with all correspondence pro tem.
>
> I must tell you in all honesty that our artists [identified] and the company as a whole are so shocked by this turn of events that there may be no need for further correspondence.
>
> We doubt somehow that there is a reasonable explanation for this unhappy step that you have taken.

The company was one with which the LSO had close contractual arrangements. It is, of course, highly unlikely that the implied threat would have been carried out: in the world of commerce, interests governing the expectation of profit are almost invariably stronger than questions of abstract justice to individuals. The reaction illustrates nevertheless the personal standing of Ernest Fleischmann and the kind of pressure recording companies feel they can bring to bear. The sentiments also show complete ignorance of the constitution of the LSO.

Barry Tuckwell, at the request of the Board, withdrew his letter of resignation and resumed as Chairman. He pressed on with his schemes of reform. That summer, at Daytona Beach, Florida, he impressed J. B. Priestley as "a strictly self-disciplined . . . and very ambitious man, still youngish and not yet fully conscious of the drive of his ambition, but for all that an agreeable companion". Priestley might have modified his view had he known that at a Directors' meeting on 3rd August, Tuckwell resurrected as an interim necessity his "Comprehensive LSO Administration Plan": the Board should dictate policy through three working sub-committees; he, the Chairman, should become Managing Director and another Board Member, Alan Jenkins, Company Secretary (in place of Ernest Fleischmann). They would represent the Board in artistic and contractual matters, and in the Orchestra's public relations. The Administrator (Alan Jefferson) should co-ordinate all the Orchestra's activities, and a special publicity agent should be appointed for close and continuous contact with the press in England, Europe, the USA and the East.

These proposals would enable the Orchestra to manage its affairs until the right full-time Secretary could be found. To a degree the proposals (which had previously been discussed) regularised a situation which already existed. For about a year, Tuckwell had been a managing director in all but name. A Secretary might conveniently be appointed from the Board *ad interim*; the sub-committee structure sought to rationalise an increasingly onerous schedule of work. Above all, the process by which the LSO now had the world for its concert hall had left a number of loose ends which required to be tidied up and created a need for co-ordinated management.

The proposals were so obviously sensible it is not surprising that the Directors took about two minutes to reject them totally. The reason lies in the psychology of LSO Boards. The history of the Orchestra shows that styles of management oscillate between having a Chairman with a maximum authority—Tuckwell fashion—and a Chairman whose task is merely to keep Board Meetings in order. The LSO's reflexes are for the minimum, if not minimal, role—the idea of a Managing Director is suspect—but changes in the Orchestra's environment impel the Chairman towards the maximum, even if temperamentally he is not as overtly ambitious as Barry Tuckwell appeared to his colleagues to be in 1967. There was no telling where his energy might lead; it was all very well to out-manœuvre Ernest Fleischmann, but "consolidation" was very recent history and . . .

Effectively, Barry Tuckwell's career in the LSO ended at this point. He resigned from the Board shortly afterwards on another issue, and, in view of the demands for his services as a soloist, from the Orchestra in the next year. His artistic leadership was vital in the LSO's success; one Member commented that when he and Gervase de Peyer were absent, the whole standard went down. This overstated the role of the two men, but not their capabilities. Tuckwell, as an artist, was one of those by whom the LSO was identified in the profession. In this respect, he recalled Adolf Borsdorf. As a Director, he was unable to translate his leadership into specific reforms of the LSO. In 1965 "consolidation" could have taken the Orchestra clear of its rivals, but was dissipated in the collective resistance of Members. In 1967, the machinery *did* need an overhaul, but his ideas came to grief in what is still known half-humorously in the LSO as "Barry's Daytona *putsch*". It is necessary to point out that these schemes were inspired by a genuine passion for reform. Neither of them would have made their originator financially better off than his leading colleagues.

In quick succession, the LSO had lost its forceful and energetic Secretary (April) and its equally forceful and energetic Chairman (August), but the month of Tuckwell's resignation was also the month from which, under the contract with the Principal Conductor, the LSO and Kertesz respectively had the right to declare their intentions about the future beyond the expiry date fixed in his original contract for the end of the 1967/68 season.

The relationship had not worked too well. Kertesz' artistic merits were fully appreciated by the players: they found him withdrawn and casual in rehearsal, but transformed when "on the box", with splendid results in performance. This trait they specially valued when they were wilting in the middle of a tour! But Kertesz never got on similar terms with the public in Britain. The Directors noted that he failed to attract capacity audiences. This presented a problem, but it was not insuperable. What compounded the difficulty was that, in the view of many Members, Kertesz had proved incapable of distancing himself from the Orchestra as a whole. So, by the autumn of 1967, he had become a controversial figure in an organisation which after the traumas of the spring and summer was not in a sweetly reasonable frame of mind. For his part, Kertesz had become impatient with the constraints on his authority, and let it be known that he considered he should participate in managing the LSO. It was neither a propitious time nor a good atmosphere in which to raise questions about the future. Nevertheless, Kertesz exercised his option to do so.

The first exchanges took place during the Edinburgh Festival, at which Kertesz conducted the Orchestra and the Festival Chorus in Kodály's *Psalmus Hungaricus*, in Hungarian. He asked for wider powers, threatening otherwise to resign, and was surprised at the alacrity with which that alternative was received. The Directors did not, however, wish to part company with their Principal Conductor if it could be avoided and subsequently examined Kertesz' proposals in detail. These related to a closer public identification between himself and the Orchestra, to extending his options of appearing with it, in Britain and on tour, and to bringing him into the management of the LSO. The Directors went some way towards Kertesz on all these major issues, but tacked on their requirements as to rehearsal methods, and Kertesz' relationship with the Orchestra and with individual Members. On the crucial management question, however, the concessions took the form of undertakings to advise Kertesz in advance of major developments and consult him on problems.

In December 1967, Kertesz submitted his "final conditions" for "a completely new basis of collaboration", adding that in his opinion, for him "to fulfil the responsibilities of a principal conductor, every single one of these points must become part of our contract with each other". The details of publicity and fee structure were much as canvassed in discussions with the Directors before, but the items under "Artistic Points" and "Personal Points" were an uncompromising series of demands which hitherto had not been explicitly formulated. Kertesz claimed the sole "right of final decision on all artistic questions, without exception", including those relating to the LSO Chorus; the right "to participate in all Directors' meetings, and meetings of shareholders in the Orchestra"; the right "to veto all decisions which, in his (Kertesz') opinion, do not serve the standard, quality and reputation of the Orchestra"; and the right to "every kind of confidential information regarding all artistic and administrative problems . . . from all appointed executives." The Directors found these stipulations unconstitutional and excessive, and Kertesz' original contract was not renewed; he ceased to be Principal Conductor when it expired in the summer of 1968.

Kertesz' motives in raising his requirements remain enigmatic. He was sufficiently familiar with the LSO's traditions or methods of government to realise that his stipulations flouted both, and on that ground alone would be totally unacceptable. Or did he consider that the critical state of the LSO would induce the Directors to concede to him rights they had hitherto reserved to themselves? The available evidence offers no definite conclusions on this point. What *is* certain is that Kertesz had disastrously overplayed his hand, when a more moderate approach might well have yielded him some of the authority he sought. The insistence on *rights*, however, in his final conditions suggests that *some* authority would not have been enough.

After this dénouement, it was some time before the Orchestra and Kertesz could resume music-making on the old footing. Relations did, however, become reciprocally warm, based on mutual artistic respect, for some time before Kertesz' lamentable death in 1973, though, to the end, he seemed to be anxious to return to a closer and more consistent working with the LSO.

During 1967, while the Orchestra triumphed in Florida and Scotland, the LSO tottered. By the end of the year, its deficit stood at about £18,000; it had no liquid resources; Decca was conferring its favours elsewhere; the Principal Conductor was departing; and the back of the administration had been broken. The situation was so desperate that there was even a move to reinstate Ernest Fleischmann. He, when approached, stipulated that he be asked formally in a letter signed by every Member of the Orchestra. The initiative petered out.

XII

After Fleischmann's departure, the Directors attempted to revert to the former style of running the LSO's business, but the formula which John Cruft had found difficult to manage towards the end of his career with the LSO was by now quite unworkable. The Orchestra's commitments and the environment in which it worked had become far more complex. An executive officer, with perhaps more carefully defined responsibilities, was absolutely necessary. Without him, the organisation was not geared to getting work for the Orchestra. The order book ran down, and the services of one important conductor were lost, through simple failure to re-engage him. The Company was virtually insolvent. A General Manager was vital, but the Board was in no mood to saddle itself with another Fleischmann, so in July 1967 it appointed a temporary Administrator, Alan Jefferson. His role was strictly that of an executive official and his authority was circumscribed accordingly. It was far less than the situation demanded, but the spectre of Fleischmann loomed large, and, as Daytona showed, Barry Tuckwell had his own ideas about executive authority in the LSO. The immediate practical consequence was that the Directors attempted to deal with business between rehearsals and performances, and the management of the LSO stumbled from one situation to the next.

There were many loose ends. The Vice-Chairman, Jack Steadman (who became Chairman after the next AGM) and his fellow Directors realised for the first time the extent to which the LSO was committed to appear in 1968 in Japan and New York. It was in no financial position to undertake either engagement. In the event, the Board was able to negotiate a release from their Japanese engagement, but the Carnegie Hall appearances had to be fulfilled, and, as the British Council does not assist in funding ventures in the United States, the LSO bore the total loss.

Kertesz' resignation created the problem of a replacement, but he had to fulfil his engagements with the LSO till the end of the season. His views still carried weight, and, in the frantic autumn of 1967, he, and one or two other conductors, expressed their dissatisfaction with the LSO Chorus. The Directors were inclined to the belief that the difficulties could be overcome, but then Decca joined in. The LSO had resumed working with that company, although on a more limited basis than before, and it was, at this juncture, the company to which Kertesz was contractually bound. The matter thus became an issue. Steadman persuaded the other parties that Chorus and trainer must be given the opportunity to vindicate themselves. The problem was postponed. As the criticism of the Chorus had formed only one item in an agenda of complaint about the LSO, Alan Jefferson suggested that the Board, who were looking for a Principal Conductor anyway, might usefully consider one who had a firm recording contract with another company. He nominated André Previn. The suggestion was received with incredulity.

There was additionally the problem of the Barbican. Fleischmann and Tuckwell had worked closely together on the details of the LSO's involvement and the future management of the Concert Hall. Now, they had both gone, and the formula under which the LSO had made its bid appeared to be likely to work against the Orchestra. The LSO lacked a consistent and authoritative voice, not only in the City, but in the concert and recording world. The remedy was to abandon the attempt to run the LSO of the sixties in the style which worked in the twenties, and appoint a General Manager.

The Directors considered sundry candidates, all of whom they decided were unsuitable. Then Neville Marriner asked off-handedly, "What about Harold Lawrence?" The Directors were impressed by Lawrence's running of their sessions for the Mercury Company, and he *did* know the recording and broadcasting business backwards. Lawrence was approached, interviewed and engaged. The Board prudently drew up a much more detailed and formal contract than it had given his predecessor, attempting to define lines of demarcation which had become fudged under Fleischmann. But Harold Lawrence's primary and immediate task was the same—to secure engage-

Pierre Monteux

"Preluding"

Rehearsal problem: (*l. to r.*) Ronald Moore, Terry Palmer, Howard Snell, André Previn, Harold Lawrence

ments for the Orchestra. To this task he brought a quiet but otherwise Fleischmann-like persistence. Above all, he had the strong reflexes which enabled him to survive the shock of encountering chaos when he arrived in the LSO office in January 1968. From then until March (for which recording sessions had been booked), getting sessions became obsessional—with a residual effect which has persisted. Even now, when their situation has become far more stable than it was in the spring of 1968, LSO players cast a nervous and wary eye on any monthly schedule with more than two or three blanks in it.

In the atmosphere of crisis, no one dissented from the proposition that the LSO needed a replacement for Kertesz as Principal Conductor.

The Board drew up a list of candidates—some of whom had been approached, others not—and methodically considered each in turn. The argument established those who were not available and those who, though available, were unsuitable. One candidate, of sub-stratospheric European eminence, had not even bothered to reply. It was felt that a somewhat younger colleague, who was very interested, "would probably have strong views on programmes and would not bring much recording business". His case foundered, however, on his request to be involved in changes of personnel and on what the Board felt to be the generally maladroit bargaining of his agent. The Minutes then record: "Mr Lawrence outlined the type of conductor the LSO needed: someone who was a serious musician, who was easy to work with, who would bring business (though this was not a prime consideration), who was good for publicity and who was forward-looking." He felt these criteria led logically to André Previn.

The subsequent lengthy discussion showed general agreement on the criteria, but rather more doubt about the conclusion. The Directors' final decision was, however, unanimously in favour. Previn was approached, and accepted on the basis that no scheduled Houston rehearsals were to be shifted. But for a number of reasons, commuting by air proved unsatisfactory, and he left Houston at the conclusion of his contract. He recalls that his first year as Principal Conductor of the LSO was "very shaky"—an opinion shared by a number of Members who were inclined to question the Board's wisdom, if not its sanity.

It is necessary to recount these facts now to show that the election of André Previn was by no means a foregone conclusion, nor was it procured by commercial rather than artistic considerations (though his recording contract with RCA did not weigh against him). Both parties were taking risks. Previn needed a job, preferably in England: he had not entirely lost his "Hollywood" background, and he had to prove himself to his new employers by conducting them in public, not by being agreeable to a Board of Trustees. Conversely, the Orchestra needed a Principal Conductor, but was acutely aware, particularly after its experience with Kertesz, that *that* role taxes relationships in a way which guest appearances do not. Previn was *not* engaged *faute de mieux*, but in 1968 the assets he brought to the Orchestra were by no means unquestioned. That the association with him would prove so mutually beneficial, artistically and commercially, no one foresaw.

The conjunction of André Previn and Harold Lawrence led some critics to dub the LSO "an American orchestra"—which induces the thought that they were perhaps deaf to the differences between, say, Chicago, Philadelphia and Boston. Certainly, the Orchestra has intensified its activity in the United States—but because it is the most important single market for classical recordings and has attractive festivals. Daytona, Ravinia and Carnegie Hall were not invented by the Principal Conductor and General Manager. In one vital sense, the LSO is the reverse of an American orchestra. The Philadelphia Orchestra, for example, spends its time being the Philadelphia Orchestra and nothing else. LSO players find themselves working in different contexts as the demand for their services develops. These include providing the musical backgrounds used in advertisements on television, known in the jargon as "jingles", or in the "backing" for pop stars in recordings. (Such engagements are commonly used to fund individual annuity schemes which the absence of a pension makes imperative for players.)

Lawrence had been engaged to fill the order book, to improve the LSO's income and its morale. As General Manager he had to create some order out of the accretion of expedients which had characterised the administration of the LSO during much of the previous year. They were not always amenable to control. In February 1968, the respite the Directors had gained over the Chorus ran out. Kertesz attributed the "friction" between the LSO and himself in part to his "complete divergence in musical views to those of John Alldis. I had an opportunity to discuss some problems with Mr Alldis . . . and we disagreed on every single point." Kersetz accordingly, "with a heavy heart", wished to withdraw from a performance of Janáček's *Glagolitic Mass*. The Board convinced him that it was too late, and he conducted the LSO and Chorus in the concert as scheduled.

The dispute rumbled on, and at the beginning of the next season, Decca weighed in on Kertesz' side of the argument. They jointly informed the LSO that they would no longer work with John Alldis. The Directors hurriedly had to engage a professional chorus to perform the Dvořák *Requiem* on 8th December and subsequently record it. The *démarche* by the record company and conductor implied that on all future occasions the LSO would have to follow the precedent established over the *Requiem*, or be prepared to dispense with Kertesz for choral concerts and record such works with another company. As will be evident by now, in such a situation there is in practice only one way out for an orchestra which depends on recordings for a significant part of its income. The Board decided not to renew John Alldis' contract, but explored with him the possibility of his sharing the work with another choir-master who would be responsible for preparing the Chorus for Decca sessions. The idea was abandoned.

When news of Alldis' dilemma spread round the London musical profession, *another* record company indicated their hope that the rumours were untrue, since they were looking forward to collaborating on various projects with the LSO and John Alldis. A *third* company insisted that the LSO Chorus would not be engaged unless Alldis were Chorus Master, since, although the LSO's decision was legally correct, the moral aspect of the matter had to be upheld. Alldis' agent expressed his disgust at the Directors' "flabbiness" and took legal advice.

But the Directors, though embarrassed, were legally unassailable, and their contract with John Alldis ran its full course.

He moved to the Bath Festival and subsequently with great success to the London Philharmonic Choir. His successor was Arthur Oldham, whose work had impressed the LSO at the Edinburgh Festival.

The episode demonstrates the more brutal aspects of reality in the world of music. Famous conductors, as a class, are not noted for compromise: the interests of recording companies do not always coincide with those of orchestras. Only a fully subsidised orchestra can be immune to this kind of pressure.

Nevertheless, the Directors were to some extent taken by surprise. The Chorus had been virtually refounded in 1966. In 1967, the Board was preoccupied by in-fighting over Fleischmann and Tuckwell and by coping with the administration of the LSO: there was little time to consider, say, whether the age limits on the Chorus should be lifted to change its tone colour. Only afterwards did Kertesz's professional disagreement with Alldis bring the question of the Chorus into the Board's agenda.

A similarly unforeseen problem arose at this time from another quarter. In 1967 turbulence in the LSO was echoed in the LSO Club. It had been founded in 1948 as a "supporters' club" for the Orchestra, on lines already pioneered by the LPO. Its purpose was "to establish closer liaison and co-operation between the Audience and the Orchestra, and Soloists, Conductors, Composers and other Artists". Over the years, this formula admitted a number of interpretations, but by 1967 had hardened into two: the first, that it was to be strictly construed in relation to the LSO; the second, that it was consistent with the idea and practice of a general music club, with a special allegiance to the Orchestra—the corollary being that the LSO should have no role in Club business. These differences were compounded by personalities, around whom factions grouped themselves.

The issue was, in fact, fundamental, but the Board of the LSO was too preoccupied with its own troubles to notice what was developing in the Club, which it had left largely to go its own way. The wrangling came to a head in 1967, with the Committee split into irreconcilable groups, discussing the constitutionality of the actions of various members, and with the dissidents taking legal advice. Eventually, at an Extraordinary General Meeting on 16th March 1968, the advocates of a general, autonomous music club carried a motion rejecting the Committee's report on its handling of Club business. The LSO Board awoke to the implication that the vote demonstrated "no confidence", not only in the Club committee but in themselves. It was not in the LSO's interests to lend its name to an organisation which tacitly repudiated the Directors. So they withdrew permission to use the LSO's name.

Harold Lawrence's circular, explaining this decision, went on to express the "Orchestra's intention to found a new club called The London Symphony Orchestra Club, as from 1st July", with a constitution which reserved to the Directors certain controlling powers to ensure that history would not repeat itself and that the new club would "go forward with much greater co-operation as well as supervision from the Orchestra's Directors and executive". The nature and extent of these powers recipients of the circular could see for themselves, since the proposed constitution was thoughtfully enclosed with the circular.

The LSO's invitation implied but did not necessarily determine that the "old" club went out of existence. *That* could only be decided by the members themselves. They held an Extraordinary General Meeting on 6th July to decide this issue. The motion to wind up the club and pay its assets over to the LSO was carried by 116 votes to 115, after a recount! The Directors, by a belated display of energy had managed to save that situation—though a change of one vote would have left them in an invidious position.

But as regards the Barbican, there was absolutely no doubt: they *were* in an invidious position.

The original estimate of the building costs of the hall had increased by 51 per cent, which destroyed the basis of the LSO's submission and of the Heads of Agreement reached two years previously. The Directors then commissioned a consultant to prepare a report examining the entire scheme for submission to the City Corporation. His estimates demonstrated that the LSO would, by the time the Barbican opened, be running a substantial deficit, apart from its liability for rent. The LSO (or any other orchestra) would therefore need a subsidy, in connection with running the hall. The Court of

Common Council blenched and indicated a preference for going ahead under the terms of the Heads of Agreement: any necessary subsidy should not come from the City. In practice, the matter went into abeyance, since the LSO's revised submissions were grist to the mill of those in the City Corporation who thought subsidising the arts to be an improper use of ratepayers' funds. The Corporation itself entered into a prolonged internal political dispute on the whole policy for the Barbican Arts Centre. The LSO having, with considerable embarrassment and regret, made its position clear, could only await the outcome.

Another significant change had taken place since the original submissions were formulated: the London Orchestral Concert Board had come into existence and was by 1968 playing an important role in the administration of funds among the four London orchestras. The possibility that the LSO might go into the Barbican changed the conditions for the other three users of the Festival Hall. More specifically, the reluctance of the City to contemplate a subsidy, other than, perhaps, through a low rental charge, raised the question of whether the LOCB might extend its activities in that direction. It seemed reasonable to suppose that with the LSO moving to the Barbican, there would be, at least transitionally, some fall in average attendances, affecting both the LSO and the orchestras remaining on the South Bank. In that case, what would be an appropriate subsidising policy? More fundamentally, would not the move to the Barbican raise again the question which "Goodman" had avoided answering?

That the proposal to move into a hall of its own should, long before it could possibly be implemented, have such extensive repercussions is itself evidence of the complexity of the world in which the LSO now had to earn its living. The Directors, however, were not wholly preoccupied with the politics of the LOCB and the intricacies of estimating in the construction industry. The ordinary business of settling programmes, arranging tours, and making records went on. Their most momentous artistic decisions concerned modern music.

Music being composed at the present time can be regarded as either "modern" or "contemporary". The distinction is, broadly, between composers who adhere to traditional styles and tonalities and those who seek to dispense with them.

Critics often accuse the LSO of neglecting the living composer, in terms from which it is clear that they do not have this distinction in mind. The crucial, and divisive, figure is Anton Webern; his work marks a discontinuity in our musical culture. After him, the "avant garde" in music is not engaged in the same kind of activity as composers before. Some of the more rigorous experimentalists do not expect their work to be performed in public—and they are likely to have their expectations fulfilled. But, of those who do intend their works for public performance, the most that can be asserted about them and their "traditional" forbears is that they both use sounds: there the resemblance ends. There is a demonstrable relationship between Shostakovich and Schumann; none between Shostakovich and Stockhausen, even though they are contemporary.

Modern composers are not of course confined by definition to traditional techniques and many have experimented with serialism and atonality in the context of works written predominantly in the traditional idioms. Of these, Tippett, Searle, Penderecki and Lutoslawski have been and are represented in LSO programmes and recording schedules. The Orchestra "adopted" Tippett's Second Symphony, helping through repeated performances to establish it with the public whose initial reaction had been coloured by the breakdown of the orchestra which played the première. It was, according to Colin Davis, "the biggest effort on behalf of Tippett that anyone had ever made and it marked a turning point in the LSO's relationship with him—and the public's". The Directors capped this enterprise by commissioning Tippett's Third Symphony. It took two years to compose: the LSO nominated Colin Davis to conduct and gave him all the sectional rehearsals he required. Through the sectionals, the players were more and more drawn in to the work. Tippett himself attended the first general rehearsal, to be welcomed by one player, "We've had a marvellous time." At the rehearsal, the Orchestra was playing the work complete for the first time. They went "through it," recalls Tippett, "like *that*"—producing a sweeping gesture of total finality. In the première, on 25th June 1972, the Orchestra, with Colin Davis and Heather Harper, also conveyed a sense of absorption and finality. It was as if the work was already part of the tradition.

While they were negotiating with Tippett for the new composition, the Directors were also elaborating a scheme which touched the limits of the possible for a "commercial" orchestra—a festival of what is conveniently described as "The Second Viennese School". The idea was Boulez'. He was puzzled by the paradox that for young musicians the works of Schoenberg, Berg and Webern were part of their heritage, whereas concert audiences had yet to become generally acquainted with them. A "retrospective exhibition", analogous to practice in the visual arts, might help to convince both students and public of the role of these composers in twentieth-century music and the virtues of their compositions. Fleischmann leapt at the idea.

The Members were not entirely strangers to this music: they had been introduced to Schoenberg and Berg by Dorati. The object now would be more than to achieve good performances of difficult music as individual items; it would be to present an authoritative *vue d'ensemble* of a "School"—and that as part of the ordinary schedule of work. It was decided to combine rehearsals (32) and recording sessions for CBS (14) and to add to the programme the first complete performance of Mahler's early cantata, *Das klagende Lied*, as representing the composer whose work is the link between the School and nineteenth-century Romanticism; "an act of homage to the Grandfather" in Boulez' terms.

The details were settled in October 1966: the concerts were to be given in 1969, five in London and two in Vienna, as part of the Vienna Festival. Financing the project proved unexpectedly difficult. The extended rehearsals and large forces for the Mahler and Schoenberg Op. 22 demanded extra efforts at fund-raising. The LOCB, the LSO Trust and the Peter Stuyvesant Foundation contributed, but in March 1969 it appeared likely that the concerts would have to be abandoned. The Directors' decision to go ahead as planned turned on one vote. A frantic campaign elicited some funds, but the ultimate deficit was borne by the LSO.

Rehearsals became occasions during which Boulez communicated to the Orchestra his own enthusiasm and commitment to the works, dispelling completely the puzzlement of many and the hostility of a few. The music was absorbed and the performances exhibited exactness and clarity (which were expected), and warmth (which was not). "In the end," remarked one player, "it was just like playing Brahms"—which was Boulez' aim, his view being that the new music should be played exactly as the old, and vice versa. He put this point to the audience in his interval talks; it was underlined by the performances themselves in London and in Vienna.

Audiences were receptive and enthusiastic. In the Konzerthaus, the Festival audiences reacted as if they had listened to Karajan and Tchaikovsky. The LSO was commended for devoting itself to the works to the point that they were revealed as part of the tradition, and for its virtuosity, brilliance, and beauty of sound.*

The concerts were epoch-making, in the sense that they changed the perspective of audiences. Neither Boulez nor the LSO conceived the project as a merely pedagogic exercise but their performances were instructive, and since May–June 1969 the horizons of public taste have been no longer the same. Aesthetically considered, such an enterprise is as essential as performing Beethoven's Fifth Symphony with the same care for someone who may be experiencing the piece for the first time.

From the Orchestra's point of view, life has not been quite the same either. Boulez had an impact on the LSO out of all proportion to the time spent on rehearsal and not confined to works performed. He affected the way the LSO thinks about music. The Company lost about £10,000 on the venture: the Orchestra thought the experience cheap at the price.

"Goodman" was a pioneer enquiry, but it derived strictly from the uncertainties of the London orchestras and deliberately left out of its purview the situation of orchestras elsewhere in Britain and all chamber orchestras. The inquiry did, however, generate a continuing discussion on the problems of orchestral music as a whole—which, in turn, became the subject of a second enquiry, entrusted in January 1969 by the Arts Council to a committee under the chairmanship of Professor Alan Peacock. The committee's deliberations were not uninfluenced by what was happening during the same year at the BBC. In June, the Corporation announced that it was

* The works which were performed are set out in Appendix II.

adopting a new style of "broadcasting in the seventies" which would require recasting its music programmes and therefore its orchestral requirements. These possibilities sent a *frisson* through the ranks of professional musicians: orchestras outside the BBC were automatically affected not only by the possible loss of engagements but also by the increase in the supply of available musicians, through redundancy in the Corporation. The Peacock Committee, in considering the problems of "orchestral resources in Great Britain" was acutely aware that the dominant user of these resources was likely to take independent decisions which would completely disrupt the assumptions on which the Committee's investigations were based.

The Committee reported in 1970. Its salient conclusion affecting the London orchestras was that the LOCB should from the beginning of the 1973/74 season financially support only two orchestras accepting contractual obligations designed to provide permanence and stability. "Peacock" not only grasped the difficult issue of "how many orchestras?" but proposed the means whereby the policy was to be carried through! This was the most disputatious of the recommendations—so much so that the Arts Council, when publishing the report in July 1970 added a preface dissenting from the recommendation on the grounds that the case that the two non-subsidised orchestras could survive on broadcasting and other commercial activities had not been proved. This argument appeared over the signature of the former Mr Arnold Goodman, who since his report had been ennobled and become Chairman of the Arts Council. There, so far, this particular controversy rests.

For the orchestras in London, the threat to their survival through a withdrawal of subsidy has subsequently never been far from the minds of their managements and has intensified the politics of concert life. The Report in its many other respects is not strictly relevant to the development of the LSO, though its general comments on concert halls and patterns of concert-giving in the provinces affect the environment in which the Orchestra operates.

As with the Goodman enquiry, the LSO's representations offer an insight into the Orchestra's view of its own situation at the end of a decade of artistic success on a world scale.

The Orchestra submitted that LOCB support represented less than 20 per cent of the LSO's gross income and did not cover the deficit on the Orchestra's own promotions. Thus the LSO had to play as many "commercial" engagements as possible to cover these deficits and the costs of foreign tours, *and* contribute towards its operating costs. This meant being prepared to work seven days a week, and up to thirteen hours a day: current schedules demanded a fifty-hour week, excluding travelling time. Support from the private sector was restricted to one major industrial sponsor (Peter Stuyvesant), despite determined efforts to locate others; until the Orchestra could develop new sources of finance, it would be compelled to compete even more strongly for "commercial" engagements. Such conditions of economic uncertainty ruled out any policy other than engaging musicians on a free-lance basis.

The Board's personnel policies were in consequence at the mercy of the players' need or readiness to accept other, better-paid, engagements, either from the BBC, which could offer Principals considerably more money for less work, or from TV and film recording companies, whose pay scales were more lavish. The LSO attempted to match individual fees in order to maintain continuity in personnel and therefore standards of playing, but of necessity it lagged behind and could always be outbid. The management could do nothing about the conditions under which the Members earned their living; engagements had to be carried out wherever the employer of the Orchestra desired—a requirement which frequently involved Members in playing in three different and widely distant places on the same day.

Economic necessity restricted the size of the Orchestra to eighty-six, discounting the Associate Members, who provided a reliable pool of acceptable extras. The LSO was thus inferior in strength to the American and Continental orchestras with whom it competed, but even so, was too large for recording companies, which habitually required only fifty of the Orchestra's sixty strings on the grounds that in reverberant halls such as the Kingsway Hall more were unnecessary. Hence, on the one hand, the LSO could not reap the benefits of being a fully constituted symphonic organisation, while, on the other, the demands of the recording companies, to whom the LSO had to look for its regular livelihood, frequently ensured that not even all the Members could be employed.

These constraints are still characteristic of the LSO's working life. They impart a sense of urgency which under some conditions keeps the players on their toes, and, under others, easily induces feelings of insecurity. Members have developed over the years an acute sense of when the first is likely to crumble into the second. *One* effect of this awareness can be detected in elections to the Board of Directors, though, as a matter of history, it has not always happened that the candidate who would "do something about the situation" found that he could. But, this, of course, is not unknown in other electoral circumstances. The problems arise from the financial environment in which the LSO works and are not intrinsic to the Orchestra itself. Thus, to take one example not covered in the Peacock submissions, the LSO is not able to take on tour the large pieces requiring more than the conventional number of players, such as *The Rite of Spring*, even though they make the technical and artistic demands which the LSO is superbly equipped to meet: touring repertoire has to be costed in terms of players required for each programme.

Not all the problems are totally intractable, short of a revolution in the scale and methods of financing the Orchestra. The rehearsal problem, as put to the Peacock Committee, now appears to have been solved, at least in principle.

The aims of the LSO Trust, as published, included the financing of facilities in which the LSO could regularly rehearse. From time to time, individual Directors or Harold Lawrence would inspect a former cinema or similar premises, but none was found to fit the Orchestra's minimum requirements, as regards working space, remoteness from traffic noise and the flight paths of aircraft, and access for the instrument van—all in a building located within easy reach of Central London for players, soloists and conductors. It was subsequently considered necessary that the rehearsal hall had to be suitable for recording purposes.

In 1969, the LSO acquired the services of an honorary enquiry agent into London real estate, in the person of Mrs Mary Morris Lawrence, wife of the General Manager. Starting from the premise that a building with a cubic capacity and the other characteristics necessary was likely to command a prohibitively high price, Mrs Lawrence concentrated her search among properties so restricted that they would not attract ordinary commercial users. This supposition drove her inevitably towards the Church Commissioners. By mid-1970, her enquiry had narrowed to a number of Anglican Churches in the Diocese of Southwark. The LSO's policy was either to purchase or lease premises for its own use or come to an arrangement to use a church where the congregation made only minimal demands on the facilities. Inspections and tests in churches gave Members a new interest in the points of ecclesiastical architecture in Battersea, Bermondsey and Wandsworth. Arup Associates, who had so successfully converted the Malt House at Snape into the Maltings Concert Hall for the Aldeburgh Festival, provided professional advice and assistance.

In the winter of 1970/71, the search finished at Holy Trinity, Southwark, a Georgian church built in 1824. It stood in a square off the Borough, designated as a conservation area under the Town and Country Planning Act. The church had been badly damaged during the war but was structurally stable and the roof was very sound. Finally, it was available, having been the first to be declared redundant by the church authorities under a newly-invented statutory process. As regards site, access to the Royal Festival Hall and the Barbican, available capacity and acoustic possibilities, Holy Trinity met the LSO's requirements admirably.

Unwittingly, however, Mrs Lawrence and the LSO walked into a situation which would have provided Anthony Trollope with subject matter for a series of novels. For some years, the future of this damaged church had been disputed between the Diocese of Southwark and the Elder Brethren of Trinity House,* who had originally donated the site and were the owners of the surrounding square. The Diocesan officials wanted to raze the building to the ground and let the land for office building. Trinity House objected, on the grounds that the site had been given for a church and not for the Diocese to make a capital gain: additionally, that offices would destroy the amenities

* Trinity House was founded in the seventeenth century as a charity for the provision and upkeep of lighthouses and lightships.

of the square in which it stood and of the associated housing. The Elder Brethren eventually took their objections to Parliament, in the form of a Petition, where they opposed a Private Bill which had been introduced by the Diocese to enable its officials to do as they wished. The Petition was upheld. The Diocese retaliated by using the new law to declare the church redundant so that it could be used for secular purposes. They entered into negotiations with a property developer who wished to convert the church into seven luxury flats, with a swimming pool in the centre of the nave. Trinity House promptly lodged an objection to the application for permission to change the use of the building. This time, the Elder Brethren lost. Meanwhile, the birds and the cats continued in undisturbed occupation.

Then the LSO appeared and offered an alternative. After an initial misunderstanding, it was supported by Trinity House—but was opposed by the Diocese. The LSO, also, applied for planning permission under the Town and Country Planning Act. This was refused, because of another misunderstanding. The LSO re-applied. Their application was supported by Trinity House. At this juncture, too, the LSO and LPO decided to join forces over the project since both orchestras had the same need, and partnership offered a chance to share costs.

The Diocesan authorities, however, did not proceed with the representations of the orchestras—indeed, they refused to entertain them—and entered into what they maintained was a commitment with the developer, subject only to the approval of the Church Commissioners and the Privy Council. In normal cases, these bodies simply "rubber stamp" a Diocesan scheme, but, in view of the Diocese's refusal to negotiate, the orchestras went directly to the Church Commissioners and launched a campaign for public support which was backed by the Master of the Queen's Musick, the Minister responsible for the Arts, the Chairman of the Arts Council, and eminent architects and conductors. In May 1972, the Commissioners rejected the Diocese's scheme and invited the orchestras to negotiate on their own proposals.

At this point, the situation passed from the Trollopian to the Gilbertian. Trinity House was anxious to secure a right to a say in any future decision about the use of the church (should the orchestras not stay). The Elder Brethren approached the Diocese, now acting for the Church Commissioners, and asked in effect if they could buy back the freehold of the church and act as landlords to the future users. The Diocese refused to negotiate with them or acknowledge that they had any standing in the matter—which left Trinity House in the same position as the orchestras had been some months previously and with no remedy but to lodge yet another appeal to the Church Commissioners, this time *against* the orchestras, even though the Elder Brethren were enthusiastic to have them in the building!

The summer and early autumn of 1972 involved the orchestras in negotiating an arrangement in which the various interests of the parties could be squared with their own practical and immediate need. By November, this had been accomplished: the orchestras set up a joint management company to receive a ninety-nine-year lease from the Church Commissioners, and assumed obligations under covenant to Trinity House, so as to protect the latter's legitimate interests in the surrounding property. At a crucial stage, Sir Jack Lyons volunteered, with Lord Shaftesbury for the LPO, to underwrite the venture.

On Sunday morning, 19th December 1972, the LSO carried out an acoustical test. John Pritchard conducted selected snippets from Bach, Stravinsky and Ravel. Conductor, players and soloist (Jill Gomez) all wore heavy coats against the cold, and construction workers' helmets were compulsory! The LPO carried out a similar test in the afternoon. The Orchestra was highly satisfied with its new quarters. Harold Lawrence declared that, could the equipment be installed, he would be prepared to start recording the same evening. All that remained was to get the building in order—which was estimated to take about eighteen months. There were the usual delays associated with the development of any scheduled building, but eventually, work was due to start on 1st October 1973. The contractors duly arrived, only to find that during the night the building had been gutted by fire.

The two orchestras decided that, when repaired and in use, the premises will be known as the Henry Wood Hall—a tribute to Wood's qualities at rehearsal, and, for the LSO, a gesture to its own past. The Henry Wood Memorial Trust, founded originally to rebuild the Queen's Hall,* agreed to donate its uncommitted funds to the new rehearsal hall, which it recognised was a project as near the original intention of the Trust as could be achieved in practice thirty-three years on.

Perhaps the most hopeful development at home has been the revivifying of interest in the Barbican. The City fought out its political battle and appointed an Administrator to the planned Arts Centre. The LSO and other intending tenants responded to this initiative from the City. In June 1973, the LSO produced yet another—and designedly final—report, putting its entry into the Barbican on the same footing as that to be enjoyed by its artistic "partners", the Royal Shakespeare Company and the Guildhall School of Music and Drama.

The logic of the argument stems from the fact that the three form an artistic triad. The LSO wants to have regular working relationships with the Guildhall School in training orchestral musicians and with the RSC, which will allow experimental concerts such as *Beatrice and Benedict* and *Joan of Arc at the Stake*; the GSM on its drama side has relationships with the RSC matching those it can develop with the Orchestra. The Shakespeare Company has already given evidence of its willingness to have the converse relationships with the other two.

The LSO argued that, as "resident orchestra", it would have to give at least forty concerts a season, of which about half would have to be repeated on account of the limited seating capacity of the Hall (2,000 seats). This of itself pointed to formally vesting artistic control in the LSO since the Orchestra would absorb a substantial amount of the time available for music. Additionally, programmes contributed by other bodies and with their own artists would affect the LSO's own planning policies. The Directors indicated the facilities which they would undertake to guarantee to visiting orchestras, chamber concerts and recitals.

The report went into the crucial problem of subsidy in great detail, advancing the hope that the Greater London Council

* See above, Chapter 10, page 129.

Verdi's *Requiem* in St Paul's Cathedral, 1970

The initial acoustics test at Holy Trinity, Southwark, 1972

might be persuaded to maintain and even extend its support, even though the LSO removed itself altogether from the South Bank. But the Directors carried their analysis one stage further, making the point that the opening of the Barbican raises the basic problems of subsidisation. "It follows that . . . the City Corporation, the GLC and the Arts Council should start now to rebuild from scratch the entire system of orchestral subsidy which will be required." If so, there is one corollary: "The LSO realises that the cost to the taxpayer and the ratepayer must be kept within reasonable bounds and it may well be that the organisation of permanent symphony orchestras working in London may have to be reviewed anew."

So, on its seventieth anniversary, the London Symphony Orchestra is within sight of an achievement which will alter the way of life it has followed hitherto. The Barbican does not imply that the LSO will work less hard: it does mean that the LSO may become a contract orchestra, with the fixed points in its schedule all in the same place. The reduction in fatigue alone may well seem to the players a reversal of the natural order of things!

But seventy years has bred certain qualities in the Orchestra—something of a buccaneering streak which may well disappear in the domesticity of the Barbican. The LSO will have to put its aggressive competitive energy into something else: should this happen, the character of the Orchestra will change.

In the last five years, the LSO has consolidated itself, if not in quite the way Barry Tuckwell intended.* The personnel has remained fairly static; there have been few resignations. Neville Marriner has established himself as a conductor, whose approach to the "Eroica" impressed his former colleagues when he conducted them recently in Lincoln Cathedral. Gervase de Peyer, likewise a conductor, has maintained a more direct link with the LSO through its wind ensemble. But the Orchestra has recruited others whom it confidently backs to attain the same degree of artistic eminence. Jack Steadman gave way as Chairman to Stuart Knussen and he in turn to the present incumbent, Howard Snell. "Principals

* The Orchestra's view of itself at this stage of its career is vividly recorded in *To Speak for Ourselves* (ed. Alan Smyth), published in 1970.

versus Rank and File" is no longer an issue in the same way as it was—a consequence of financial reward and prudent management. On tours, the Orchestra invariably receives the same kind of reception that, say, the players from Berlin or Vienna (to take the two orchestras mentioned in the original LSO prospectus) get in Britain.

The most impressive overseas venture for the Orchestra was its appearance at the Salzburg Festival in 1973. It gave five concerts in fifteen days with no other sessions—which for the LSO almost comes into the category of "working holiday". Audiences were enthusiastic and the critics commented on the Orchestra's virtuosity, phrasing and vitality. But they also noted a "joy in the music", which appears to sum up the impact of the Festival concerts on the LSO. It was not just a matter of the stimulating encounter with Karl Böhm, or of the triumph of the première in Austria of Shostakovich's Eighth Symphony, under André Previn. Perhaps the Salzburg concerts mark a new stage in the development of the Orchestra; do they indicate the qualities it can reveal when it can afford to relax?

Salzburg was the last major LSO venture associated with Harold Lawrence, who shortly before it opened, resigned his position to become Manager of the New York Philharmonic Orchestra. His contribution to the LSO can be measured in terms of the difference between the Orchestra's order book when he arrived and when he left.

The style of the administration changed yet again. The Board appointed an Administrator, Stephen Reiss, whose professional antecedents were in Aldeburgh—not, however, as an interim measure to avoid a chaotic hiatus, but because the move to the Barbican would demand additional management. In the event, the Directors did not proceed to appoint a General Manager but are now experimenting with a new arrangement in which Stephen Reiss and June Hall (concerts manager) are concerned with planning and administration, with André Previn more closely associated with artistic policy.

Previn's is a novel relationship in LSO terms, since it brings him into artistic planning as an act of deliberate policy at a time when the Orchestra is being successful. The interventions of Coates and Harty were made in adverse circumstances.

Previn accepted on condition that he gets "some of the praise, and not all the blame". Another departure from precedent has been the decision to make his contract open-ended. This does not mean that the present Directors have committed the Orchestra indefinitely to an autocratic conductor: merely that they prolonged the period of notice which they would have to give their Principal Conductor should they ever wish to dispense with his services. From an orchestra with the traditions of the LSO, this is a great vote of confidence.

His appointment has naturally strengthened the LSO's connections in the United States. It is good to note that its thirteenth tour, which took place in September 1974, opened in Los Angeles at the Hollywood Bowl at the invitation of Ernest Fleischmann, manager of this famous open-air concert hall as well as of the Los Angeles Philharmonic Orchestra.

EPILOGUE

THE LSO EXHIBITS a marked sense of continuity. If Borsdorf, Busby, Vander Meerschen and John Solomon could return to the organisation they founded, they would find it working fundamentally as they designed it. Members are still the only shareholders and, as such, still elect Directors who are responsible for setting the policy of the Orchestra in music, administration and finance. That they have chosen to delegate the execution of some of these responsibilities is a difference of degree, not of kind. The founders might, perhaps, find a more assertive democracy than they themselves experienced—attitudes to leadership have altered since 1904—but nothing beyond the limits which they then set. The scale of work is larger—the LSO now itself promotes as many concerts as filled the entire season in the Orchestra's first full year—but the philosophy is unchanged.

If they turned to the world in which the LSO operates, the founders would find that it has changed not only in scale but in character since 1904. Then "live" concerts were the Orchestra's sole form of activity, and the task of the Board was to maximise the number of occasions on which it might profitably appear. The Directors still have this same general aim, but have to realise it in a wholly different environment. Public concerts now share the Orchestra's schedule with studio work, either for records, radio or television. A large proportion of Members' work involves them in no direct contact with the public. Moreover, through air travel, concert platforms may easily be located anywhere in the world. The Orchestra still proudly bears the title of "London" but metropolitan audiences are only a small minority of those who, through one medium or another, listen to the LSO.

These changes pose problems within the Orchestra unimaginable by the original Board. The LSO was founded by men of determination and character—and has continued to find room for both qualities within its ranks. This is disadvantageous, if the organisation is to be run tidily: not every Member can easily arrive at the balance between freedom and responsibility; nor does every player interpret these two terms in the same way. Ultimately, under the LSO's constitution, management must aim to create the conditions in which Members can achieve that balance, in their own interest and that of the Orchestra. For, although the LSO is a company, its shareholders are not laymen in regard to the company's activity: nor are they removed from the Directors. Every time the Orchestra assembles, in principle the Directors of the Company are necessarily present. The Board is on view and can be button-holed. Individuals can and do take different views on what "the good of the Orchestra" entails, so the success of the LSO at any juncture depends on the Board's formulating an operative consensus on that highly subjective topic. If the Directors cannot define it, there are many outside the LSO who will define it for them. Their predecessors in 1904 were not faced with this contingency at all.

The immediate sources of external definition may be traced by looking at the LSO's sources of income. Gramophone recordings account for more than half its income but, conversely, the requirements of recording engineers bear on the personnel policies of the Orchestra and can infringe the independence of its management.

The problem is originally technical. The LSO archives show that from the beginning of electrical recording, gramophone companies have expressed dissatisfaction with particular instrumentalists. Before then, as Wynn Reeves shows, sound quality hardly mattered. The advent of long-playing recordings and the consequent rise in costs raised the problem more acutely. It is possible that George Stratton's career as Leader was nearing its end, but the final move began with the management of Decca. This is only an exceptional and drastic outcome but it represents the ultimate reality for any orchestra wishing to make recordings.

More customarily, the record companies' point of view emerges in day-to-day discussions about contract conditions and recording problems. Some of these may be limited, as, for example, the request by a recording company that the LSO tympanist use natural skins for recording, because they give the kind of results its technicians require.

Other representations range wider over the sound qualities of the orchestra and thus bear on general policy. The general approach may be demonstrated by comments from a source over ten years old:

> As far as the composition of the Orchestra is concerned, there are certain weaknesses of which you yourself are no doubt well aware. In my opinion, the LSO needs a first-class solo flute, one who is not merely competent, but who is exceptional in his own right. . . . (How easy it is to write this, and how hard it is to find them.) If you listen to our . . . recording . . . you cannot help being struck by the very unsatisfactory playing of the cor anglais, who was not, as erroneously stated . . . that fine artist Roger Lord. You need a good cor anglais. In my opinion you also need an outstandingly good solo trumpet. Another notable gap in the Orchestra is caused by the absence of a really outstanding solo cellist. As a matter of fact, the entire cello section needs strengthening.

The point is not whether these assertions were true to fact, or not: it is that the interests of recording brought them into the relationship between the company and the Orchestra—and still does. In this particular conflict of interest, the balance of power is tilted towards the record companies, since they have the alternative of using another orchestra or assembling one *ad hoc* in the studio. Recourse to either, however, raises difficulties.

Using another orchestra depends on its contractual commitments and the demands of conductors, whose relationships with the alternate orchestra may not be such as to withstand the proximity and tensions of studio working. Assembling a body of players *ad hoc* deprives the recording company of the vital quality of *ensemble* and would tend to prolong the recording time and, therefore, its cost. Above all, under Union agreements going back many years, recording fees for *ad hoc* bands are significantly higher than for regular orchestras. These constraints mean that, in practice, it is easier for recording companies to prod orchestral managements into improving their personnel. As the LSO has found, success does not eliminate these pressures, though it does make easier the task of retaining an identity in the face of a technology which tends to operate against it.

The second main outside source from which "the good of the Orchestra" may be defined are the organisations disbursing public funds. That the arts have to be subsidised and that such subsidies have to come, in part, from public funds, are two propositions which generally no longer have to be argued, even in Britain. The extent of public funding and the basis on which it is given still cause debate not only among the taxpayers at large but also between government departments and the recipients: in the present discussion, orchestras. The specific point at issue is the proportion of subsidy to other earnings. The proportion for the four London orchestras is 20 per cent on average, as compared with 80 per cent in Amsterdam, Berlin and Paris. The answers bear on the artistic policies of the orchestras as well as their employment prospects for their players, since they govern decisions as to whether a metropolitan orchestra should take Tchaikovsky to the Outer Hebrides or undertake a new work by Penderecki at the Festival Hall. The idea that an increased subsidy must carry with it corresponding restrictions on the recipients is one which appeals to the bureaucratic mind, but is, otherwise, by no means axiomatic.

The pressures from these outside bodies occur in day-to-day policy making and only rarely in the form of direct confrontation. They are experienced by all four London orchestras, which, however, respond to them in different ways, since their interests are not identical. For, as well as competing collectively with more heavily subsidised bodies such as the BBC Symphony Orchestra and with orchestras in the Common Market, they are, after all, competing severely with one another. This domestic competition originates in the well-canvassed fact that opportunities in London for performances of the highest quality extend not to four orchestras but at most to three-and-a-half. The problem has been with us for some time and is one to which "Goodman" gave no clear answer and "Peacock" one which is, so far, unacceptable. All the orchestras have survived crises—the LSO having developed considerable expertise in doing so. Before Krips, it could plausibly be urged that if any London orchestra had to disappear, the LSO could the most easily be spared. In 1957, the LPO nearly sank without trace and only saved itself by scrapping its contract basis and pension fund; in 1961/62, the Royal Philharmonic Orchestra presented itself as a natural candidate for dissolution; while in 1964, the New Philharmonia was struggling to survive. Yet all these orchestras, by changes in personnel, by reorganisation, by finding conductors to attract the public and regain prestige, have survived. The fact of survival has strengthened the will to live. There are unlikely to be any administratively convenient suicides. The orchestras have all found themselves work and subsidies and, as long as they can continue to do so, there is a case for their going on as they are. This was, broadly, Goodman's conclusion: it has the additional merit of obviating the need for unpleasant and, quite possibly "wrong", administrative action now.

The fact of survival is, of course, no guarantee of continued survival, as operating circumstances, particularly increases in costs, become more stringent. Additionally, having to grab at every session that is going ignores the question of standards and the relationship between them, the location and number of engagements and the strain on the players. LSO players are gluttons for work—they sometimes give the impression of regretting that the Parliamentary abolition of Christmas in 1652 was ever rescinded—but they are aware of the demands on their health and therefore their alertness and performance. In the longer term, the present policy links the future of the orchestras to the rate of technological innovation and obsolescence in the recording industry. Quadraphonic systems will probably require a complete re-recording of the whole repertoire, which will be profitable only if the system is not confined to the sound enthusiast but becomes general among those interested in music. If the public is attracted or can be induced to convert to the new system, all will be well for the orchestras for the next decade, including especially the LSO, though the influence of recording companies' requirements on the orchestras' personnel policies is likely to grow. Ultimately, this *could* dissolve completely the identity of orchestras too closely dependent on them for income.

The most immediately relevant consideration, however, stems from decisions which have already been taken. The entry of the LSO into the Barbican will change the situation not only for that orchestra but also for all the others. It would raise a case for the GLC's emulating the City and putting an orchestra in the Festival Hall, with predominant but not exclusive rights. The two which did not become established could either fight to the death or emigrate to Kensington, whichever is preferred. Who gets what, at that stage, depends not so much on positions taken now as what happens to the orchestras by the time the question becomes "actual". The least favoured candidate now might well have discovered a reincarnated Toscanini in the meantime.

The probable future effect of the Barbican suggests that the problem of "too many orchestras" can conveniently be considered not in terms of organisations and loyalties but of the centres in London for orchestral music. There then appear to be four: the Barbican, the South Bank, Kensington and the opera houses, offering prospects for five orchestras. Of the concert halls, the Royal Albert Hall is economically the most difficult to fill, except for the Proms. It is unrivalled in London for performances of Mahler's Eighth and the Berlioz *Grande Messe des Morts*, but such works can hardly provide a regular income between summers. It also provides a place for impresarios whose business requires them to put on at least a minimum of concerts for a maximum audience with minimum rehearsal (frequently in three-four time or with cannon effects).

These five orchestras could provide regular engagements for upwards of 500 players and would enable each orchestra to be permanently enlarged, but the solution to the problem cannot be to take the number of London-based players and spread them over the concert halls and opera houses. The immediate objection arises from the number and standards of string players and *that* aspect ramifies into the system of education and training for musicians. Then again, the halls are not equal in value to either orchestras or entrepreneurs. The Barbican is, in some respects, an unknown quantity, but the LSO's entire approach rests on the confidence that what it has to offer and the standing it has built up internationally over the past decade will overcome any hesitations the public may experience in going to the new hall. Of the others, the Royal Festival Hall is very much a going concern with international prestige which it would automatically confer on any resident orchestra. Whoever inherited the Albert Hall would, on present showing, collect the warmest acoustics in compensation for the worst economics.

There are no clear-cut solutions, because the problems are interdependent and no one authority is willing to enforce its own panacea. One infers that rising costs will ultimately enforce some rationalisation, either in the direction of keeping the same number of orchestras with smaller forces, or fewer orchestras with larger forces, or by enlarging the available financial resources by tax remissions for private support of the arts, or through lotteries, or through higher grants from public funds. One or other of these factors may well have to change as it is unlikely that additional costs could wholly be recovered through the box office.

These are the main features of the environment in which the LSO operates, or which it is likely to encounter in the years after its seventieth birthday anniversary. They have been sketched in here only to illustrate the scale and complexity of the problems which its Directors and Members now face, in the knowledge, drawn from the LSO's past experience, that the margin between success and failure is very small.

They realise, however, that there is more to fulfilling the LSO's function in society than prudent management of its resources and opportunities. The public position of an orchestra is not a question simply of where it can be heard and how frequently, but involves considerations of quality, taste and style—all necessarily subjective elements in the judgements of audiences. The successful orchestra is one which latches on to these variable responses and which can "explain" to audiences, perhaps unaware of their aesthetic preferences, what their preferences explicitly are or where they lead. Arguably, the current success of the LSO, not only in Britain but throughout the world, rests on the Orchestra convincing publics, of widely differing backgrounds, that it can offer musical insights which extend or deepen their aesthetic experience and that this results from attending LSO concerts: it is not enough to watch television or listen to records, however technically excellent. The core of the matter is personal experience of music.

An orchestra's ability to sustain this kind of success with audiences across the world depends on its ability to develop its personality through performing works over a period of time and the degree to which the players can identify themselves with music of a wide range of periods and styles. This personality is not fixed and immutable but varies with the tastes, standards and preferences of whoever is responsible for auditioning and training the players—in the LSO's case, the LSO.

The instinct for independence which has and does distinguish the policies of LSO Ltd has also been reflected in the approach of the Orchestra to its work. Collectively, it tends to be tough-minded with conductors: "What can we get out of this man, artistically?" If it appears that the man has little to give (which may, at a rehearsal take from ten minutes to an hour but *before* a break will have given the players a chance to exchange ideas verbally), then the reaction can range from mild impatience to outright contempt. The Orchestra's one-time reputation for conductor-baiting derives from this demand for artistic insight. As a matter of history, it does not like conductors who play for safety.

In individual players, the instinct makes itself evident in the desire of soloists to make personal artistic statements, within the limits of the score. This leads players to gamble with their skills, not just in the bandroom but on the platform. Unvarying unanimity of thought and phrase is not characteristic of the LSO: the drive to experiment or to develop is too strong. It is part of the LSO's tradition. Nikisch once stopped a rehearsal and asked Borsdorf to repeat a passage simply to savour the individuality of his playing, and Francis Bradley demonstrated to the author how John Solomon put his own stamp on performances through his imaginative phrasing.

The experiments do not succeed every time. Both Josef Krips and André Previn remember vividly occasions when particular players' desire to experiment has called on all their resources as conductors and the collective reflexes of the Orchestra to prevent disaster. But in this respect, the LSO spares itself no less than its conductors; it is profoundly uninterested in the idea of settling on a particular "reading", or giving stereotyped performances.

The history discussed in this book shows that the LSO does not operate in a world of ineffable beauty; nor is it composed of bloodless aesthetes. It is a working democracy in an intensely competitive environment. Its perennial problem is security to do what it wants to do. But what it wants to do lies in the realm of artistic values. A concert is simply an opportunity to enlarge the experience of the audience, and its awareness, through music. This is what the audience has a right to expect, and is therefore the *raison d'être* of the Orchestra. Members of the LSO do not usually put the point as explicitly as this ("Last season we played X concerts, and from time to time music emerged"), but it governs all their policies and actions. Commissioning new works, trying out rotary trumpets to give the warm, dark sound for Brahms and Bruckner, arguing cases to impresarios and officers of recording companies, discussing the fee structure of Members, all derive their meaning only from the drive to communicate a technically better, and possibly richer, experience. Whether it is in fact richer or not will depend on the audience: after the applause has died down, the Orchestra cannot know what the performance has meant to those who have heard it. But it is the recognition that they are concerned with values which gives LSO Members higher ambitions than achieving a reputation for sheer brilliance, technical virtuosity and alertness of response.

APPENDICES

NOTES

BIBLIOGRAPHY

INDEX

APPENDIX I

London Symphony Orchestra Tours 1960 Onwards

1960	*Holland*	The Hague
		Amersfoort
		Amsterdam
		Haarlem
		Rotterdam
1960	*Israel*	Haifa
		Tel Aviv
		Jerusalem
1960	*Greece*	Athens
1961	*Vienna Festival*	
1962	*Portugal*	Lisbon
		Braga
		Oporto
		Coimbra
1962	*Switzerland*	Basle
		Berne
		Zurich
1962	*France*	Paris
		Strasbourg
1963	*Japan*	Osaka
		Hiroshima
		Yawata
		Shizuoka
		Tokyo
		Koriyama
1963	*Austria*	Vienna
		Salzburg
		Innsbruck

1963	*Germany*	Freiburg
		Stuttgart
		Munich
		Augsburg
1963	*Italy*	Perugia
		Milan
		Venice
1964	*Switzerland*	Zurich
		Basle
		Berne
		Biel
		Lausanne
1964	*Germany*	Dusseldorf
1964	*America*	Elmira
		Rochester
		Ann Arbor
		Toledo
		Urbana
		East Lansing
		Columbus
		Charleston
		Raleigh
		Charlottesville
		Washington
		New Brunswick
		New York
		Boston
		United Nations, New York
		Los Angeles
		San Diego
		San Francisco
		Seattle
1964	*Japan*	Tokyo
		Osaka
		Nagoya
1964	*South Korea*	Seoul
1964	*Hong Kong*	
1964	*India*	Calcutta
		Bombay
		Delhi

1964	*Iran*	Teheran
1964	*Israel*	Tel Aviv
		Ein Gev
		Haifa
		Jerusalem
1964	*Turkey*	Istanbul
1965	*European Tour*	West Berlin
		Hamburg
		Hanover
		Stuttgart
		Linz
		Budapest
1965	*Prague Spring Festival*	
1965	*Vienna Festival*	
1966	*Hong Kong*	
1966	*Singapore*	
1966	*Australia*	Perth
		Adelaide
		Melbourne
		Sydney
		Brisbane
1966	*America*	New Brunswick
		New York
		Washington
		Daytona
1966	*Switzerland*	Geneva
		Basle
		Zurich
		Berne
1967	*America*	New York
		Daytona
1967	*Belgium*	Brussels
1968	*America*	New York
1968	*Israel*	Tel Aviv
		Haifa
		Jerusalem
1968	*America*	Daytona
1969	*America*	Daytona
1969	*Austria*	Vienna

1970	*America*	Storrs
		New Haven
		Syracuse
		Northampton
		Hartford
		Boston
		White Plains
		Philadelphia
		Charlottesville
		Raleigh
		Richmond
		Washington
		New York
1970	*Switzerland*	Berne
		Lausanne
		Geneva
		Zurich
1970	*Europe*	Brussels
		Ghent
		Bucharest
		Cluj
		Bratislava
		Prague
		Brno
		Budapest
1971	*Russia and Far East*	Moscow
		Leningrad
		Osaka
		Tokyo
		Nagoya
		Seoul
		Hong Kong
1971	*Italy*	Milan
1972	*America*	Boston
		New York
		Philadelphia
		Washington
		Norfolk
		Greenville
		Raleigh

		Charlottesville
		Asheville
		Columbia
		Atlanta
		Miami
		Fort Lauderdale
		Miami Beach
1972	*Germany*	Lubeck
		Salzgitter
		Mulheim
		Bonn
		Cologne
		Dusseldorf
		Ludwigshaven
		Munich
		Nuremberg
		Stuttgart
		Heilbronn
		Frankfurt
		Kassel
		Hamburg
		Hanover
1973	*America*	Columbus
		Indianapolis
		Madison
		Ames
		Peoria
		Lafayette
		East Lansing
		Ann Arbor
		Providence
		Boston
		New York
		Washington

APPENDIX II

The programmes given by Boulez and the LSO in London in 1969 under the rubric of "The Crossroads of 20th Century Music" were:

Berg	*Three Fragments from Wozzeck, Op. 7*	1915–21
Webern	*Cantata, Das Augenlicht, Op. 26*	1935
	Cantata No. 2, Op. 31	1941–43
	Cantata No. 1, Op. 29	1939
Schoenberg	*Four Songs, Op. 22*	1913–16
Berg	*Three Pieces for Orchestra, Op. 6**	1913–14
	soloists: Halina Lukomska, Yvonne Minton, Barry McDaniel, John Alldis Choir	

Schoenberg	*Film Music, Op. 34**	1930
	*Five Pieces, Op. 16**	1909
Webern	*Symphony, Op. 21**	1928
	Three Pieces, Op. posth.	—
	*Variations for Orchestra, Op. 30**	1940
Berg	*Violin Concerto*	1935
	soloist: Isaac Stern	

Webern	*Concerto for Nine Instruments, Op. 24*	1934
	Entlief auf Leichten Kaehnen, Op. 2	1908
	Two Songs, Op. 19	1926
Schoenberg	*Three Pieces, Op. posth.*	—
Berg	*Chamber Concerto for Violin, Piano, and Thirteen Wind Instruments*	1923–25
	soloists: Sachko Gawriloff, Maureen Jones John Alldis Choir	

Mahler	*Adagio from Symphony No. 10*	1910
	Lieder eines fahrenden Gesellen	1883–84
	Das klagende Lied	1888
	soloists: Evelyn Lear, Grace Hoffmann, Hermann Prey, Stuart Burrows, LSO Chorus	
Webern	*Five Pieces for String Orchestra, Op. 5**	1909
Berg	*Seven Early Songs**	1905–8
Webern	*Six Pieces for Orchestra, Op. 6*	1909
Schoenberg	*Erwartung**	1909
	soloist: Evelyn Lear	

* Also played in Vienna

NOTES

Chapter I

1. Quoted in A. W. Ganz, *Berlioz in London*, p. 91.
2. Quoted in R. H. Elkin, *Queen's Hall*, p. 38.

Chapter II

1. Sir Henry Wood, *My Life of Music*, p. 112.
2. Sir Henry Wood, *My Life of Music*, p. 278.
3. Sir Henry Wood, *About Conducting*, p. 44.
4. Reginald Pound, *Sir Henry Wood*, p. 270.
5. J. B. Priestley, *Trumpets over the Sea*, p. 142.
6. M. D. Calvocoressi, *Musicians' Gallery*, p. 286.
7. M. D. Calvocoressi, *Musicians' Gallery*, p. 18.

Chapter III

1. Josef Szigeti, *With Strings Attached*, p. 231.

Chapter IV

1. Josef Szigeti, *With Strings Attached*, p. 63.

Chapter V

1. See chapter on Coates in Bernard Shore, *The Orchestra Speaks*.
2. Michael Kennedy labels the episode "a permanent disgrace to British music" and commends Ernest Newman for fixing "the blame where it belonged", on the Orchestra. (See *Portrait of Elgar*, p. 235.) One infers from the warmth of Elgar's continuing association with the LSO that the composer was less worried about the "permanent" effect than his biographer.
3. F. W. Gaisberg, *Music on Record*, p. 134.
4. Sir Eugene Goossens, *Overture and Beginners*, p. 184.

5. Sir Ivor Atkins, "The LSO and the Three Choirs Festivals, 1899 to 1938" in Hubert Foss and Noel Goodwin, *London Symphony*, p. 197.
6. Sir Arthur Bliss, *As I Remember*, p. 73.
7. Roy Henderson, letter to author, 14th June 1973.
8. C. G. C. Hector, letter to author, 20th June 1973.
9. Charles Reid, *John Barbirolli*, p. 87; Michael Kennedy, *Barbirolli, Conductor Laureate*, p. 84.
10. Gerald Jackson, *First Flute*, p. 36. He gives an astringent view of the LSO in the mid-twenties, suggesting that by this time its famous democracy had degenerated into jobbery (p. 37).

Chapter VI

1. Charles Reid, *Malcolm Sargent*, pp. 220–8.
2. Sir Henry Wood, *My Life of Music*, p. 94.
3. Ernest Newman in the *Sunday Times*, 15th November 1931.
4. Quoted in Asa Briggs, *The Golden Age of Broadcasting*, p. 184.

Chapter VII

1. For the background to this decision, see Harold Rosenthal, *Two Centuries of Opera at Covent Garden*, pp. 476–94.

Chapter VIII

1. See Gerald Jackson, *First Flute*, pp. 44–5.
2. Spike Hughes, *Glyndebourne*, p. 46.
3. Roy Henderson, letter to author, 14th June 1973.

Chapter IX

1. Elisabeth Lutyens, *A Goldfish Bowl*, pp. 104–5.
2. Ferrucio Bonavia, "London Concerts 1944–45", in *Hinrichsen's Musical Yearbook, 1945–46*.

Chapter X

1. Thomas Russell, *Philharmonic Project*, p. 39.
2. Thomas Russell, *Philharmonic Project*, p. 51.

SELECT BIBLIOGRAPHY

Foss, H. and Goodwin, N., *London Symphony*, Naldrett Press, 1954.
Priestley, J. B., *Trumpets over the Sea*, Heinemann, 1968.
Smyth, Alan (ed.), *To Speak for Ourselves*, William Kimber, 1970.

Elkin, R. H., *Queen's Hall 1893–1941*, Rider, 1944.
Elkin, R. H., *Royal Philharmonic*, Rider, 1946.
Nettel, Reginald, *The Orchestra in England*, Cape, 1948.
Russell, Thomas, *Philharmonic Decade*, Hutchinson, 1945.
Russell, Thomas, *Philharmonic Project*, Hutchinson, 1952.
Young, Kenneth, *Music's Great Days in Spas and Watering Places*, Macmillan, 1968.

Arts Council, *Report of the Committee on the London Orchestras*, 1965.
Arts Council, *A Report on Orchestral Resources in Great Britain*, 1970.
Arts Council, *Report of the Committee of Enquiry into Seat Prices*, 1973.
Hinrichsen's Musical Yearbook, 1944 onwards.
London Orchestral Concert Board, *Annual Reports*, 1967 onwards.
Russell-Cobb, Trevor, *Paying the Piper*, Queen Anne Press, 1968.

Briggs, Asa, *The Golden Age of Broadcasting*, Oxford University Press, 1965.
Gaisberg, F. W., *Music on Record*, Robert Hale, 1946.
Manvell, Roger and Huntley, John, *The Technique of Film Music*, Focal Press, 1967.
Wood, Sir Henry, *About Conducting*, Sylvan Press, 1945.

Journals and Newsletters of the London Symphony Orchestra Club.
Files of *The Musical Times*, *Music and Musicians*, *The Penguin Music Magazine*.

Aldrich, Richard, *Concert Life in New York*, Putnam, NY, 1941.
Beecham, Sir Thomas, *A Mingled Chime*, Hutchinson, 1944.
Bliss, Sir Arthur, *As I Remember*, Faber, 1970.
Ganz, A. W., *Berlioz in London*, Quality Press, 1950.
Godfrey, Sir Dan, *Memories and Music*, Hutchinson, 1924.

Goossens, Sir Eugene, *Overture and Beginners*, Methuen, 1951.
Heemskerk, E. B., *Over Willem Mengelberg*, Uitgeverij Heuff, Amsterdam, 1970.
Hughes, Spike, *Glyndebourne*, Methuen, 1965.
Jackson, Gerald, *First Flute*, Dent, 1968.
Kennedy, Michael, *The Hallé Tradition*, Manchester University Press, 1960.
Kennedy, Michael, *Barbirolli, Conductor Laureate*, MacGibbon and Kee, 1971.
Kennedy, Michael, *Portrait of Elgar*, Oxford University Press, 1968.
Lutyens, Elisabeth, *A Goldfish Bowl*, Cassell, 1972.
Neel, Boyd, *The Story of an Orchestra*, Vox Mundi, 1950.
Pound, Reginald, *Sir Henry Wood*, Cassell, 1969.
Reed, W. H., *Elgar as I Knew Him*, Gollancz, 1936.
Reid, Charles, *Thomas Beecham*, Gollancz, 1961.
Reid, Charles, *Malcolm Sargent*, Hamish Hamilton, 1968.
Reid, Charles, *John Barbirolli*, Hamish Hamilton, 1971.
Rosenthal, Harold, *Two Centuries of Opera at Covent Garden*, Putnam, London, 1958.
Schnabel, Artur, *My Life and Music*, Colin Smythe, 1970.
Shore, Bernard, *The Orchestra Speaks*, Longmans, 1938.
Szigeti, Josef, *With Strings Attached*, Cassell, 1949.
Wood, Sir Henry, *My Life of Music*, Gollancz, 1938.

INDEX